EXPLORING
COASTAL
MISSISSIPPI

Best wishes,

Scott Williams

EXPLORING COASTAL MISSISSIPPI

A Guide to the Marine Waters and Islands

SCOTT B. WILLIAMS

University Press of Mississippi / *Jackson*

www.upress.state.ms.us

The University Press of Mississippi is a member of the
Association of American University Presses.

12 11 10 09 08 07 06 05 04   4 3 2 1

Library of Congress Cataloging-in-Publication Data

Williams, Scott B.
    Exploring coastal Mississippi : a guide to the marine waters and
islands / Scott B. Williams.
    p. cm.
Includes bibliographical references and index.
    ISBN 1-57806-423-6 (cloth : alk. paper)—ISBN 1-57806-424-4
    (pbk. : alk. paper)
1. Gulf Coast (Miss.)—Guidebooks. 2. Mississippi—Guidebooks.
3. Waterways—Mississippi—Gulf Coast—Guidebooks. 4. Islands—
Mississippi—Gulf Coast—Guidebooks. 5. Outdoor recreation—
Mississippi—Gulf Coast—Guidebooks. 6. Boats and boating—
Mississippi—Gulf Coast—Guidebooks. 7. Navigation—Mississippi—
Gulf Coast—Guidebooks. I. Title.
    F347.G9W55 2004
    917.6'20464—dc22   2003022077

British Library Cataloguing-in-Publication Data available

This book is dedicated to the loving memory of my mother, Barbara Burgin Williams, who spent her childhood in Biloxi and passed on her love of the coast to me. And also to my father, Frank Williams Jr., who taught me to appreciate nature and the outdoors from my earliest memory.

CONTENTS

Part 3
Mississippi's Barrier Islands

ACKNOWLEDGMENTS

I would especially like to thank Ernest Herndon, who, after writing *Canoeing Mississippi*, convinced me that there was a need for a boater's guidebook to Mississippi's marine waters and urged me to send a proposal to Craig Gill at the University Press of Mississippi. Ernest also accompanied me on research trips to the Lower Pearl River, Horn Island, Back Bay and Bernard Bayou, and Round Island and the West Pascagoula River. I am greatly indebted to Jeff Hudson for dropping everything and flying to West Palm Beach to help me sail my boat back to home waters when I suddenly found myself without crew. We bypassed every hamburger joint in Florida and sailed 800 miles with only one shore visit. Jeff also helped out on research trips to the Pascagoula River and Horn Island. I would also like to thank my brother Jeff, of Gulfport, for providing a couch to crash on for countless nights and weekends while I worked on my boat and did the research for this book. My sister Jenny, of Florence, also frequently provided a place to stay while I was writing the book and working in Jackson. Thanks also to my brother Frank and my sister-in-law Cathy, of Tampa, for their help when I was searching central Florida for a suitable boat to buy and sail back to Mississippi for restoration and preparation for cruising.

This book would not have been completed without the love and encouragement of Michelle Calvert, who was there for me like a promise of sunshine after the darkest storm and always kept me motivated to write when

I thought I couldn't go on. I would also like to thank her daughter, Jasmine, for sincerely trying to hold down the noise level while I was writing!

I would like to thank Dr. F. W. Tripp, pastor of the Prentiss Presbyterian Church for the years of youth group trips to Pensacola that introduced me to boating on the Gulf and cultivated my fascination with the sea. I would like to thank Dek Terrell of Baton Rouge, for helping me out of a tight spot off of Cat Island; otherwise I might not be here to write this today. Special thanks also to David Sanford of Sumrall for the opportunity to fly over Horn and Petit Bois Islands in his Cessena 152 for some aerial photography and a chance to see the islands from a new perspective.

I would also like to thank Jack Waldrip and all the crew at Discovery Bay Marina; Dave and Marie Parker, for advice on refitting *Intensity*; Kenny and Louis Skrmetta of Ship Island Excursions; T. J. Covacevitch and JoLyn Covacevitch, of Covacevitch Yacht and Sail; Todd Read of Da Beach House; Nina Kelson of Gulf Islands National Seashore; David Halladay of Boatsmith; Mike Neckar of Necky Kayaks; Christopher Cunningham, editor of *Sea Kayaker* magazine; Mike Jones, of the Mississippi Department of Wildlife Fisheries, and Parks; Robert Stallworth Jr. for information on the Scranton Museum; David Watts, editor of *Mississippi Outdoors*; and Brian Nobles, Steve and Robbie Cox, Phil Hudson, Ernest Herndon, and other customers who have bought my hand-built wooden boats; John Whitfield, of *Sundancer*, for navigation into Old Fort Bayou; Danny Prine, of the motor-vessel *Audacity*; and Laurie Bryd for information on the catamaran *Yellowbird* and Deer Island.

INTRODUCTION

Why the Mississippi Coast?

The resident boaters of Mississippi's Gulf Coast already know that this unique area is a paradise for those who love the water. Most other Mississippians and certainly nonresidents of the state may not be aware of the opportunities for adventure and relaxation that await at the southern boundary of our state.

When I was growing up in inland Mississippi, I thought of Florida when I thought of beaches and marine water sports. Year after year I made countless trips to Pensacola or Destin, feeling myself drawn by the Gulf, but finding

Miles of uninhabited island beaches lie just over the horizon from the Mississippi mainland.

mostly crowds and condominiums on the beaches there. Until I acquired my own boat to take me to Mississippi's barrier islands, I drove blindly past what was practically in my backyard.

I had, of course, made many excursions to the mainland beaches of Mississippi's coast, and had even taken a few trips on the tour boat to West Ship Island. But it was not until I paddled a sea kayak to the wilderness shores of Horn Island that I realized just how special the islands of Mississippi really are.

Fifteen years of countless trips to the islands and explorations of the coastal rivers and marshes have led to putting what I have learned of the area into this book. The more I traveled to other islands and coastal areas of the Gulf of Mexico, as well as parts of the Caribbean, the more I realized how hard it would be to find anything to rival what Mississippi's natural coastal areas have to offer.

Mississippi's barrier islands are perhaps the most remote and unspoiled of any along the Gulf Coast, from the Florida Keys to the Yucatan Peninsula in

A permanent resident of a barrier island beach

Mexico. Unlike most of the barrier islands in the other states that border the Gulf, Mississippi's islands are quite distant from the mainland. This and Mississippi's poorer economy have saved them from being connected by causeways and developed as tourist resorts like those of Florida, Alabama, Louisiana, and Texas. Then in 1971, the Gulf Islands National Seashore was established, preserving the pristine quality of these islands and protecting the fragile ecosystems found there. The inclusion of these islands in the National Park System assures that they will be kept in a natural state for future generations to enjoy.

The distance from shore that discouraged commercial development of these islands makes them perfect for exploration by anyone with a boat capable of reaching them. A variety of small craft are seaworthy enough to negotiate the ten miles or so of open water between these islands and the mainland. So while the islands are far enough removed to be inaccessible to the masses, those adventurous enough to find their own way can do so without needing an expensive or large vessel. Many of the passages described in this book will require a basic knowledge of seamanship and navigation, but none are long, uncomfortable voyages requiring lots of money or equipment.

The information presented here will enable those willing to look beyond the hotels and casinos of the mainland to find the quiet beauty of deserted islands and unspoiled estuaries. Though the mainland coast is only about seventy miles long, there are nearly two hundred and fifty miles of coastline if you follow the convoluted shores of the bays and islands. There are eighty miles of undeveloped shoreline to be found on the seven main islands. Two major river systems empty into the Gulf along this coast, and the bayous, marshes, and bays associated with them offer a world of places to explore besides the offshore islands.

This book not only will serve as a guide to specific areas of the Mississippi coast but will also include how-to information on boating, camping, and related topics as they apply to the region. My hope is that this information will make it easier for those wishing to find their way to these places to have a safe and enjoyable trip. Much of what I learned about coastal exploring has been through trial and error, over many years in a variety of boats. By passing on some of what I have learned, perhaps I can save the reader from repeating some of my mistakes. I have had numerous encounters with other boaters over the years who demonstrated little if any knowledge of seamanship, safe boating practices, or common courtesy. Hopefully some of the information here will help those who wish to explore by boat to see the importance of learning everything they can about safety, navigation, and the basic Rules of the Road for boating.

For those armchair adventurers who are not able or so inclined to visit these places described, there will still be much of interest in these pages. I have included some of the history of these waters and islands, from the time of the first Native American inhabitants through the discovery and exploration by the first European sailors, and later settlement. There is also information on the wide variety of marine and island wildlife, and the unique natural ecosystems found here.

Some readers who do not have their own boats will still want to see some of these areas, and for them I have included a variety of destinations that can be reached by road. There are also many opportunities to get out on the water by chartered boats and tour boats, and details of these are included in the descriptions of areas where such services are available.

Though some longtime residents and experienced boaters in the region might not like to see a guidebook like this to their favorite hideaways published, I believe that making people aware of these resources will in the long run benefit all who visit them. Though much of the area is already included in the National Seashore, there are still relatively untouched areas desperately needing some sort of protection from development, especially now, in a time when the coast is booming economically due to the gambling industry. Steps to save what is left of the natural world can only be taken if the public knows what wonders there are left to save. In an area so vast and diverse, there will always be room for the relatively few who are able to get to the really remote places. The harsh realities of scorching sun, rough waters, and insect hordes will all play their part in discouraging overcrowding on these windswept barrier islands.

This book is divided into three main parts. In the first I include general information on exploring the entire region, including some history, weather patterns, navigation, safety, camping techniques and a discussion of gear, and something of related activities such as fishing and hiking. There is also a chapter on various boat types that can be used to access these areas, which might be helpful to would-be boaters wanting to get started but not really knowing what is required.

In the second part of the book, I give detailed descriptions and access information to each of the major areas of the coastal mainland, beginning at the western boundary of the state and working eastward to Alabama. Each area is described so that readers can decide if they would like to go there. Pertinent details are given, so that with the right nautical chart,

Aerial view of a barrier island, showing muddy waters of the sound to the north, and the clear Gulf beyond

readers will be able to explore it for themselves. My intention is not to describe every mile of coastline in great detail, but to outline the main points of interests, point out the hazards or downsides, and then leave it up to the reader to go there and get his own impressions. Some information, of course, is subject to change, such as the names and phone numbers of marinas, charter boat operations, and so forth, but all of this is as up to date as possible at the time of this writing. In a hurricane-prone area such as this coast, even geographical details can change over a short time, as seen in 1969 when Hurricane Camille cut Ship Island in two. Underwater obstructions such as sandbars are always subject to change, even in lesser storms, so it is up to the prudent mariner always to have the latest editions of nautical charts. Sources for applicable charts and other information will be given in the appendices in the back of the book.

In part 3, I take the reader offshore on a tour of the barrier islands, leaving the mainland on the eastern boundary of the state, where part 2 left off.

Beginning with Petit Bois Island, we work our way back west along the chain to complete the circle at Cat Island.

Let's begin our exploration of this fascinating area by taking a look at the many seafaring explorers who sailed and paddled these waters in times long past, from the pre-Colombian natives to European colonists and immigrant fishermen and boatbuilders.

Part 1

GENERAL INFORMATION FOR EXPLORING THE REGION

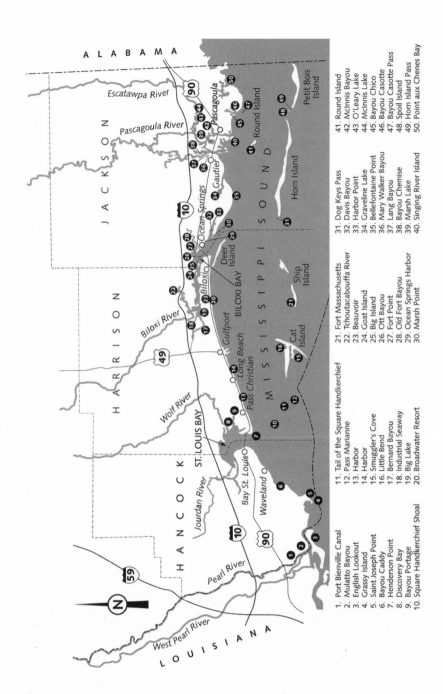

A L A B A M A

Escatawpa River

Pascagoula River

Pascagoula

Petit Bois
Island

Round Island

Horn Island

M I S S I S S I P P I   S O U N D

Gautier

Ocean Springs

Deer
Island

Biloxi

BILOXI BAY

Ship
Island

Gulfport

Long Beach

Cat
Island

Pass Christian

Biloxi River

J A C K S O N

H A R R I S O N

Wolf River

St. Louis

ST. LOUIS BAY

Bay St. Louis

Waveland

Jourdan River

Pearl River

H A N C O C K

West Pearl River

L O U I S I A N A

N

1. Port Bienville Canal
2. Mulatto Bayou
3. English Lookout
4. Grassy Island
5. Saint Joseph Point
6. Bayou Caddy
7. Henderson Point
8. Discovery Bay
9. Bayou Portage
10. Square Handkerchief Shoal

11. Tail of the Square Handkerchief
12. Pass Marianne
13. Harbor
14. Harbor
15. Smuggler's Cove
16. Little Bend
17. Bernard Bayou
18. Industrial Seaway
19. Big Lake
20. Broadwater Resort

21. Fort Massachusetts
22. Tchoutacabouffa River
23. Beauvoir
24. Goat Island
25. Big Island
26. Ott Bayou
27. Fort Point
28. Old Fort Bayou
29. Ocean Springs Harbor
30. Marsh Point

31. Dog Keys Pass
32. Davis Bayou
33. Harbor Point
34. Graveline Lake
35. Bellefontaine Point
36. Mary Walker Bayou
37. Lang Bayou
38. Bayou Chemise
39. Marsh Lake
40. Singing River Island

41. Round Island
42. McInnis Bayou
43. O'Leary Lake
44. McInnis Lake
45. Bayou Chico
46. Bayou Casotte
47. Bayou Casotte Pass
48. Spoil Island
49. Horn Island Pass
50. Point aux Chenes Bay

1

A BRIEF HISTORY OF
THE MISSISSIPPI COAST

Long before Europeans arrived on the Mississippi Gulf Coast, Native Americans inhabited the mainland shores and coastal riverbanks. In addition to the abundant game animals and plant foods they found in the inland forests, they foraged for a variety of fish, crustaceans, and shellfish in the Gulf waters. With the combined abundance of seafood and game, living off the land in this region would have been easier than in the interior to the north. These early coastal inhabitants did not confine their hunting to the mainland and made regular trips to the barrier islands in their dugout canoes. The islands, however, were probably not as desirable for permanent settlement as the mainland, due to the shortage of freshwater and the difficulty of traveling between them in unsettled weather.

Stone spear points and other tools used by the Paleo Indians have been found along the Gulf Coast, indicating that these people arrived in the region before 8,000 B.C. Many of these Paleo sites are underwater now, as the sea level along the Gulf Coast was much lower then. During the Archaic Period, from 8,000 B.C. to 500 B.C. native people lived on the Gulf Coast in large villages from the Pearl River to the Pascagoula.

Ceramic vessels and stone effigies of animals and humans found in the area date to the later Woodland Period, which lasted until about A.D. 1,000. During this time a complex religious culture emerged, with burial mounds and ceremonial areas becoming a central part of the villages. Cultivation of crops such as maize was also becoming an important part of the lifestyle of these more settled people. The last period of pre-European contact is known as the Mississippian period, and this lasted from A.D. 1,000 until February 13, 1699.

On this day everything changed for the native peoples of the Gulf Coast when the French explorers Sieur d'Iberville, Jean-Baptiste Le Moyne, and Sieur de Bienville landed on the mainland. They had come ashore from the anchorage at Ship Island, where the expedition's four ships were secured after sailing from Hispaniola with plans to establish a colony near the mouth of the Mississippi River. Spanish ships sailed this coast long before, as early as 1519, when Alonzo Pineda set out on a mapping mission to establish the limits of Florida. Another Spaniard, Cabeza de Vaca, was shipwrecked on an island in the northern gulf in 1537. He may have visited the Mississippi islands at that time, but no Spanish settlement was established.

Iberville's landfall was on the Biloxi Peninsula near Deer Island, where they found footprints and later spotted a canoe crossing to the island. Iberville followed the natives, who fled from the strangers, leaving behind an old man who was too sick to travel. When the Frenchmen fed the old man and offered him no harm, other members of the group came to meet Iberville and so began a long friendship between the people known as the Biloxis and the French.

Villages of the Biloxi, Pascagoula, and Capinan were located on the Pascagoula River. Another tribe known as the Acolipissa lived around the mouth of the Pearl River. The Biloxi Indians wore little if any clothing but did have elaborate feather headdresses, nose rings, earrings, and tattoos.

These coastal people lived in houses of mud and thatch, their villages probably more closely resembling those of the jungle tribes of Central and South America than what most people picture as typical North American Indian villages. Like present-day Native American inhabitants of Amazonia, they relied on water travel as part of their daily life, and the canoe was obviously their most important means of transportation and food gathering. The French explorers called these hollowed-out log canoes *pirouges*, a term that is still used today for a canoelike boat that is popular in the Deep South swamps.

Though the waters of the Gulf, the marshes, and the rivers provided abundant seafood, and the forests were rich in game, including deer, turkey, and buffalo, some aspects of life here must have been hard. Mosquitoes, deer flies, and swarms of tiny sand fleas must have been quite troublesome to these people at times, in the days before mosquito netting and insect repellant. When I made a couple of long river trips in Central America, where the local Indians still live in primitive villages, I remember wondering how they coped with the insect problem in open thatched huts with no walls. We carried insect-proof tents with us. Without insect screens and repellants, the only remedy these people had was to keep a smoky fire going all the time in an attempt to keep pests at bay.

Shortly after making contact with the native Biloxi people, Iberville set out on February 28 to find a large river to the west that the natives told him about. He successfully navigated the North Pass into the Mississippi River and explored upriver as far as present-day Baton Rouge.

When he returned to Biloxi Bay, he had his men build a fort on the eastern shore of the bay at present-day Ocean Springs. The fort was protected by deep natural gullies on its sides and the bay on its front. Fort Maurepas was completed on May 4, 1699, and Iberville set sail to France to report on his discoveries and to secure more men and supplies.

The men left behind at the fort further explored the coastline and the Mississippi River. The early French settlers no doubt found life on this coast challenging, but they quickly adapted to native ways and lived in similar primitive dwellings and fashioned their own canoes and larger boats for further exploration.

Iberville returned to Biloxi in January of 1700, and then again in December of 1701, each time with new colonists and supplies, further strengthening the French foothold on the Gulf Coast. The main colony was relocated to Mobile Bay, where Fort Louis was established, because of its proximity to the Spanish settlement at Pensacola. This fort soon thereafter became the site of an alliance between the French and the Choctaw and Chickasaw nations, to unite against the English.

Iberville left the coast for the last time in 1702, leaving the colonies at Biloxi, Mobile, and the Mississippi River to the command of his brother

Bienville. During this period the English took over uninhabited Dauphin Island, but this was their only threat to the French colony at the time. Bienville was later appointed official governor of the Louisiana colony, and Biloxi once again became the capital of the territory, replacing the Mobile Bay settlement. In 1720 the capital was established as "New Biloxi" and a new fort was built on the peninsula separating Biloxi Bay from the Gulf. New Biloxi was the capital for only a short time, as the rapidly growing city of New Orleans became the permanent capital in 1722.

In 1744 war broke out in Europe between France and Britain, and the consequence for the New World was a blockade of French supply ships. The inability to import manufactured trade goods made it difficult for the French to maintain their alliances with the Indians throughout North America. Many tribes invited the English to supply the goods they had come to depend on. The French and Indian War that began in 1754 finally resulted in a treaty between France and Britain in 1763. As a result of this treaty, France turned over to Britain all of Canada and territory east of the Mississippi except New Orleans. The remainder of French territory in North America, including New Orleans, went to Spain.

Present-day Mississippi south of the 31st parallel was included in the newly formed territory of British West Florida. The seat of government was established at Pensacola. The territory remained sparsely populated, and residents did not join the 1776 rebellion of the original thirteen colonies against Britain until several years after the fighting had begun. In 1779 the Spanish joined the French in opposition to Britain during the American Revolution, and this led to them defeating the British at Baton Rouge and Natchez, and later Mobile and Pensacola. Under the Treaty of Paris of 1783, which ended the American Revolution, Spain was given back its old Florida territories plus the lands of British West Florida. The Spanish governor-general of the territory established Natchez as the commercial center.

Settlers in Mississippi eventually favored a challenge to Spanish rule and in 1810 assisted Americans living in the Baton Rogue area in a revolt against the Spanish. This was followed by annexation of all the area from the Mississippi River to Pensacola into the United States. The United States did

Fort Massachusetts was built on West Ship Island in 1859 to guard the approach to New Orleans. Photo by Michelle Calvert.

not have the military strength at the time to enforce this, and the Spanish refused to cede any coastal territory. Spain retained control over coastal Mississippi until the War of 1812, when General James Wilkinson took over and occupied Mobile by force.

The British again entered Mississippi's coastal waters when they amassed a huge fleet at Ship Island in 1814. By 1815, after suffering defeat in New Orleans, the British ships were withdrawn from the Mississippi Sound, and in 1817, Mississippi was admitted as a state into the Union.

Because of the British fleet's use of the excellent natural harbor at Ship Island, American military leaders recognized the importance of fortifying this strategically located island and construction of a fort was begun in 1857. Details of the fort and its role in the Civil War are given in chapter 13, in the description of West Ship Island.

Throughout the 1800s, outbreaks of yellow fever plagued coastal areas, but especially New Orleans, which had by this time grown into a large, dirty city where rainwater stood for long periods of time, creating the perfect breeding ground for mosquitoes. Ships arriving from the Caribbean carried people already infected with the disease, and it rapidly spread in the city. Wealthier New Orleans residents began traveling by steamboat to the smaller communities of the Mississippi Gulf coast, where more regular breezes kept the mosquitoes and the heat somewhat at bay. This began a grand era of the building of mansions, hotels, and boarding houses to accommodate summer visitors and residents.

In 1849, an event took place in the Mississippi Sound off Pass Christian that began the long tradition of recreational boating on the coast and earned Pass Christian the title of "the birthplace of yachting in the South." This event was the first sailing regatta held in these waters. Twelve sailboats from different towns competed, with the *Flirt* of Biloxi winning the race.

This race led to the organization of the Southern Yacht Club that same evening in Pass Christian. The only older yacht club in the United States is the New York Yacht Club, organized in 1844. Following the lead of Pass Christian, Biloxi held its first regatta later that same summer. This led to the formation of other yacht clubs, including the Biloxi Yacht Club, Bay-Waveland Yacht Club, and the Gulfport Yacht Club. By 1919 the Gulf Yachting Association was formed and sailboat racing was firmly established on the coast. Today there are still many races held in the area, including the Gulfport to Pensacola race and the "Regatta Al Sol" from Gulfport to Isla Mujeres, Mexico.

A specialized type of sailing vessel that often participated in regattas but had its origins as a working vessel was the Biloxi schooner. Biloxi schooners evolved to suit the particular requirements of the commercial fishing industry in the Mississippi Sound. These schooners were fast under sail, could haul heavy loads, and were inexpensive to build out of locally available materials, mainly cypress and long-leaf yellow pine. They were characterized by their broad beam and shallow draft, which enabled them to work the oyster reefs and shallows of the sound.

The Biloxi schooners were continually refined and improved, becoming faster and better able to sail to windward. They averaged 45 to 50 feet in length, but some were up to 65 feet. In addition to working in the shrimp and oyster industry, some of these schooners were used to haul freight along the coast between New Orleans and Mobile.

The working rig consisted of three sails, but when the boats were used for racing, as many as six sails were set, including topsails. The schooners came to be known as the *White Winged Queens* of the Gulf Coast, and from 1888 to 1933, races would be held every Sunday afternoon during the summer months.

Today there are two full-sized replicas of the Biloxi schooners operating as charter boats on the Mississippi coast. Information about these boats and their construction is given in chapters 7 and 8.

In 1933, the Mississippi Seafood Conservation laws were changed to allow motorized boats to dredge for oysters, and the Biloxi schooners were destined for extinction as working vessels. A few of the old ones are still at work, but hardly recognizable with the masts removed and bowsprits gone.

Another major change to the commercial fishing industry of the Mississippi coast came about in the 1970s when large numbers of Vietnamese refuges moved into the area. They brought many of their traditional methods with them but quickly adapted to local conditions and built or refurbished large vessels and began a highly successful shrimping and fishing operation.

A shadier type of boating that was widespread on the Mississippi coast in the mid-1920s was rum-running. When the prohibition against liquor was enacted in 1920, every kind of alcoholic beverage imaginable began arriving by ships from Cuba and other islands in the Caribbean. The ships would lie just south of the barrier islands, beyond U.S. waters, to rendezvous with smaller power boats and fishing vessels that would take the illicit cargo and run it through the Mississippi Sound to pick-up points along the rivers and bays. More illegal alcohol entered the United States at the Gulf Coast than at any other point of entry, including Canada.

Some geographical features that were present in the Mississippi Sound in earlier days are now gone forever. Barrier islands and the shoals found in the shallow waters of the sound are in a constant state of change, as will be seen in the following chapters about each specific island. Before the 1930s, two islands existed in the present day pass between East Ship Island and

Horn Island. Today this pass is called Dog Key Pass, referring to these islands then known as the Dog Keys. The largest of the two, Dog Island, was 3 miles long and more than a quarter mile wide. Like the other barrier islands, it had high sand dunes clothed in sea oats and oleander bushes.

In 1925, local businessmen looking for a place to locate a new resort playground to attract more tourists to the area acquired Dog Island and began dredging operations to accommodate a pier and boat dock. An artesian well more than 600 feet deep was dug to provide fresh water.

Some residents warned the investors that the island was nothing more than a shifting sand key, citing old Indian legends that spoke of the island periodically disappearing beneath the waves. In 1925, however, the land was solid beneath their feet, so these businessmen were not to be deterred by local legends.

Developers built a raised pavilion large enough to house a casino, dance hall, restaurant, and bathhouses. They also built cabanas to accommodate overnight guests and installed generators to provide electrical power. The name Dog Island, deemed unsuitable for a luxury beach resort, was changed to Isle of Caprice Amusement Company.

The company ran newspaper ads announcing a formal opening on May 30, 1926. The ads promised 5½ miles of the world's finest beaches, music by the best orchestras, and splendid dining. Three converted schooners, running three times per day, provided transportation to the island. The island became so popular that a larger vessel was needed, so in 1927 the company bought and outfitted the 100-foot *Nonpareil*, a double-decked passenger ferry.

Visitors to the island enjoyed roulette wheels, dice tables and card games in the casino. Swimming marathons, concerts, and beauty contests provided family fun. The island became a magnet for pleasure seekers, and the investors' grand schemes were coming to life. For six years the island attracted visitors from all over the South. Many college fraternities and sororities, as well as other organizations, chose the resort for their annual outings. Visitors picked the sea oats on the island and used them for home decoration until it was eventually stripped bare.

By 1930, when the water rose during storms it never receded completely. The island seemed to be shrinking, but the crowds kept coming and the resort was booming.

By the end of the summer of 1931, land over much of the island was submerged, and in the fall of that year, a fire broke out and the casino and the nearby cabanas all burned. The cause of the fire was not known. By the summer of 1932, when the resort would normally be open for the season, the Isle of Caprice was gone, reclaimed by the sea. The only thing left was the pipe of the artesian well that still stood, gushing fresh water into the sea for many years after the lost island faded into memory.

2

REGIONAL WEATHER, NAVIGATION, AND SAFETY

GULF COAST WEATHER

Weather is, or should be, foremost in any boater's mind as he prepares to go to sea. Conditions that might cause a minor inconvenience or discomfort on land can ruin a boat trip, or worse, bring it to a disastrous end. Throughout the long history of seafaring, a sailor's survival depended on keeping an eye to the sky and being an expert weather forecaster. People who spend most of their lives at sea, making a living in all seasons and conditions, cannot afford to be ignorant of the natural signs that foretell a change in the weather. Some commercial fishermen and other mariners continue the traditions of the old sailors and have the long experience that this kind of understanding is built on. Most of us, however, as recreational boaters going to sea for pleasure rather than for a living, have not spent enough time on the water to learn the skills of weather predicting. As in most aspects of our modern lives, we rely perhaps too much on technology to give us the answers, and we leave the forecasting to the professional meteorologists. But even the old salts listen to the broadcast weather information, for the fact is the experts can now see bad weather coming from much farther away than was ever possible before, and as a result many lives are saved by early warnings.

To be prepared for the conditions likely to be encountered while exploring a particular region by boat, it helps to know something about the climate and the seasonal patterns that bring different weather systems. Compared to other shores of North America, the Mississippi coast is, for the most part, an area of benign weather and sea conditions. The Gulf of Mexico should never be underestimated by those going far offshore, but its size is limited compared to the Atlantic and Pacific Oceans that border our other coasts. This accounts for the fact that the swells coming into shore are smaller and surf breaking on the island beaches is not as violent as it is in places like northern California. The chain of barrier islands that makes this area so appealing to explore prevents any significant waves from reaching the mainland shores, except, of course, when hurricanes score a direct hit on the area. Water temperatures are also warmer than on the West Coast and much of the East Coast, and this makes boating safer because of the reduced risk of hypothermia.

The climate of the Mississippi coast is considered subtropical, based on its latitude, but summers can feel decidedly tropical with oppressive heat and moist, humid air sometimes stirred by light southeasterly breezes from the Gulf. Rainfall is plentiful, averaging 60 inches per year, but much of this in warm months comes in short, torrential downpours, usually accompanied by thunderstorms. These thunderstorms can be expected 70 to 80 days out of the year, from spring through fall, but most commonly in late summer.

The summer months are the time of lightest wind activity in the region, and this can be good or bad for boaters. It's good for those in small powerboats or sea kayaks, because light wind means calm seas and no headwinds to fight. The Mississippi Sound and even the open Gulf beyond the islands is sometimes as calm as a farm pond, the surface of the water like a mirror. For sailors, of course, this can be frustrating, so if your vessel is wind-powered, don't count on getting to your destination on a tight schedule in the summer months, unless you have some type of auxiliary engine, which is a good idea any time.

This general rule of light southeast winds in summer does not apply during the numerous thunderstorms that seemingly spawn out of nowhere and move through the area with unpredictable fury. These storms can sometimes

Sea kayaker Brian Nobles of Brandon about to be caught in the heavy rains of a Gulf thunderstorm

pack winds of 50 to 60 knots, along with hail, torrential rain, and raging lightning. Being caught out on the islands or in the marshes in such storms is bad enough, but being caught far out on the water with nowhere to run can be terrifying. I had no choice but to sail through line after line of these vicious squalls when I made the mistake of bringing my sailboat, *Lightning Struck*, home across the Gulf from Tampa, Florida, in the month of August. Even a 26-foot bluewater cruiser with a cabin is little comfort when the daytime sky turns black under towering clouds, lightning rains from the sky like fire, and the boat is heeled over nearly 45 degrees from the wind even with all sails furled! These storms were so big—many miles across—that I could not dodge them or run from them, but often you can get out of the path of smaller thunderstorms by being watchful and taking quick action. Though it was certainly frightening, my only real concern when caught in these storms on *Lightning Struck* was that she would live up to her name and be hit again. Her previous owner in Florida had rechristened her with this dubious name after a bolt of lightning struck the aluminum mast while she was tied up in the marina and completely fried the electrical system, melting all the wiring inside. I kept telling myself the name was lucky and would protect my little ship from being hit again, and I tried to trust the grounding ability of the piece of chain that I kept dangling over the side from the rigging. A metal chain or wire of some sort connected to the metal mast on one end and submerged in the water on the other is supposed to help reduce the potential for the electrical charge that occurs during a thunderstorm, thereby preventing the resulting strike to the charged object. Perhaps it worked. *Lightning Struck* has not been hit again—so far.

Those caught out in such a storm in a smaller boat might be in more trouble from the wind and the rough waters that result from it. Every year on the Mississippi coast, the U.S. Coast Guard rescues boaters who venture miles from land in open, unseaworthy boats and get caught in conditions that result in their vessels being overpowered and swamped by breaking waves. In the next chapter on boat choices, we will look at design considerations and discuss what makes some small boats quite seaworthy, while other, much larger vessels are suitable only for protected lakes.

Strong winds associated with summer thunderstorms can also be disastrous for those camped on the exposed barrier islands. I once made camp on East Ship Island late one afternoon in July, on a perfect sunny day with a light breeze and not a cloud in the sky. There was not a soul in sight, and I went to bed after dark thinking I was alone on the island. Around ten o'clock that night, as I tuned into a mainland radio station on my Sony Walkman, I heard a surprising weather report. The forecaster said dangerous thunderstorms were moving through the New Orleans area and heading my way. The storm was bringing 60-mile-per-hour winds that had already done damage to homes in Louisiana. I was out of my tent in a flash, cutting larger stakes from driftwood and frantically pounding them deep into the sand in an attempt to anchor my meager shelter to its unstable foundation. Then I sat and watched with helpless fascination the spectacular light show to the west that was fast bearing down on my camp. With my sea kayak and all my possessions as secure as I could make them, I crawled into the little mountain tent and hoped for the best. Howling gusts of wind flattened the tent on top of me, but it held together, and I spent a long, restless night mopping up water around my sleeping bag and listening to ground-shaking thunder. By daylight, I had fallen asleep to the sound of steady rain on the tent fly, when I heard a voice calling from somewhere out on the beach. I stuck my head out to see a man with his small son, standing drenched in the rain and looking to me as their only hope of salvation. The man asked if I had a VHF radio, which I did. He said they had been camped about a mile down the island, on the other side (which is why I had not seen them). The storm had torn their 22-foot powerboat loose from its anchor, tossing it high and dry upon the beach. I walked with them back to their camp. Their cheap dome tent had fared far worse in the storm than mine. It was now nothing more than a flattened, soggy mass of wet nylon and broken fiberglass poles. They had spent the entire night out in the open in the rain. Their heavy, outboard-powered boat would require a dozen men to move it back to the water. I radioed the Coast Guard on my handheld VHF, requesting assistance, and luckily, there was a patrol boat close to the island. The big vessel could not approach too closely, so they sent a party of men over in an inflatable. They soon had a strong winch cable connected to the grounded boat, so that the ship was able to drag it back across the sand and into the water. When I paddled back to the mainland a couple of days later, I learned that the storm did quite a bit of damage to houses and trees in Biloxi.

Chances are you can pick your days and happily explore the Mississippi coast all summer without being caught in a bad thunderstorm, so don't let the prospect of encountering one keep you on the shore. Most of these brief summer storms occur in the late afternoon, so morning hours are a good bet for short trips.

While we are on the subject of summer weather and storms, the ultimate boater's nightmare, the hurricane, must be mentioned. The official season for tropical storms and hurricanes in the Gulf and Caribbean is June through November. Statistics show that for the northern Gulf coast region, mid-September is the peak of the season, and after mid-October, chances of storms here are rare. On August 17, 1969, Hurricane Camille devastated the Mississippi Gulf coast with one of the worst storms on record. More than

Ominous clouds preceding Hurricane Isidore as seen from the deck of a sailboat secured in the Biloxi River

250 people were killed. Winds of 210 miles per hour were recorded before the instrument used to take the readings broke. The storm surge reached 25 feet above sea level.

No sane person has to be told to get off of the water when one of these storms is approaching. Thankfully, with modern storm-tracking technology, there is usually plenty of warning when a hurricane threatens the coast. Those with large, nontrailerable boats in the coastal marinas usually make a mad scramble for safer anchorages in the upper reaches of bays and estuaries as far as their draft will permit. Some stay aboard in an attempt to save their vessels as anchors drag, mooring lines snap, and other free-floating vessels become battering rams. Some of these folks live-aboard their boats and have everything they own tied up in them. It is a personal decision, but one must weigh the risk and realize that it can be a matter of life and death. Those boaters with small, trailerable boats or car-toppable kayaks should have nothing to fear from hurricanes, as there is no reason for them to be anywhere near the coast when one is coming. These megastorms are easily avoided, so for our purposes, there is no reason to dwell on them. In the aftermath of a big hurricane, there may be further difficulties for boaters, as these storms sometimes make major changes on the landscape, such as cutting barrier islands in two, as Camille did to Ship Island. These are changes that are impossible to predict, other than to say they will, at some point, occur again, as they always have.

In the fall of the year, as hurricane season passes, the occasional cold front from the west reaches the Gulf coast. Most of these fronts that do make it to the region don't bring much in the way of cold weather until late November, but they can bring thunderstorms and possibly, tornadoes. When the fronts start moving into the region, expect winds out of the north. The light south-easterlies that prevail between fronts begin to clock around to the south-west as the weather system approaches, and then shift to northwest and north. Depending on the strength of the front, these sustained north winds can blow from 10 to 30 or more knots. Small craft advisories are issued in the area when sustained wind speeds reach 18 to 33 knots. These winds can create choppy to rough conditions on the Mississippi Sound, especially on the south side near the islands, since the wind can blow unimpeded ten or more miles over open water. Near the mainland, in the lee close to shore, strong north winds and calm sea conditions can make for some exciting sailing conditions for those willing to push their boats a little toward the edge.

A note about wind speeds and direction should be made here, since forecasts can be confusing and the terminology used by sailors may be unfamiliar to new boaters. The first thing a would-be mariner should know is that when wind speed is discussed in terms of knots, it is not half-hitches, bowlines, and square knots that are being referred to. For landlubbers, wind speeds are given in terms of miles per hour, a concept that most people can easily relate to. On land, a mile is measured as 5,280 feet. This is called a statute mile. At sea, nautical miles are the accepted unit of measure. A nautical mile is just over 6,000 feet. This measure is used by mariners to simplify navigation, since one minute of latitude is equivalent to one nautical mile. A degree of latitude contains 60 minutes, or 60 nautical miles. Therefore every degree of latitude given on the chart corresponds to 60 nautical miles of distance north of the Equator.

Since a nautical mile is somewhat longer than a statute mile, wind speeds given in knots are a bit faster than speeds given in miles per hour. For example, a forecast for 30-knot wind speeds would be the same as 34 miles per hour on land. The knot is also the preferred unit of measure when discussing boat speed over the water. It is wise to become familiar with these units and get used to using them when on the water.

The wind direction given in a forecast can also be critical, not just for sailors, but for all boaters trying to determine if conditions permit going out. As mentioned, a strong north wind will result in calm conditions near the mainland, and rougher seas the farther south you go. The distance that the wind can blow over open water is referred to as fetch. So if you are out on the north side of the barrier islands, the ten or more nautical miles of fetch possible in a northerly blow can result in steep, choppy whitecaps of 3 feet or more. If you are on the south side of the islands, however, with strong sustained winds out of the south, winds blowing across more than 500 miles of fetch can result in huge swells, with breaking seas of 10 feet or more. It is this fetch that causes large surf to sometimes break on the exposed south beaches of the islands. Sailors and marine forecasters toss around terms like leeward, windward, and lee shore, frequently to the confusion of landsmen and less experienced boaters. To be in the lee of an island means to be on the safe, sheltered side, protected from the wind. The windward shore is the exposed side, such as the south side of Ship Island, when 20-knot winds are blowing in from the Gulf and 6-foot breakers are pounding the shore. This exposed side of the island would, however, be a lee shore if you were out there south of it in your boat. That's because the island is now on the lee or downwind side of your vessel, to your north. The south side of your vessel in this instance is the windward or weather side. Mariners always fear getting too near a lee shore, as this is an exposed shore downwind of their position, and without care, the vessel can be blown downwind into the surf and wrecked. Good anchorages are always in the lee of land, protected from the prevailing winds.

The wind speed and sea conditions that you can go out boating in are, to a large extent, determined by the type of boat you have and your own tolerance for discomfort. Only by experience can you learn to interpret weather forecasts so that you know just what to expect out there from the numbers given.

The cold fronts that begin moving into coastal Mississippi by late fall become more frequent and often stronger during the winter months. These stronger fronts sometimes linger in the area longer, so that the north winds associated with them last several days. Winds of longer duration blowing over a given fetch will cause rougher sea conditions since the wave heights increase steadily in the influence of sustained wind. These fronts in the winter months bring colder temperatures as well, with the thermometer sometimes dropping well below freezing, especially at night. Freezing temperatures usually don't last more than a couple of days, but combined with 20 or more knots of wind blowing over the water, these conditions can make for some miserable boating or island camping. Those who have the right gear, especially clothing to stay warm and dry while boating, may enjoy going out in such weather. Anyone seeking solitude and a wilderness experience is sure to find it by crossing to a barrier island ahead of a major front and then camping there for the duration until sea conditions permit an easy return crossing. A few of these winter cold fronts bring days of dreary gray skies and steady drizzling rain that seem like they will never end. Few campers will be happy in these conditions. Forecasters in the area are usually pretty accurate in predicting winter fronts and rain so such trip-ruining conditions can be avoided.

Thick fog can sometimes factor into winter conditions on the Mississippi coast. Usually such fog occurs in the mornings and burns off by noon. Fog, of course, severely limits visibility, making navigation more difficult, as well as making it hard to see other vessels and obstructions that might present dangers. A compass is essential on all boats that venture out in coastal waters because of this possibility. A GPS receiver is an excellent aid as well, allowing you accurately to determine your position no matter what the visibility. Many larger vessels are equipped with radar, and though expensive, these units are the ultimate safety tool for low visibility, allowing you to "see through" fog and rain and track other vessels in the vicinity.

Other than cold fronts and occasional fog and rain, winter conditions on the Mississippi coast are often fine for boating. There are usually many warm days even in December and January, with plenty of sunshine and mild winds. By keeping up with the forecasts, boaters can avoid the worst winter days and enjoy getting out on the water year round.

Despite the many fine boating days available in winter, many boaters on the coast don't go out during these months, and marinas crowded with unused vessels don't see much activity until spring arrives. People start thinking about the water again by March and especially April, and boat sales are brisk from then until about the end of May. Strong cold fronts continue to pass through the area in March and April, bringing thunderstorms and sometimes tornados. By April these fronts don't drop the temperatures that much, and between the fronts the light southeast winds of summer prevail over the region.

NAVIGATION

Being able to find your way to where you are going and then back home again is a concern that ranks a close second behind getting caught out on the water in bad weather. Beginning boaters, especially, might worry more about this until they have confidence in their navigation skills. Navigating across open water is a bit more involved than, say, making your way around the shore of a small, inland lake, or following a stream from the put-in point at a bridge to the take-out at a boat ramp.

On clear, good-visibility days, you will be within sight of some land almost anywhere in the Mississippi Sound. Though the barrier island you are heading toward may be out of sight as you leave the mainland, on a 10- or 12-mile crossing you will see it before you lose sight of the land you left. Even so, the wide-open spaces can make it difficult to tell where you are in reference to the distant land you can see. Especially when you're traveling at the slower speeds of a kayak or sailboat, it may seem as if you are making no progress at all in relation to the land. From several miles out, the shoreline will all look the same, unless you know specific landmarks to look for from local knowledge or from nautical charts of the area.

Since a complete discussion of navigation would fill an entire book this size, it is not my intention to teach navigation here. Those boaters not already adept at this necessary skill should refer to the books on the subject that I have listed in the appendix. My purpose here is to stress the importance of navigational skills and to look briefly at navigation methods and equipment. Learning navigation is a straightforward process, so there is little reason for anyone traveling along this or any other coast not to know his or her location at all times. This is imperative for safe boating.

Keeping track of where you are is simple if you know the basics of piloting and dead reckoning. Piloting is the formal name for the usual way of getting around—using known landmarks for references. When you're boating, this means finding your position using charted landmarks. Having the proper nautical chart on board is the first step in navigation. Nautical charts are maps designed specifically for marine navigation. They show water depths, shoreline composition, obstructions and underwater hazards, and navigation aids such as lights, buoys, and daybeacons. Also shown is the direction that compasses point to in the charted area and other aids to navigation such as buildings and towers on the shore that may be used as landmarks. Latitude is given in the left and right margins and longitude at the top and bottom margins. Distance between any two points on the chart may be found by measuring with the latitude scale, remembering that one minute of latitude equals one nautical mile, or approximately 6,000 feet. There are detailed charts available for every section of the Mississippi coast and its islands and estuaries. A list of available charts and a description of the area each covers is listed in the appendix.

When piloting with charts, you know where you are on the chart anytime you pass close to a buoy or other landmark on the chart. When well away from landmarks, however, it's not as simple to pinpoint your position on the chart just by looking. To find position with only one distant landmark in sight requires a compass direction to the landmark and a measurement of how far away it is. If you can identify two landmarks on the chart that are in different directions from your present location, you can accurately determine your position on the chart by taking compass bearings to each landmark. Your position is the point where these two bearing lines intersect on the chart.

If no identifiable landmarks are in sight, position must be found using the procedure known as dead reckoning. This is not just guessing, but rather a way of figuring position from speed and time elapsed. To navigate by dead reckoning, a present position is deduced from the distance and direction traveled away from a known location. For example, suppose you start out for East Ship Island, traveling due south from the mainland, and it starts to rain when you are halfway across, so that you can no longer see the island or the mainland. There should be no problem if you have been keeping up with the time you have traveled, your average speed, and your compass heading. Knowing your speed to be, say ten knots (ten nautical miles per hour), and the elapsed time to be 30 minutes, you can deduce that you have traveled five nautical miles south of your starting point. From the measured distance on the chart, you know that East Ship Island is another 5 miles to the south. At the present speed, maintaining the same compass course, you will arrive at the island in 30 more minutes. For short crossings such as this, dead reckoning is quite accurate. When the distance between known landmarks increases, the potential for error increases because of other factors like cross currents that might be imperceptibly moving your vessel at an angle away from your destination.

For these longer crossings, it is necessary to back up dead reckoning deductions with other methods of position finding. Until recent technological developments, this meant celestial navigation, which is a method of determining position by taking sightings of celestial bodies with an instrument known as a sextant. The sextant is used to measure the angle between the sun at noon and the horizon, or at night the angle between certain stars and the horizon. Then, through a series of complicated mathematic deductions using a nautical almanac, a position fix can be pinpointed. This method is still used for ocean navigation, especially as a back up for those venturing far offshore. While interesting to study, celestial navigation is not much use for coastal navigation in areas such as those covered in this book, as the sextant fix can be off by a mile or more due to operator error, and overcast skies or rain may make taking the sight impossible anyway.

Radio direction finders and LORAN (Long-Range Aid to Navigation) receivers were commonly used in coastal navigation until recently. Both of these methods used radio signals from land-based towers to provide an identifiable reference for boaters within range. Range was the major limiting factor, and signal coverage was limited to areas that had the necessary network of towers and transmitters in place.

Today precise navigation is as simple as pushing the keypad of an electronic device as small as a compact cell phone. This miraculous device is the GPS (Global Positioning System) receiver. The Global Positioning System is a network of satellites that are in geosynchronous orbit above the earth's surface. This means that each satellite is placed at the exact altitude so that it remains stationary over a fixed point on earth, even though the earth is rotating. Each of these satellites transmits to earth a powerful signal that can be received by the handheld unit that you carry on your boat. The computer built into the receiver unit works out the exact location of the receiver by triangulating the signals of three or more of these geosynchronous satellites, which are received simultaneously. This is the same principle as you use in piloting by taking visual compass bearings to two or more charted landmarks and plotting your position by drawing these bearing lines until they intersect. The GPS is the intersect point for multiple bearings coming directly from the satellites in space. The entire process is practically instantaneous. Position is given on the unit's digital display in degrees, minutes, and seconds of latitude and longitude. The position fix is being continuously updated as long as the receiver is working, so that if you are using the unit in a moving boat, you can watch as your latitude and longitude change and your average speed is displayed. If your boat is moving, your present compass heading is also displayed. Pre-set points called waypoints can be programmed into the unit using the latitude and longitude of any location on a chart. If, for example, your destination is the west tip of Horn Island, you can obtain the latitude and longitude for this point by measuring from the chart, then enter this data into the GPS unit to create a waypoint. Most units can store hundreds of waypoints, which can be named for easy identification. Now when you are cruising along in your boat with the GPS constantly updating your present position, it is also giving you a constantly corrected bearing and distance to the waypoint that you have selected, in this case, the west tip of Horn Island. Along with your average speed information, an estimated time of arrival is also given. Positional accuracy is within a few meters.

Basic units that can perform all the above functions are now priced as low as $100. When the technology was first made available to the public, the same unit was around $3,000, a bit steep for most casual boaters. At today's prices, anyone who ventures out in open water or in confusing marshes and swamps should consider investing in a GPS. The new units are small and rugged enough even for kayakers and canoeists, and most operate on disposable batteries so an on-board charging system is not necessary. More expensive and sophisticated units eliminate the need for carrying paper charts altogether by using electronic charts that are available on CD-ROM or special cartridges. These units have high-resolution screens that display the charts and your position on the screen, so that you can actually see your boat as a moving blip passing by the landmarks on the chart as if you were watching it from a bird's-eye view. It would be quite difficult to get lost with this sort of technology. Even so, GPS users should remember that electronic devices can fail or be dropped overboard and ruined, so basic piloting and dead reckoning navigation should always be practiced as a backup on any trip.

Keeping track of where you are at all times and being able to find your destination are the most obvious reasons to develop good navigation skills. Equally important is knowing how to navigate in the presence of other marine traffic. In a busy area like the Mississippi Sound, you cannot travel far by boat without coming into close proximity to other vessels, ranging from ships, tugs and barges, and commercial fishing boats to other recreational craft from yachts on down in size to jet skis. Close encounters with other vessels while on the water are always potentially hazardous because of the possibility of collision. To avoid collisions and embarrassing maneuvers that mark you as a landlubber to professional mariners, it is necessary to have an

The author steers his sailboat, Intensity, through the channel of an opening drawbridge.

understanding of the laws that govern the interactions of all vessels, known collectively as the "Rules of the Road." These rules are federal regulations similar to highway regulations in that they specify which vessel has the right of way in certain traffic situations common in busy waters.

The rules are detailed in the Coast Guard publication called *Navigation Rules* and in other general boating books such as *The Annapolis Book of Seamanship*. On any sunny weekend in Mississippi's coastal waters or practically anywhere else, it is common to see a large percentage of the boaters on the water flagrantly violating the Rules of the Road. The main reason for this is that most of these violators are ignorant of the rules and probably even of the fact that they exist. Since there is no licensing requirement for recreational boaters in Mississippi and most other states, anyone who has the money can go out and buy a high-performance powerboat or personal watercraft can take off across the water. Many people are attracted to boating in the first place by the obvious freedom that taking to the water represents, and since there are no stop signs, red lights, or marked traffic lanes, some assume this means they can do whatever they please. Others know about the rules but ignore them anyway, thinking that the risk of being caught by the Marine Patrol or Coast Guard is slim. Boaters should be aware, however, that if they do get caught, the fines for negligent action that endangers life or property can amount to thousands of dollars and may include imprisonment. Ignorance of the Rules of the Road is no excuse. Boaters should be knowledgeable of the rules that apply to their type of vessel, as many of these rules are specific regarding right-of-way issues in various situations for vessels under power, under sail, or limited in maneuverability. A number of these rules that apply to recreational boaters pertain to situations where they might impede or endanger larger, commercial vessels that are restricted to deep-water channels and require much more room to stop or change course. Though in certain situations the recreational boater may technically have the right of way, this matters little if he is run down by a 100-ton tow. Recreational boaters, especially those in small, hard-to-see vessels such as kayaks and personal watercraft, should be aware that they may not even be visible to the captains of larger craft who rely mainly on radar to alert them to the presence of other vessels.

The issue of visibilty to other vessels becomes even more important for those boaters operating at night. Anytime you venture out on the water, you should be prepared for nighttime navigation, as any number of factors such as the weather or mechanical difficulties can delay your return from a day trip. There are detailed U.S. Coast Guard regulations for navigation lights that specify which lights are required to be shown for different sizes and types of vessels. These light requirements are different depending on whether the vessel is moving under power, moving under sail, or lying at anchor. These different lighting configurations make it obvious whether a distant vessel is moving toward the observer, away from him, or across his path to the left or right. Without this system, it is difficult to avoid collisions at night, as it is surprisingly hard to tell if a large vessel is even moving in the darkness. The smallest vessels, such as kayaks and daysailors, are exempt from the requirement of carrying navigation lights but are required to carry a bright, handheld lantern or flashlight that can be used to alert other vessels of their presence.

VESSEL SAFETY EQUIPMENT

In addition to navigation gear such as charts, compass, GPS, and proper lighting, there is a list of Coast Guard-required safety gear that must be carried on board, and many other items not required but that should be considered by the prudent mariner. Anyone venturing far from land should remember that the sea is an unforgiving environment and should never be taken lightly, even by experienced mariners. Chances are, nothing will go wrong during your offshore adventures, but when things do go wrong, the problems can quickly compound and turn into disasters, so every trip should begin with preparations for the worst-case scenario. Much of this preparation simply involves having the right safety gear on board and knowing how to use it.

Staying afloat is the number one priority when out at sea, and doing so in your boat is the preferred method. This means having a seaworthy vessel in the first place, then the knowledge to stay out of dangerous weather situations and to navigate clear of situations that could cause structural damage and sinking. If the worst should happen and you find yourself in the water with no boat, staying afloat is much easier with a proper PFD (personal flotation device). This is why the Coast Guard requires that a wearable flotation device for each person on the boat must be on board at all times. While it is not required by law that the occupants actually be wearing these PFDs, they will do little good if you should suddenly find yourself in the water without one on. The boat does not have to sink for this to happen. Falling overboard is another distinct possibility. This can be especially bad if you happen to be boating alone. In this case, especially aboard sailboats, which require a good bit of moving about to operate, a safety harness and tether become even more important than a PFD. If the sail control lines are cleated fast and the boat is under way, a solo sailor who accidentally falls overboard can do nothing but tread water as he watches his vessel vanish over the horizon. While kayaking in the U.S. Virgin Islands many years ago, I met a yachtsman who was lucky enough to have survived just such an incident. He had left Puerto Rico in good conditions, sailing east to St. Thomas, a passage of about 35 miles. Midway across, he had fallen overboard and had watched helplessly as his 40-foot sailboat continued on her course. This particular passage is exposed to the open Caribbean Sea to the south and the Atlantic Ocean to the north. The water is thousands of feet deep there, and the only thing that saved this sailor from certain death was a granite pinnacle three miles away that juts from the ocean like a giant shark's tooth. He was able to swim to this isolated rock, thanks to his good physical conditioning, but the smooth cliffs offered no place to climb out of the sea, so he had to cling there for a day and a night until he was rescued by a passing boat. His sailboat turned up two months later off the coast of Scotland.

Falling overboard even in the Mississippi Sound can have equally serious consequences, especially if you are alone, in bad weather, or navigating at night. Staying on board your vessel is therefore a prerequisite to safe boating, and you should take every measure possible to make this easier, including installing safety rails or lifelines and nonskid surfaces on the decks.

In addition to wearable PFDs for each person on board, the Coast Guard requires boats over 16 feet in length to carry at least one throwable Type IV PFD to assist a person who has fallen overboard until he or she can be rescued. Some of the better devices of this type include a man-overboard pole that floats in an upright position and features a highly visible flag several feet above the water. This makes it much easier to find a person in the water while the crew is attempting to turn the vessel around and go back for a rescue. It can be extremely hard to find someone even a short distance from the boat in rough sea conditions and breaking waves. For nighttime boating an additional safety device is a compact waterproof strobe light that is attached to an armband or directly to the PFD. These lights are highly visible and should be worn by everyone on board while under way at night. Each PFD should also include an attached whistle, which can serve as an audible aid to searchers looking for a person in the water.

All vessels operating in coastal waters are required to carry visual distress signals, including a minimum of three pyrotechnic flares suitable for day or night use. For day use the distress signals also include orange smoke devices, red marker dye to put in the water to aid aerial searchers, and an orange distress flag. For night use, a high intensity white light flashing at regular intervals is considered a distress signal. All of these visual distress signals are only useful if someone happens to see them when you are using them. Flares reach high altitudes and are visible from quite a distance, but last only a few seconds, so care must be taken not to waste your supply when no other vessels are near. They can certainly be a lifesaver, though, as I learned firsthand while sea kayaking in the Caribbean. I had landed and made camp for the night on an isolated beach on the island of Culebra, which is about 18 miles east of Puerto Rico. The sun was setting as I cooked rice on my campstove and stared out to sea while resting from an exhausting day of paddling against the tradewinds. Suddenly, from out of the sea, a bright red stream of light climbed in a high arc and disappeared in a matter of seconds. I knew it was a flare, and it obviously originated from a boat several miles away in the passage between the islands. I knew I wouldn't be able to help anyone that was in trouble with just my single-seater kayak. I ran a couple of miles down the beach to the only other people in sight, a group of Puerto Rican guys who had set up a tent and settled in for a night of beer drinking and fishing. They had a seaworthy open powerboat with dual outboards, and we all jumped in and sped off in the direction I had seen the flare. Sure enough, there was a boat out there in trouble. It was an open fishing boat occupied by a young couple clad in bathing suits and equipped with nothing but an ice chest and a picnic lunch. They had set out from Puerto Rico on a day trip, and their outboard motor had failed midway in the open ocean passage, leaving them adrift in six thousand feet of water where it was impossible to anchor. They had no radio, no shelter from the tropical sun, little food and water, and had used all three of their emergency flares. They were lucky I had seen one of them. The current would have carried them north into the Atlantic, but they seemed oblivious to the danger, and seemed to take it for granted that someone would come out and tow them to safety, which we did.

In much shallower waters such as the Mississippi Sound, which averages only ten feet deep, anyone in a similar predicament would be able to at least stop the vessel's drift by anchoring. This would make it much easier to be found by searchers while preventing the possibility of being swept out to the open Gulf. At least one and preferably two anchors and lines matched to the size of your boat should be considered essential safety gear and should always be on board.

One of the major blunders this young couple from Puerto Rico committed was setting out on such a major passage with no VHF radio on board. A VHF marine radio should be considered essential for anyone boating in coastal waters. These are two-way radios that can be used to communicate with other vessels, the Coast Guard, or the marine operator to make telephone calls. They are useful not only in emergencies but to communicate with other vessels about traffic situations and other navigational concerns. These radios also include channels for continuous, 24-hour-a-day weather forecasts. Most boats with charging systems on board will be equipped with more powerful fixed-mount VHF radios and antennae for maximum transmitting range. On smaller craft, the handheld VHF units are the way to go. These function the same as the fixed units, and most are rugged and waterproof enough to use even in kayaks and personal watercraft.

Another means of communicating in coastal waters that has become recently available is the cellular telephone. Most of the areas described in this book are near enough to shore to be under excellent coverage by the cellular tower network, so boaters can enjoy the convenience of calling anyone they wish directly, or calling the Coast Guard in emergencies. Even so, VHF radios are still the preferred means of marine communication, and should still be on board regardless of whether you have a cell phone.

Another emergency communication device to consider is the class C EPIRB (Emergency Position Indicator Radio Beacon) transmitter. This device transmits a one-way distress signal upon activation that is monitored by the Coast Guard and other vessels on VHF channel 15. The signal can be tracked by the Coast Guard to your position and is useful as a backup to VHF or in situations where you may be unable to communicate your position. Many of these units are activated automatically by immersion in water, such as would happen if your vessel sinks. Other safety gear essential to have on board is a means of removing water quickly in a situation where your boat may be taking on water and in danger of sinking. On small boats, this may be as simple as a handheld bailer or bucket to scoop the water out. A bilge pump may be more practical on decked boats or deep-bilged boats where access to the water is difficult. Most larger boats will be equipped with electric bilge pumps, but these should always be backed up with manually operated pumps.

A fire on board a boat at sea can be as serious as taking on water and sinking. The Coast Guard requires fire extinguishers on board all vessels with any of the following: inboard engines, closed compartments where portable fuel tanks may be stored, double bottoms not completely filled with floatation materials, closed living spaces, or permanently installed fuel tanks.

Several other items can greatly contribute to your comfort and safety on a boat trip, especially if things go wrong and plans get changed. A first-aid kit should always be on board to handle unexpected injuries and should include such items as motion-sickness preventatives. Extra food and water should always be carried by those venturing out to remote areas such as the barrier islands. I learned this the hard way once when I kayaked to Petit Bois Island with just enough food to camp one night and got stormbound there for four days. It was in the winter, so I was all alone on the island and got pretty hungry, but I did have extra fresh water. Boaters should be aware that there is no fresh water available on the uninhabited barrier islands, so it is essential to bring plenty, especially in hot weather. Foul weather gear and sun protection are other necessities to have on board. The young couple adrift off of Puerto Rico in nothing but their bathing suits would have been in serious trouble after a day or more of exposure to the tropical sun. In the summer months, the heat in Mississippi can be equally disabling and dangerous, so sunscreen, adequate clothing, and a good hat are essential. In colder weather, good foul weather gear is necessary to stay warm and dry and reduce the risk of hypothermia.

Dealing with the weather, navigating, and staying safe while boating all boil down to preparation and knowledge. Knowledge is gained through experience and from reading about the experiences of others. Preparation is half the fun of boating, and studying the charts, going through your gear, and working on your boat while planning your next voyage can occupy many enjoyable hours when you cannot be out on the water. Successfully completing the planned voyage will result in a great feeling of accomplishment. Every mariner should strive to be as competent and self-reliant as possible. Don't make the mistake so many beginning boaters do and assume that you can just call the Coast Guard when things go wrong because of your lack of preparation or knowledge. Their job is hard enough as it is, and they shouldn't be bothered except by those in a real crisis and as a last resort.

The sea is indifferent to our insignificant passages, and its power can be awesome, but if we learn as much about it as possible and always have a respect for this power, then even those of us who venture out in small boats have nothing to fear.

3

BOATS

Many of the best places described in this guidebook cannot be reached without some sort of boat. Almost any boat will do on the protected waters of some of the bayous and rivers, but to reach the barrier islands that lie across the Mississippi Sound, a seaworthy vessel is required. The spectrum of pleasure boat types that are available is so vast that this alone is the subject of countless books, as well as an array of specialty magazines. For many, boat ownership is a passion and an end in itself that becomes much more than just a means of water transportation. Most of these boaters are not satisfied with just one boat or even one type of boat, but may own and use many different kinds of vessels over a lifetime of waterborne recreation.

In this chapter I will attempt to help those readers who want to get into boating but may not be sure where to start. I will describe boats that are suitable for use in these waters and compare the advantages and disadvantages of each. All of us who are experienced with boats know that every boat is a compromise, and there is no one perfect vessel for every need, situation, and place. Therefore we will examine the merits of many types, from the simplest paddle-propelled kayaks to the complex and expensive offshore power cruisers. Hopefully, the information provided here will help some would-be mariners to make an informed decision and find the right vessel to get out and experience the pleasures of navigating to unfamiliar and new shores.

The boats described here are grouped into three categories: human-powered vessels, such as sea kayaks and rowing craft, sailing vessels, and those vessels driven by internal-combustion engines, known collectively as powerboats. From these three groups, there should be a boat to fit every age, taste, and budget.

SEA KAYAKS, CANOES, AND ROWING CRAFT

If simplicity is your style, watercraft that rely on muscle power as their primary means of propulsion will certainly appeal to you. These boats, while small and generally less expensive than sail or powerboats, are still quite capable vessels worthy of serious consideration. Some of these, especially sea kayaks, are in many ways more able than larger craft, especially in extreme conditions that would keep most mariners in port. Kayaks and canoes have been around much longer than any other type of watercraft. With the materials that nature provided, primitive native people fashioned themselves a means of taking to the water in order to claim new territory and to aid in the never-ending search for food. Over thousands of years, the designs were perfected and constantly put to the test. Now these simple designs are executed in space-age materials—kevlar, fiberglass, and wood composites—the main advantage being durability and simplicity of mass production rather than any improvement in design or concept. It is easy to dismiss these simple boats as toys or day boats for an afternoon paddle on the lake, but nothing could be farther from the truth.

Sea kayakers have successfully completed major expeditions in some of the most hostile coastal and ocean environments of the globe, including rounding Cape Horn and circumnavigating most of the world's large islands and even the continent of Australia. Kayakers have crossed the North Atlantic and the Gulf of Mexico, among other seemingly impossible blue-water passages. There is no other boat more seaworthy and yet so simple. This is a vessel that you almost wear, rather than ride on or in. It is an extension of your body that allows you to take to the sea and move though the waves as easily as you would walk on land. It is the only vessel ever designed which

The author in a fully-loaded sea kayak equipped for expedition paddling.
Photo by Pete Hill.

you can cross an ocean in and then, when you're done, pick up and carry away with one hand.

A sea kayak is the ultimate escape vehicle. Like a magic carpet, a kayak allows one to glide in silence and with little effort over water—whether quiet stream or open ocean. When you slip into the cockpit and seal the sprayskirt, you are no longer a shore-bound, two-legged creature that must follow paths and roads. You are free to go anywhere that water flows, and given enough time, you can reach the farthest horizon. It costs nothing but a little muscle energy to operate, a steady paddle stroke that, with experience, is as easy as walking, and much more relaxing.

In recent years, sea kayaking has been one of the fastest growing segments of the watercraft industry worldwide. As a result many new types of kayaks have been designed and manufactured for a wide variety of uses. These kayaks range in price from a few hundred dollars for the simplest sit-on-top models to more than five thousand dollars for some of the touring models built of high-tech materials. Regardless of cost, for what they are capable of, sea kayaks represent the most boat for the money of any type of watercraft on the market, and their simplicity and rugged durability means little if any maintenance is required.

Many readers unfamiliar with sea kayaking may think of the short, highly maneuverable river kayaks they have seen shooting the rapids and plunging over waterfalls on television. Some paddlers do use this type of boat to play in surf zones, but most sea kayaks are specifically designed to paddle for longer distances with less effort, and to track in a straight line on open water. This requires a longer hull than that typical of river kayaks. Sea kayaks are now generally divided between two types—those with an open cockpit, known as sit-on-tops—and the more traditional decked boats. In these enclosed kayaks, you slide down into the cockpit and then seal yourself in by means of a sprayskirt that fits around the waist and seals to the boat to keep water out.

Sit-on-tops are the easiest kayaks for beginners to paddle. Little special equipment is needed. You just climb on and sit in the molded cockpit and start paddling. These boats are mainly used for casual day paddling close to shore, and are popular as rental boats because they are so user-friendly. Some of the larger models have seats for two paddlers, and some have watertight storage compartments in the bow and stern like the more serious touring kayaks. Sit-on-tops are favored by some expert paddlers who like to surf big waves with them, as there is no cockpit to flood in a capsize. The main disadvantage of the sit-on-top kayaks is that they offer little protection from the elements. These boats are best used in warm weather and warm water, as those who paddle them will be wet from spray and chop and totally exposed to rain and cold wind. The hull designs of most sit-on-tops also make them slower than good touring kayaks, and the wider beam makes them somewhat more difficult to paddle for long periods of time. Overall, sit-on-tops are good for casual paddling off the beach, exploring a lazy bayou, fishing, or for fitness paddling, which is also quite popular. What these kayaks are not as suitable for are long, multiday tours such as a kayak trip to the barrier islands would entail.

For an entry-level boat that can be taken out in choppy seas, the sit-on-top is about the cheapest boat you can buy. They start at around $300 and even the best ones are rarely up to $1,000. I have a 9-foot model I paid $300 for that fits nicely on the deck of my cruising sailboat. This kayak is a useful addition to the regular dinghy and can be used by one person for trips to the beach, or just to get off the boat to explore and get some exercise. I tow it astern on a long line during offshore passages as a last-ditch rescue aid that might be grabbed by anyone unlucky enough to go overboard.

The other type of sea kayak, the touring kayak, is the modern derivative of the traditional sealskin kayaks developed by the Eskimo people of the far north. The original Eskimo kayaks were always long and extremely narrow in beam for their length. Most modern touring kayaks are designed with a little more beam to increase load-carrying capability. A typical single-seater touring kayak will be 17 feet long with a maximum beam of 24 inches. A kayak this size will have the capacity to carry a solo paddler along with camping gear and a week's supply of food and water. Other kayaks will vary these dimensions, some in favor of fast day trips without as much gear, and others designed to carry loads for major expeditions of a month or more. There are also tandem-decked kayaks for two paddlers, and a few companies even market three-seaters.

A touring kayak set up for sea use typically has watertight bulkheads fore and aft of the cockpit area. These essentially divide the boat into three compartments, making it much safer for open water use since the boat cannot sink unless all three compartments become flooded, which is highly unlikely. The spaces fore and aft are used to store gear and supplies, and these are accessed through watertight hatches on the deck. When the paddler seals the spayskirt around the cockpit coaming, this area also becomes watertight. The kayak is now totally sealed against intruding water, and even loaded with gear the hull is designed with immense reserve buoyancy. This allows kayakers to paddle through breaking surf with no problems. The whole boat may be temporarily buried under an avalanche of whitewater in a wave crest, but handled correctly, it always resurfaces on the other side, with the cargo inside staying secure and dry.

Sea kayaks are designed to ride low in the water and the decks are low to minimize the effects of strong headwinds and crosswinds that are frequently encountered on open water. Some designs track well in beam winds without a tendency to turn upwind, but many paddlers prefer a foot-controlled rudder mounted on the stern. This is not used so much to turn the boat as to keep it tracking straight in winds and seas that would tend to turn it off course. By using a rudder the paddler can focus all the energy put into the paddle stroke on forward motion, rather than having to waste effort correcting the boat's heading with the paddle.

Those who paddle a sit-on-top kayak for casual day use will require little special equipment. A double-ended kayak paddle and a life jacket or PFD are the main items required. Touring kayakers will eventually accumulate quite a collection of specialized gear. In addition to the paddle and PFD, a sprayskirt to seal the cockpit is needed. A spare paddle that breaks down in two pieces and can be carried on the deck is always a good idea. With a decked kayak, a paddle float device is also required in the event of a capsize. This is an inflatable float that fits over one end of the paddle so that it can be used as an outrigger to stabilize the kayak and allow the paddler to climb back into the cockpit from the water. Most sea kayaks are far too unstable to reenter from the water without this essential safety aid. A hand-operated bilge pump must also be carried to pump out the flooded cockpit after reentry. Other safety items include a loud distress whistle, a set of aerial flares, and a handheld VHF marine radio. Serious paddlers will usually install a deck-mounted compass on their kayaks where it can be easily seen and read in the roughest conditions, and most will carry a handheld GPS receiver for navigation.

Packing a touring kayak for an expedition is an art in itself. John Dowd, who is perhaps one of the most experienced long-distance kayakers in the world, says that "sea kayaking has infinite potential for those who like putting things into small bags and sealing them tightly". This is exactly what is required if you expect to arrive at your destination with gear and supplies dry. Even though the watertight hatches on most good kayaks are reliable, they should never be trusted without the backup of waterproof bags. I once loaned a sea kayak to a photographer acquaintance who casually put more than $1,000 worth of gear into the rear compartment without a second thought. When he opened the hatch at our lunch stop, his camera and lens were awash in a puddle of water. Always use plastic bags inside the storage compartments. Zipper seal bags are great for small items. A variety of purpose-made high-quality dry bags are sold at kayaking and camping stores for large items such as sleeping bags, clothing, and food.

I found it possible to travel for months at a time with the gear that I could fit into a 17-foot touring kayak. The key is to sort out what you really need from the things you might bring without a second thought in a bigger boat. The essentials for island camping are discussed in the next chapter. In the appendix at the end of the book, you will find my gear checklist for kayak touring. Travel by kayak is not difficult, but successful trips do require planning.

Anyone who is new to kayaking should attend at least one instructive course to learn the basic self-rescue techniques, such as how to reenter the kayak from the water after a capsize. A competent instructor can quickly show you how to maximize the efficiency of your paddle stroke, how to maneuver, and how to brace with the paddle to negotiate large waves. Information on where to find such instruction is included in the appendix on resources.

Kayaks are not the only human-powered boats to consider if you want to get some healthy exercise while exploring coastal waterways. While open canoes are not generally suitable for long, open-water crossings such as a trip the barrier islands, they are more capable than many people think. If a canoe is the only kind of boat you have access to, you can still reach many of the places described in this book, especially the more protected bays, rivers, and bayous. Some canoes are capable of handling open water and rough chop as well, if equipped with sufficient floatation in the form of air bags or sealed compartments to prevent swamping or sinking. Canoes vary in design almost as much as kayaks, but for most of the waters in this book, there are a few general qualities to look for in a canoe. Most of these waters have little if any current and are not as twisty or obstructed as smaller inland canoeing streams. There are also powerboat wakes to consider, even in areas where wind-driven waves might not be a factor. The best canoes for this type of paddling are long and narrow, which means they can be easily driven over still water or against headwinds. This type of canoe should have

A decked canoe on the beach at Deer Island

adequate freeboard to prevent choppy waves from filling it easily, but the ends should not be too upswept, as they can act as a sail and make it difficult to paddle a straight course in windy conditions. Canoes that are designed for the open lakes of the far north, along the lines of traditional Native American canoes, are the best type to consider for paddling coastal waters.

To get anywhere on open water paddling a canoe, you will have to become proficient in at least one basic correction stroke. This is a paddle stroke that allows you to paddle continuously on one side of the boat, rather than inefficiently switching sides as most casual river paddlers do. To learn this stroke, seek the guidance of an instructor or experienced canoeist, or learn on your own from a good book on the subject. Ernest Herndon describes the basics and provides a wealth of other information about canoes in his guidebook, *Canoeing Mississippi*.

The last category of human-powered boats we will consider are boats that are propelled by rowing with oars. This is completely different from paddling canoes or kayaks, as the rower faces backwards and propels the boat by pulling on an identical pair of oars fixed to the gunwales of the craft by

An 8-foot rowing dinghy ashore on Cat Island

oarlocks. Though not commonly seen these days on the coast of Mississippi, rowing vessels were prominent on the waterfront before the widespread use of outboard motors on small skiffs. Rowing is not as difficult as it may appear, and good rowing craft are capable of long voyages and of handing rough water, almost as well as sea kayaks. The late Ocean Springs artist Walter Inglis Anderson used row to Horn Island regularly in a 12-foot open boat. He also rowed to Chandeleur Island, which is nearly 25 miles offshore from the Mississippi coast. On the deck of my 26-foot sailboat, I carry a rowing dinghy that is 7 feet, 9 inches long and less than 4 feet wide. This tiny dinghy can easily carry 3 adults and their duffle bags to and from shore from the anchored sailboat. I have often rowed it for miles, exploring shallow waters off limits to the sailboat when in a new anchorage. I would feel confident in rowing this dinghy from the mainland to the barrier islands, and the trip would probably take only a little longer than it would in a sea kayak. Peter Tangvald, a famous world-voyaging sailor I met many years ago in Puerto Rico, once survived a sinking sailboat in a similar 7-foot-long dinghy. A hundred miles east of Barbados, in the open Atlantic Ocean, his sailboat struck some floating object and was holed, leaving him to row this entire distance in the dinghy. It is the hull design and light weight that makes such a small dinghy so seaworthy. These boats simply bob over large breaking waves like a cork, the flare of the hull's sides causing them to slide down wave faces rather than flip upside down. I usually carry mine on the deck of my sailboat when offshore, but I have towed it in rough seas, even in the open Atlantic, with no problems.

Like canoes, longer rowboats are faster and more efficient. My brother, Jeff, built a 15-foot wooden rowboat that is also less than 4 feet wide, and it is much easier to row and tracks straighter than my shorter dinghy. Rowing shells are even more efficient and can easily outpace sea kayaks when propelled by experienced athletes. Shells are limited to fitness rowing and racing however, as they don't have any storage space for cruising gear.

SAILBOATS

Kayakers find their thrill in the simplicity of their craft and in gliding silently over the water using nothing but their own muscle power. Sailors, however, get their pleasures from harnessing the wind and skimming effortlessly over the waves in what is perhaps the most romantic form of water travel.

Paddlers or powerboaters usually take to the water with a destination in mind, and steer that course until they reach it. Sailing is different. Often, just being under way on a good reach is satisfaction enough, and consequently, on a breezy day, one often sees many sailboats of all sizes tacking back and forth on the waters of the Mississippi Sound. Some go to the islands or the offshore waters beyond, but many just cruise back and forth along the beach.

The variety of sailboat types is seemingly infinite when compared to simpler boats like kayaks. Sailing has been around for thousands of years, and as a result, a wide variety of sail craft has evolved to suit different purposes. Beginners who would like to get started in sailing might be put off by the apparent complexity of it, as I was for years when kayaks were the only boats I was interested in. Anyone can become a sailor, however. There are

The author sailing his hand-built 19-foot outrigger canoe, <u>Seldom Seen</u>

hundreds of books in print on every aspect of sailboats and sailing, and some of the better ones are listed in the back of this book.

The types of sailboats can first be sorted out by the number of hulls that they have. The most popular and common are the monohulls, which are conventional boats with just one hull like a powerboat or a kayak. Multihull sailboats include catamarans and trimarans, with two or three separate hulls, respectively.

Small monohull sailboats are the simplest and least expensive for the beginner to get into and learn the principles of sailing. Few are as simple as the ubiquitous Sunfish, or the newer Hobie Escape. These are the most basic dayboats, with a shallow, planing hull to carry the skipper and maybe one crew. Such boats are excellent vehicles in which to learn the intricacies of sailing maneuvers such as coming about, which is a way of changing direction by either tacking or jibing. These boats are good for experiencing the pure joys of sailing off the beach on a windy day, but there are other small sailboats that are quite capable of exploring farther afield and carrying a few supplies, such as a picnic lunch or even beach-camping gear. A deeper-hulled day-sailing boat such as the 12-foot O'day Widgeon has room for such gear and can carry her crew through a chop without soaking them on every wave.

Sailboats of this type are all "open" boats—that is, they have no cabin and offer no pretense of shelter or accommodation. Despite this, epic voyages have been made in open boats of suitable design. Webb Chiles, a hardy adventurer famous among sailors for his extraordinary voyages, sailed an 18-foot open boat three quarters of the way around the world. The design was the Drascombe Lugger, which has excellent sea-keeping abilities, but despite this, open boats are not intended for long offshore voyages. They can, however be quite suitable for the kind of beach cruising and exploring that is discussed in this book. Open boats with enough stability can be rigged at night with a boom tent for sleeping aboard, if you don't want to camp on the beach. Since they have no cabin full of gear they are generally lighter and can be dragged ashore or trailered more easily.

Another open boat that has been used for long coastal cruises of this type is the Wayfarer dinghy, which at just under 16 feet and with a beam of 6 feet makes a stable platform and offers lots of room to store gear. There are many other good open boat designs, such as the 21-foot Sea Pearl, which is a sailing dory design built in Florida. This model is offered with an optional boom tent supplied by the builder. It has also been proven in long coastal cruises.

The next step up from an open boat, at least from a comfort standpoint, is a boat with a small shelter called a cuddy cabin. These boats offer a dryer space to store gear and a minimal space for sleeping and cooking aboard. Most boats that have cuddy cabins need to be at least 15 feet long or there is little point in having fixed accommodations. These are by no means luxury cruisers, but in most of them there is enough room to sleep two adults and a place to sit out of the weather. A famous design of this type is the 15-foot West Wight Potter. This little boat, which weighs only 500 pounds, has been proven on many ocean voyages, including crossing the North Atlantic and the passage between California and Hawaii. The boat certainly was not designed for that kind of sailing, but if you sail in a small boat, it's reassuring to know that it has seagoing abilities if you're caught out when the weather turns nasty. The Potter would certainly be suitable for exploring Mississippi's barrier islands, with an advantage over many bigger boats because you can go almost anywhere with such shallow draft.

Draft is a subject much discussed among sailors, because in order for a boat to sail well into the direction of the wind, she must have some type of fin or keel protruding deep beneath her hull. This keel grips the water and prevents sideways drift. The keel can either be permanently affixed or it can be in the form of a retractable centerboard or daggerboard. Small daysailors and trailerable cruisers like the West Wight Potter almost always have some form of retractable keel. This facilitates loading and launching from the trailer, and not having heavy ballast keeps the overall boat weight down. The disadvantage of this type of keel is the loss of some stability in rough conditions. Larger offshore boats usually have fixed keels of iron or lead that provide ballast down low, where it is needed to prevent capsizes. A compromise is found on some larger sailboats that have heavy, ballasted centerboards that are still retractable by means of a winch and cable. The Catalina 22 is a good example of a small cruiser that has this setup. Thousands of these boats were built over a period of many years, which means there are plenty of bargain examples available in the used boat market.

The ability to retract the keel by whatever means is a great advantage in areas with lots of shallow water like the Mississippi Sound. With many of these boats you can get right up to the beaches on the barrier islands or explore far up into the bays and bayous. There are so many good areas in the scope of this book that are off-limits to deep-keeled vessels, that I would recommend a shallow draft boat to anyone whose primary interest is limited to this region.

The builders of traditional working sailcraft of days gone by were forced by the shallow waters of the sound to design a type of boat suitable for the region. This need is what gave birth to the Biloxi Schooners, which, with a draft of about 4 feet with their retractable centerboards, were quite shallow for vessels 50 feet long or more on deck.

Despite the sensibility of shallow draft for the local waters, most of the larger sailboats seen on the coast are traditional fixed-keel cruisers. Above about 22 feet in length, the majority of manufactured production boats are

The author's deep-keeled sailing sloop, Intensity, dry-docked at Covacevich Shipyard, Biloxi

fitted with fixed keels. Draft is in proportion to length, so the larger the boat the more she will draw.

Most of this book has been written on a laptop computer in the cabin of my 26-foot, fixed-keel sailboat, *Intensity*, which for the past year has been my home. This is about the minimum-sized cruiser that is comfortable to live-aboard for extended periods of time. *Intensity* draws 4 feet, 3 inches, which is not excessive, but sailing the waters described in this book, I often long for a boat with half that draft. This type of boat offers quite a bit of comfort for her size, however, allowing me full standing headroom down below even though I am over 6 feet tall.

Intensity is capable of taking me almost anywhere I care to go offshore, but when exploring near shore I often have to be content with anchoring far from the beach and taking a good long row in the dinghy. Those who desire even larger and more comfortable sailboats of this type will be much more severely limited in where they can explore near shore.

There is another option, however, for sailors who want shallow draft, both in small daysailors and in oceangoing, live-aboard cruisers. This is the multihull option, which consists of catamarans and trimarans. Multihulls are based on a totally different principle than monohull type boats. Multihulls are actually descended from rafts, which primitive peoples in many parts of the world fashioned by lashing logs together to form a stable, floating platform. When they were later able to combine this idea with the technology of shaping hollowed out logs into canoes, the multihull boat was formed. This type of boat was developed to its pinnacle by the people who explored and colonized the far-flung inlands of the Pacific Ocean around 4,000 years ago. Modern sailing catamarans have only been around a few decades, as it took a long time for people of monohull sailing traditions to accept that these strange and frail-looking craft could be seaworthy.

Well-designed modern catamarans and trimarans are in fact quite seaworthy and safe. These boats get their stability in rough seas by having the hulls widely separated but attached by strong connecting beams. The result is a craft much like a raft, able to slide down the sides of waves and resist turning over by its width. No heavily ballasted keel is needed to keep such a boat upright; therefore they can be lightly built and unsinkable. A hole in one or more parts of the hull will not result in certain sinking as it would in the keelboat, and even if it is capsized by waves or wind, the multihull will stay afloat upside down.

Since they do not need ballasted keels for stability, multihull sailboats can be designed with retractable daggerboards or centerboards to enable them to go to windward when at sea, and right up on the beach with the boards up. Some designs use only a deep V-shaped hull form to achieve windward sailing ability, and therefore have no retractable boards to fuss with. This shallow-draft combined with seaworthiness and safety is perhaps the best argument for owning a multihull. Even huge catamarans and trimarans in excess of 50 feet can be built so that they can explore thin-water hideaways and anchor right within wading distance of the beach.

Because multihulls have no ballast and can be so lightly built, with two or three long slender hulls barely skimming the surface, they are easily driven by the wind. This means that with the right rig most multihulls can easily

Ernest Herndon preparing to leave Deer Island on a 17-foot James Wharram catamaran, built by the author

outpace conventional ballasted sailboats of the same size, and many are capable of truly astonishing speeds. Speed is the main attraction for many multihull sailors, but speed advantages can easily be lost if these lightweight boats are overloaded.

Before buying and restoring *Intensity*, I built a 17-foot James Wharram-designed catamaran of wood and epoxy. This catamaran is ideal for the sort of beach cruising and exploring discussed in this book. Each hull has more storage space inside than a sea kayak, and a wide deck between the hulls provides a place to pitch a tent for sleeping aboard if I don't want to camp ashore. I have sailed to the barrier islands several times aboard this catamaran, occasionally maintaining speeds of over twelve knots, which is double that of *Intensity*. This catamaran is over 10 feet wide when assembled but can be broken down and stored on a trailer for highway travel. I am confident that the design can handle rough conditions, but the boat's limitation is not having enough load-carrying capacity or enclosed sleeping accommodations for long voyages. Wharram's next size up, the Tiki 21, has been sailed around the world by a young and adventurous Englishman. In my spare time I am currently working on the construction of a Tiki 26, an even larger catamaran by the same designer. This one only draws 15 inches and has adequate cabin space in each hull for sleeping and cooking and carrying everything needed for a cruise. Such a boat should be the perfect vehicle for exploring Mississippi's marine waters.

One drawback to multihulls that discourages many newcomers to sailing from considering this type of boat is the cost. Because more than one hull has to be built, along with the connecting structures and spars, multihulls cost more to produce. Another major factor in the cost is the relatively limited number of production boatbuilders that build multihulls. Those looking for used monohull sailboats can choose from literally hundreds of models of older, fiberglass production boats that have been neglected and can be purchased for a low price and restored. Used multihulls at bargain prices are much harder to come by. The only exceptions are in the smaller, beachable catamarans like the Hobie Cat 16. These are common, and good used ones can sometimes be found for a few hundred dollars. Those who want larger cruising catamarans and trimarans will have to be prepared to spend some money or consider building their own. Multihulls are well suited to backyard boatbuilding, as they are lightweight and plans for many excellent designs are offered. Many of these boats can be built of marine plywood with an epoxy and fiberglass sheathing, a method that does not require expensive moulds, yet produces a strong and durable modern wooden boat. The Tiki 26 that I am building can be completed and outfitted for much less than the price of the average new car. Yet it is a capable offshore sailboat that has been proven in long voyages and in single-handed races across the Atlantic. A production catamaran of this size would cost many times as much.

Whatever type of boat you sail, whether monohull or multihull, daysailor, or cruiser, if you are new to sailing expect to invest some time in learning the intricacies of sail trim and boat handling. Before sailing far from shore in a new or rented sailboat, be sure that you know how to come about, slow down, stop, and make the boat go to windward. Otherwise you may find yourself unable to return, especially if it is a small boat with no auxillary engine. The best course for someone new to sailing is to go with a more experienced friend, or take a course from a qualified instructor. Sailing is not difficult, and it is easy to get an understanding of what makes sailboats work in just a single afternoon of sailing with someone who knows how. What keeps sailors involved in the sport for years or often a lifetime is that no matter how much you learn, there is always more to learn and new skills to develop.

POWERBOATS

For many people, the primary objective of going out on the water is to get somewhere, whether for the purpose of fishing or to camp or picnic on one of the islands. If this is your approach, then the type of boat to consider is the powerboat. Modern powerboats are more reliable than they have ever been and can usually be depended on to get you where you are going. They are, of course, the only vessels used these days by commercial fishermen, and most recreational fishing is done from some type of powerboat. The broad spectrum of powerboat types ranges from the simplest open skiff with an outboard to the palatial multimillion-dollar cruising yachts that are becoming more common on U.S. waterways.

The simplest powerboat is the flat-bottom skiff. Many of these skiffs are old rowboat designs to which an outboard was added. The Johnboat is a type with blunt ends on the bow and stern. The purpose of this shape is to utilize the full load-carrying capability of the hull right out to the ends in the shortest possible length. A skiff with a pointed bow is designed to part waves and handle open water a little better, especially if it has a V-shaped section in the hull at the bow. Johnboats and many small flat-bottomed skiffs are fine for use on coastal bayous and protected areas of bays. They should not be used to make crossing to the islands, however, except on the calmest days when no changing conditions are forecast by the weatherman. These boats often lack sufficient freeboard to handle choppy conditions without taking on water. A change in weather far from land could be disastrous in a boat like this, if there is no way to keep breaking seas out.

Another type of small powerboat is the inflatable boat, commonly referred to as a Zodiac, which is the name of a popular manufacturer of inflatables. Many people use small inflatables with outboards as yacht tenders, but they can also be an ideal boat for apartment dwellers and others who don't have the space to keep a larger boat. Small inflatables can be stored in the trunk of a car, along with the outboard, and quickly made ready for use at the water's edge. Larger inflatable boats are also available, and many of these are capable of carrying powerful outboards and traveling far offshore at high speeds. The most sophisticated ones are the RIB (Rigid Inflatable Boats) type with a rigid V-hull bottom and center-console steering stations. Some of these are as large and well equipped as their fiberglass counterparts. These larger inflatables are not portable or collapsible, of course, and will require a regular boat trailer for highway transport.

Small, low-cost skiffs, whether V-hulled or flat-bottomed, are likely to be made of aluminum. Once you move up in size to boats 16 feet or longer, and to more complex hull forms, almost all production boats are built of fiberglass. Fiberglass powerboats from 16 feet and up are offered in a staggering array of choices from hundreds of manufacturers. Anyone new to boating who is considering something of this size range or larger would do well to spend some time researching the various models in order to find the best match according to the requirements and budget. Some of the most versatile and useful powerboats are the center-console, outboard-powered open boats that are equally at home in a backwoods bayou or trolling offshore for bluewater gamefish. Most of these are equipped with large single or dual outboard engines and are capable of high cruising speeds. Dual outboards are a good safety measure for open boats that venture well offshore, since one engine will get you home in the event of a breakdown. Boats of this type in the 16-to-25-foot range can still be easily trailered to save on slip fees and to allow exploring on faraway waters within driving distance.

Like sailboats, powerboats above 16 feet or so are also offered with cabins and sleeping accommodations. Some of the smaller ones are still trailerable, but since all boats are a compromise, you give up one thing to get another. A small boat with a cabin will not have as much deck space for fishing, and of course it will weigh more and therefore be slower with the same horse-power.

If cruising on a powerboat is your objective, then speed will not be so much of a concern as comfort. Many power cruisers are designed to move along at a displacement hull speed, rather than come up out of the water on a plane like speedboats. These cruisers might be fitted with an inboard diesel, rather than gasoline outboards, and have extremely long cruising ranges at a modest speed of 8 to 12 knots. Most of these are still faster than the average sailboat and are sometimes preferred over sailcraft by cruisers who don't want to bother with all the string tweaking and sail handling of a wind-driven vessel.

Boaters new to cruising should carefully select a design that is suitable for the intended use. Many powerboats designed for lakes and sheltered waters are built with comfortable accommodations taking priority over everything else. Houseboats are a good example of this type. Though they provide maximum cabin space for a given length, and homelike amenities inside, most are top-heavy and poorly balanced. Boats of this type, though large, are not as safe crossing the Mississippi Sound as many much smaller boats of a better design. Seaworthy boats have a hull form that resists capsize, as well as watertight decks and self-bailing cockpits that prevent swamping in breaking seas.

Though many power cruisers are seaworthy enough for offshore voy-ages, they are most popular for traveling inland waterways and for routes like the Intracoastal Waterway. Sailboats are still the choice for long blue-water voyages, such as crossing a whole ocean. It would be impossible to carry enough fuel for such a voyage on a small power cruiser, and depend-ing entirely on an engine far from any help would not be a wise idea. Any engine can fail, and those who venture offshore, even to islands as close as the Gulf Islands National Seashore, should carry tools for minor repairs and know how to use them. In the event of major breakdowns that cannot be repaired on site, powerboat cruisers should be prepared to shell out some bucks for a towing service. This is simply a fact of life if you cruise in a boat with no alternative means of propulsion.

For those who happen to have plenty of money to spend, there are larger powerboats that can accommodate even the healthiest of budgets. There are the Sportfishermen, those large offshore fishing machines that range from 25 feet on up and combine luxurious interiors and high speed. Then there are the super-charged offshore racing boats, or cigarette boats, that are built to do nothing but practically fly across the water and burn prodigious amounts of fuel. Finally, there are the large motor yachts, which resemble sleek floating palaces and range up to 100 feet or longer.

One other type of power craft that has become overwhelmingly popular in recent years is the personal watercraft, commonly referred to by the trademark names Jet Ski or Waverunner. These watercraft are not really boats, since the operator does not sit within a hull but rather sits astride the seat like a motorcycle or rides in a standing position. Personal watercraft have been roundly cursed by fishermen, environmentalists, and professional mariners alike because of the irresponsible manner in which many operators use them. Because they have a jet drive rather than a conventional prop, personal watercraft are shallow in draft and capable of going almost anywhere at high speed. Many owners purchase these powerful machines without having any prior knowledge of boating, and this is what causes most of the problems. Some of these operators like to buzz close by other vessels or jump the wakes produced by larger boats. Many of them disregard all the Rules of the Road, zip through No Wake Zones at full throttle, and endanger swimmers and others in or on the water.

This behavior has resulted in all personal watercraft being banned from National Park Service waters, including the waters surrounding the barrier islands in Mississippi. In other states, they have been banned from commercial harbors and the waters off public beaches.

Personal watercraft can be operated in a responsible manner, and those who do so receive the respect of other mariners. If you are interested in this type of water vehicle, please take the time to learn the principles of navigation and the Rules of the Road. Also be aware that these watercraft are not boats and were never intended for long offshore trips. Although many people ride miles offshore to the barrier islands and even out to Chandeleur

Island, this can be asking for trouble. Most of these vehicles have engines that are difficult to access from the water even in calm conditions, much less in a rolling seaway. This results in lots of unnecessary rescues by the Coast Guard, and more than one personal watercraft operator has been found adrift many miles from land after an engine failure.

From the descriptions in this chapter, you can see that selecting a boat involves many choices and that all boats are a compromise in one way or another. In the back of this book you will find a list of recommended books to further expand your knowledge on the subject of boats. Just try to remember that the boat is the means to the end and not the end in itself. The important thing is to get out there, whatever your preference is. The islands and surrounding waters are yours to explore, whether you arrive in a $500 plastic kayak or at the helm of a multi-million-dollar luxury yacht.

4

CAMPING, FISHING, AND OTHER ACTIVITIES

Mississippi's barrier islands offer a unique opportunity to experience an island lifestyle, even if only for a few days. Camping on a deserted beach on a moonlit night is an experience that will not soon be forgotten. On these empty expanses of white sand, with the dark waters of the Gulf on one side and forests of tall pines on the other, it is easy to imagine that the mainland and all the civilization associated with it are much farther than 10 miles away. Sitting among the dunes and listening to the surf rolling in, one can easily imagine these beaches are on some remote Pacific atoll or Bahamian cay.

ISLAND CAMPING

Beach camping, especially on a remote island, requires some different techniques that otherwise experienced campers might not be familiar with. Scorching sun, relentless winds, and fierce insect hordes can all conspire to make these islands seem anything but paradise to those who are not prepared for such conditions.

On my first overnight excursion to one of the barrier islands, I packed my sea kayak with the discount store camping gear I had used for weekend canoe trips. I had a cheap dome tent, which had worked fine for fair-weather camping in the woods along my favorite streams. I had never even bothered to use the flimsy metal stakes that came with the tent. In the deep woods, it was unnecessary to secure the tent to the ground. In those early days of my camping career, I didn't bother to carry extras like sleeping pads. I thought camping meant roughing it, and that included sleeping on the hard ground.

On the soft beach sand of Horn Island, I found that sleeping without a pad or inflatable mattress is not a problem. Your body settles in and the sand conforms to the contours. The wind was a problem though, and during the first night there, my tent was battered by a steady 15- to 20-knot breeze, and I kept expecting it to collapse under the strain. The next morning while digging about in the storage compartments of my kayak in search of breakfast, I looked up to see my unoccupied tent rolling across the sand like a Texas tumbleweed. My sleeping bag and some of my clothes were still inside, so I made a mad dash to catch it before it reached the water's edge.

When I had moved my errant camp back to where I had wanted it in the first place, I found that the thin metal stakes supplied with the tent were useless in the deep sand. I used my full water jugs and other miscellaneous heavy pieces of gear to weight the tent down from the inside, but the wind still threatened to drag it away.

Since that first night on a windswept island, I have worn out half a dozen expensive "expedition-grade" tents on my long kayak journeys and on various backpacking trips. I have found that even the best tents can be damaged by gale-force winds, but these better quality models could be repaired at least well enough to continue the trip. Better tents come with aluminum poles, which are much stronger and lighter than the hollow fiberglass poles supplied with cheap tents. The aluminum poles can be bent, but they rarely break under stress, and bent ones can be straightened.

As I gained more beach camping experience, I discovered that using heavy objects to weight the corners down is not the solution to camping in high winds. It's inconvenient to search for something heavy enough, especially on the Gulf islands where there are no large rocks to be found. I found that staking the tent down works in all conditions, providing that the stakes are long enough to be driven deeply into the sand and thick enough so that they maintain their hold. They can be made of pieces of driftwood scavenged off the beach, but the best ones are the wide plastic stakes sold at camping supply stores. They should be at least a foot long, and T-shaped in cross-section for strength. These hold firmly even in soft sand if they are driven in deep enough. A chunk of driftwood can be used as a hammer if you don't want to carry a mallet for this purpose.

Sometimes in extreme conditions I have found it necessary to stake two corners of the tent down before even unrolling it, and especially before trying to erect it. In high winds a lightweight tent will fill like a sail and be torn from your hands if you don't secure the windward edge first.

Most high-quality modern tents were designed for mountaineering expeditions where not only wind but heavy snowfall is expected. These perform well for their intended purpose, which is to withstand the weight of snow and ice, but many of these are dome-shaped, or some variation of this shape. This means that the doors and windows slope up toward the apex of the roof, which is not the best design for shedding heavy rain. Any good tent will have a separate rain-fly that fits over the top of the tent to allow air circulation, but many of these mountain tents are designed in such a way that you cannot open the doors even partially during a downpour. This is a real disadvantage in the hot, rainy conditions frequently experienced when camping on the Gulf coast and other subtropical areas.

The tents that have worked best for me have been the A-frame or modified A-frame shapes that have zip-out doors with windows in both ends. These have a fly that overhangs the door to allow partially open windows even during heavy rain. Tents of this type are available in many levels of quality, from the discount store variety to expedition-grade.

Tent size, of course, depends on the number of people who will be sleeping in it, as well as the duration of the trip. Many tents are advertised as "one-person," "two-person," or "four-person" tents. These classifications might be accurate for hard-core mountaineers who have to watch every ounce when they select their climbing gear. But most people will find that a "four-person" tent is more comfortable for two and a "two-person" model is better suited as a solo tent than most of the tiny ones sold for solo camping. Of course a lot depends on whom you will be sharing your sleeping space with and for how long. On long trips where there is a possibility of being confined for hours or days by bad weather, space is always at a premium, and the bigger the tent, the better. Conversely, on longer trips in small boats such as kayaks, there will be less room for larger tents because more of the valuable storage space will be needed for food and other supplies.

When selecting a tent for camping on the barrier islands, there is one more critical feature that ranks perhaps higher in importance than the ability to withstand wind and to shed rain. This is protection from insects. Being caught out on one of these beaches on a windless, warm night would be a form of torture that few could endure. Swarms of mosquitoes would quickly find an unprotected camper on any but the windiest nights. A variety of biting flies work the day shift, while hordes of almost invisible "no-see-ums" or sand flies materialize at dawn and dusk. These last are the most difficult to defend against. Insect repellants have little effect on them, and they can easily pass through the mesh of ordinary mosquito netting found in cheaper tents. I found this out during my first kayak excursion to East Ship Island, in the month of July. I made camp on the Gulf side of the island, and at dusk there was a nice sea breeze that made the whole experience quite pleasant. I turned in for a good night's sleep and was doing fine until about 3 A.M., when the wind died. I awoke itching all over. It seemed that millions of these no-see-ums had invaded my tent and were biting me all over. They get into your hair, eyes, nose—everywhere. It is no mild itching, but rather an intense feeling of being attacked. I had to have some relief. The tent was no protection at all, so I bolted out to the beach and jumped into the surf, submerging my entire body to get rid of them. I couldn't stay out there all night, so I went back to the tent to repeat the cycle all over. Needless to say, I didn't get any more sleep that night. And that was the last night I ever spent in that tent. Fortunately, most tents now come with "no-see-um" netting in the doors and windows. This finer mesh limits air circulation somewhat, but it is a trade-off you must live with if you intend to camp on the beach.

Barrier island campsite with tent and additional tarp for shade on a summer day

No-see-ums and other insect pests can often be avoided if you take care to make trips to the islands when there is plenty of wind in the forecast. Windy conditions mean rougher seas, though, so this might not be practical for everyone, depending on the type of boat used to get there. The least buggy places to camp on any of the islands are on the long sand spits that extend from the east and west tips of each island. Since there are no trees on these ends, even the slightest breeze can help keep insects at bay. Most island campers know this, so these are not the places to camp if you seek seclusion. These sandy ends are often full of tents on fair-weather weekends.

In addition to a tent for sleeping, I also like to carry a small tarp that can be set up to provide shade in the daytime, or a place to cook in rainy conditions. This is especially important for longer excursions. I find that the 6-by-8-foot size is plenty. The smaller the tarp, the easier it will be to set up, especially if it is windy. You will need extra stakes and some lengths of line to set up a tarp, as well as a convenient tree or some piece of driftwood scrounged up on the beach for a pole.

Many beach campers also like to carry the large screen houses that are available where tents are sold. I've never bothered with these because most of my camping has been out of kayaks, and I did not have the room. But those traveling in larger boats may enjoy the comfort of having an open, breezy shelter free of insects for daytime lounging.

As I mentioned earlier, I never carried a sleeping pad or mattress of any sort when I began camping. On sandy islands, sleeping without any padding is not too bad, but even so, these days I never leave home without my self-inflating air mattress. Made for backpackers, this mattress is only 22 by 72 inches long and 1 inch thick. It rolls up into a tight package and takes up very little space, even in a kayak. With it, I can sleep comfortably even on a hard cement floor, so I can see no reason to be without it again.

A good sleeping bag will be needed if you camp on these islands in winter. The rest of the year it will generally be too hot at night to sleep inside one. For warm weather trips I carry a very minimal type of sleeping bag made like a thin blanket with a zipper in the side. When I expect cold nights, I carry a backpacker-type mummy bag rated to keep you warm down to 15 degrees. Don't underestimate the potential for cold on these islands just because they are on the Gulf coast. When a winter cold front comes through with temperatures in the high 20s or low 30s, accompanied by north winds over 20 knots, you may think you are much farther north. These islands offer little shelter from winter winds, but you can move your camp away from the beach and into the forests, sometimes in the hollows behind the dunes, to find some protection.

It goes without saying that you should pack adequate clothing for cold conditions. Layers are best, with the outer one being some type of jacket that stops the wind from penetrating. I also find a wool watch cap necessary for sleeping in cold conditions.

In warm weather, protection from the sun is the biggest concern. Those seeking an island tan will wear as little as possible, and for many, on these deserted islands that means nothing at all. But there will come a time when you will have had enough sun, and something besides sunscreen is needed. I always pack shorts and T-shirts, as well as beach sandals for my main camp clothing. But even in summer it is essential to pack some kind of long pants and long-sleeved shirt. The best ones are loose-fitting, lightweight cotton garments. These not only serve as sun protection but are a good defense against insects as well. My favorite camping pants are the military-issue BDUs that have drawstring cuffs and lots of pockets. They dry fast when wet and are not too hot to wear on summer days.

A good hat will also be essential. Baseball caps are not really adequate for sun protection. The best island hats are wide-brimmed, made of straw or canvas, and have chin straps or a cord to prevent them from being carried away by the wind.

Island cooking can be done with an open fire, but be aware that fires are permitted in the Gulf Islands National Seashore only in the sand below the high tide line. A portable campstove is a simpler option. I find the kind that uses disposable propane bottles to be the most efficient and reliable. Cookware and utensils exposed to salt water should be of stainless steel. Beach sand makes a wonderfully efficient pot scrubber for quickly cleaning up after the cooking is done, as long as your pans are not Teflon-coated. If you are in a small boat or kayak, fresh water will be too limited to use for dishwashing.

The fresh water you do carry should be in leak-proof containers. Since you can't get more of this precious commodity out on the islands, it is imperative that it is not wasted or spilled. When kayaking, I carry a minimum of one gallon of water per day. This allows enough for drinking and cooking. I use well-rinsed, empty bleach containers for my water supply. One-gallon jugs divide the supply, which makes it easy to distribute it throughout the storage compartments. These jugs are also opaque white, which means they will reflect the heat and keep your water cool enough to drink if inadvertently left out in the sun. And most important, they don't leak. All washing up and bathing will have to be done in seawater on this minimum supply. Those in larger boats can, of course, carry more. Nothing can make camping on the beach more pleasant than having a hot, freshwater shower before you turn in. This can be a reality with a solar shower. With less than a gallon of water, you can enjoy a good shower with one of these.

Many people don't realize that they can travel light, camp in remote places, and still be comfortable. To me, part of the pleasure in wilderness travel is feeling at home wherever I may stop for the night. And feeling at home means being sheltered, well fed, and comfortable. Compact items such as a hammock and a good book can make a campsite so relaxing that you may not want to leave for a long time. Although I camp to get away from the distractions of civilization, on longer trips I usually carry a compact Sony Walkman and some tapes or CDs. These can be nice comforts on a sleepless stormy night. I appreciate the magnificence of the lightning shows that sometimes occur over the Gulf, but there are times when I want to just drown out the sounds of bad weather and get some sleep. Items that I have found invaluable for my island excursions are listed in the beach camping checklist in the appendix. Your list may be different if you are already an experienced camper, but this should serve as a guideline for those new to camping in this kind of environment.

HIKING

In addition to camping, there are many other activities to pursue and enjoy on the barrier islands and waters of the Mississippi coast. Those who like to hike and explore on foot will find miles of dunes, forests, and seashore to lure them. Birdwatchers, photographers, and other nature lovers will find no shortage of subjects to hold their interest here. There are good places for swimming and playing in the surf, and even a few spots that offer decent snorkeling in the right conditions. And of course, for the saltwater angler, there is something to be sought out in every area covered by this book.

Hiking on the coast can be as casual as a stroll on the mainland beaches that front Highway 90, or as arduous as a backpacking trip around the 27-mile perimeter of Horn Island. Those who set out on long hikes on the islands should be aware that walking in deep sand is tiring, and five miles of island hiking may seem like ten miles on harder ground. The islands are relatively flat, but some, especially Horn Island, offer large areas of rolling dunes, some barren and desertlike, while others are covered in dense pine forests. The dune areas are relatively easy to traverse, but all the islands

Dunes and forests of Horn Island provide miles of hiking opportunities.

have large marshes that will prove to be a formidable barrier to all but the most intrepid of explorers. The late Walter Inglis Anderson was not to be deterred by these inhospitable marshes. He waded right in up to his neck and sometimes spent whole days eye-to-eye with herons, frogs, and other subjects of his paintings. Exploring these marshes requires a high tolerance to biting insects and black, slimy mud, as well as a bit of disregard to the dangers. These dangers are chiefly cottonmouth snakes and some very large alligators that make these grass-choked lagoons their home. Of course, alligators are not supposed to be all that aggressive toward man, but entering their habitat on their terms is tempting fate a bit. One park ranger I spoke with on Horn Island said that there was no way he would enter any of the interior lagoons, based on the number of big 'gators he'd seen. The cottonmouths are also plentiful. They like to act aggressive and will stand their ground sometimes when confronted, but they rarely bite unless they are really cornered or molested in some way.

For most hikers sensible enough to stay out of the marshes, heat stroke and dehydration are about the only other serious dangers to be encountered on these islands. Just as in desert hiking, backpackers will have to carry all their water, as there are no freshwater sources to be found for resupply. A good hat will go a long way in preventing overheating, but most important, hikers should slow down to a reasonable pace and drink plenty of water.

It's possible to hike these islands barefoot, especially if you stick to the shoreline, but be aware that there are lots of painful things to step on. Most common are sandspurs, tiny little green burrs that grow on low-lying grass and have needle-sharp spines protruding in all directions. These are nuisances, but broken glass, rusting bits of cans and other metal, and fish bones can do serious damage. A friend of mine stepped on the skeleton of a catfish that was half-buried in the sand. A bone penetrated his heel, requiring more than one surgery over the years and causing him lots of long-term difficulties.

But, despite all this, there is nothing quite like the pleasure of a long nighttime walk, splashing barefoot in the edge of the surf on a deserted Gulf island beach. The next best thing is a pair of hiking sandals designed to be worn in or out of the water. But even these don't offer enough protection for serious bushwhacking back in the woods away from the beach. For that you need atleast a good pair of walking shoes, or better yet, hiking boots.

SWIMMING AND SNORKELING

Many visitors to the Mississippi coast might be put off by the dark brown color of the waters of the sound as seen along the beaches of Highway 90. The water may appear dirty and uninviting to swimmers. It is, in fact, somewhat muddy, this color and opaqueness caused by the sediments carried into the sound by major rivers such as the Pascagoula and the Pearl. The offshore islands inhibit free circulation of the sound's waters, hence the dark color and low salinity level. These waters are only about half as saline as the waters of the open Gulf.

People do swim and wade off the mainland beaches despite the dirty appearance, and it is perfectly safe to do so. The bottom slopes away so gradually from the beach, however, that anyone wanting to do some serious swimming will have to wade a long way to find sufficiently deep water.

The waters around the barrier islands offer better opportunities for swimming and snorkeling. On the south side off all the islands, where the beaches are exposed to the open Gulf, those who like to play in the surf will often find good wave conditions. During periods of strong surf, particularly after storms, there may be dangerous currents in the surf zone. The beach on the south side of West Ship Island offers surf swimming under the watch of a lifeguard when the excursion boats are operating.

Areas to avoid swimming around on all the islands are the ends of the islands in the passes where strong tidal currents flow between the sound and open sea. These currents can be strong enough to sweep even the best swimmer out to sea, and there are often confused, choppy seas as a result of wind blowing against the current. In addition to these dangers, large sharks are often spotted and sometimes hooked by anglers in these passes. The tidal flow brings a steady, fresh supply of food to both large and small sea creatures, and sharks often congregate in these areas. More than once I have seen 5- to 6-foot sharks cruising over the sand flats in just 2 to 3 feet of water. Most likely these small sharks will avoid humans, but you never know what might be out there in these passes. Sailing my 17-foot catamaran between Horn and East Ship Island one day when the water was particularly clear, I passed directly over a huge shark that was cruising just a few feet below the surface. The sudden appearance of my fast and silent catamaran startled him as much as seeing him surprised me, and he quickly darted away into deeper water.

In recent years there have been several well-publicized shark attacks in Gulf waters, though not in Mississippi. Attacks like these should not prevent swimmers from enjoying the water, but they are reminders that sharks are there, and should convince you to avoid the passes and swimming at night or in excessively murky water.

Stingrays and jellyfish are other animal hazards to be aware of in these waters. Stingrays can often be seen in the shallows just off the beach. One can avoid stepping on them by shuffling through the sand. They spook easily and will quickly get out of the way as long as they know you are coming. Jellyfish are harder to avoid. Occasionally, there will be a population

A wrecked barge forming a haven for marine life off the south coast of Horn Island

explosion of these creatures, making it difficult to get in the water without making contact with one and getting a sting. Most of the time they are less numerous, and the stings are not all that painful but could be dangerous for someone who has allergic reactions to stings. Some organisms of this type have much more potent stings. While kayaking several miles off of the Florida Keys, my paddle accidentally scooped up a long strand of stringy tentacles from a Portuguese Man of War. The result was instant pain and then a paralyzing numbness in my entire arm that made it extremely difficult to get back to shore. Though I carried Benadryl in the kayak for just such a sting, it was stored away deep inside one of the dry compartments and inaccessible from the cockpit. I have since kept some handy.

For those who want to try snorkeling, the waters on the north side of West Ship Island around the fort and the pier are sometimes clear enough to offer some underwater visibility. Just off the beach north of the fort there are piles of concrete rubble under just a few feet of water, and one can usually observe schools of fish congregating around this debris. There are also fish around the pilings of the pier, but if you snorkel there, watch out for anglers and their hooks, and don't venture out near the end of the pier where the excursion boats dock.

The water can sometimes be exceptionally clear around East Ship Island. The key to finding good snorkeling is to locate some kind of underwater debris or structure that attracts fish. Most of the seabed around these islands is an underwater desert of nothing but sand, so marine life is hard to find.

Another possible snorkeling site is around an old wrecked barge that lies partially exposed on the south side of Horn Island, near the eastern tip. If you happen to catch the conditions right, when the water is clear and the surf is down, this wreck is teeming with marine life, including schools of large fish.

FISHING

Fishing is one of the main reasons many people want to explore Mississippi's coastal waters and is, of course, the main reason many people are attracted to boating in the first place. These waters certainly have their share of excellent fishing opportunities, for both the sporting angler and the professional commercial fisherman.

The variety of fish and other edible marine life, such as shrimp, oysters, and crabs, to be found in these waters is extensive. Fishermen new to saltwater angling would do well to purchase a guidebook, such as *Sport Fish of the Gulf or Mexico* by Vic Dunaway, for a complete description, as well as colored illustrations of each species. For more details on fishing methods, try *Saltwater Fishing Tactics* by the editors of *Saltwater Sportsman Magazine*. For those who think that saltwater fishing is beyond their reach because of the prohibitive cost of boat ownership, the recently published *Kayakfishing: The Revolution* by Ken Daubert opens up a whole new world of ideas for fishing from sea kayaks.

Though I am certainly no expert on the subject of fishing, despite prodigious amounts of time spent on the water, both salt and fresh, I will briefly describe the most sought-after species found in these waters, as well as some information on the methods used to catch them:

The *spotted seatrout* (usually called "speckled trout") is perhaps the favorite light-tackle species on the Gulf Coast. They usually range from a half-pound to 3 pounds in weight, but the local record is over 10 pounds. Speckled trout are found in all area waters throughout the year. During winter months they are common in deeper, warmer waters of the bays and bayous and are usually caught by anglers in skiffs. In the spring and summer, they can be caught by wadefishing off the beach, especially in areas of seagrass beds. The best time to fish for trout off the beach is during the first hour of a falling tide and the last couple of hours of a rising tide. Speckled trout are fun to catch and delicious to eat as well.

The *cobia* (commonly called "lemonfish") is one of the most respected big game fish in the northern Gulf. Cobia are found worldwide in tropical and temperate waters and move into Mississippi's coastal waters during the warmer months. They prefer waters 68 degrees or warmer. Ninety-pounders are not uncommon, and the local record is 106.8 pounds, for a cobia caught off Horn Island.

Cobia are hard-fighting game fish, known for their determination and tenacity. They are taken by trolling with artificial or natural baits and by bottomfishing. They are often found near the oil rigs south of the barrier islands and around buoys and other shade-producing structures. Cobia are also good to eat.

Jack crevalle is another saltwater species found throughout the world that is frequently caught in Mississippi waters. They reach up to 55 pounds and are aggressive feeders and fierce fighters once hooked.

Jack crevalle are a migratory pelagic species, meaning that they are constantly on the move. Like cobia, they prefer water warmer than 68 degrees, but they have a higher tolerance for salinity variations and can be found in the brackish waters of rivers and bayous as well as offshore. Jack crevalle are not considered good to eat.

The *red snapper* is another much sought-after species in the Gulf of Mexico. Red snapper are reef fish, preferring areas of high salinity, such as the offshore banks near the edge of the continental shelf. They are commonly caught on charter boat trips to the artificial reefs and offshore oilrigs off the coast of Mississippi. The red snapper is considered a delicacy and is the favorite fish of many seafood lovers.

The *red drum* (locally referred to as redfish) is another extremely popular local game fish. Red drum are common in the Mississippi Sound and around the barrier island passes. Like speckled trout, redfish can be taken near shore by wadefishing. They are usually caught near the bottom, over mud, sand, or oyster reefs. Redfish are powerful fighters and are excellent for eating as well.

Another popular fish taken by an entirely different method on the Mississippi coast is the *flounder*. Flounders can be caught with hook and line, but are most commonly taken by one of the oldest methods of fishing, with a spear or gig. Flounders are hunted at night, when they come in near the beach and bury themselves in the sandy bottom to await unsuspecting prey. A flounder will not move unless you step on him, so finding one entails carefully searching the bottom with a bright light, looking for the two eyes, which are both located on the same side of the head. The gig is then used to impale the fish, which will usually make no effort to get out of the way. Floundering is usually done by wading in the shallows right off the beach. A variation of this in areas where the water is clear enough is to hunt flounders in deeper water with an underwater light and SCUBA or snorkeling gear. Stuffed flounder is considered among the finest of seafood delicacies.

Another fish that is often taken near the beach by a method other than angling with hook and line is the *mullet*. The mullet is a big-eyed, silvery fish that is seen in large schools, often jumping completely out of the water in the sound, and in brackish bayous and rivers. Mullet will not readily take a hook and line, so the standard method of catching them is with a cast net, which is thrown by hand either while wading, standing on a pier, or standing in a boat. Throwing a cast net successfully requires some skill, and the technique is best learned with instruction from an experienced local. Experts can catch a bucketful of mullet in a short time with a cast net.

Although many people do not eat mullet because of the many bones, the fish was a staple food on the coast during the Civil War and the Great Depression. Smoked mullet often replaced bacon at the breakfast table, and came to be known as Biloxi Bacon. Today mullet is still commonly eaten in Mississippi and is also popular in parts of Florida. Fishermen seeking bigger game also use cast nets to secure mullet for use as bait.

Other game fish caught off the coast of Mississippi include dolphin (a pelagic fish not to be confused with the marine mammal of the same name) southern kingfish, black drum, Spanish mackerel, bluefish, Atlantic croakers, sheepshead, ladyfish, king mackerel, bonito, wahoo, amberjack, and a variety of sharks.

In addition to fish, there are also abundant blue crabs, shrimp and oysters. These three are usually taken by commercial fishermen, but can also be sought by recreational fishermen.

Fishing regulations and licensing requirements and fees are subject to change from year to year. Generally, a saltwater fishing license is required to fish the waters south of U.S. Highway 90. Mississippi offers a free salt-water fishing day on July 4 each year. Questions regarding regulations and licenses should be addressed to the Mississippi Department of Marine Resources at 228-374-5000.

Part 2

THE MISSISSIPPI MAINLAND, BAYS, AND COASTAL RIVERS

5

THE PEARL RIVER
TO BAY ST. LOUIS

Mississippi's coastal lands are bounded on the west by the open marshlands of the lower Pearl River. From its beginnings at Nanih Waiya (Choctaw for Rock River) in Neshoba County, the Pearl flows more than 400 miles to the Gulf of Mexico, making it the longest river entirely within the state of Mississippi. The lower reaches of this river encompass some of the largest and most inaccessible wildlands remaining in Mississippi and Louisiana. Where the river divides into the East, Middle, and West Pearl Rivers, the resulting maze of bayous both large and small becomes a 5-mile-wide corridor of wilderness known locally as Honey Island Swamp.

Canoeists and other boatmen who visit a large river delta like the Pearl for the first time might find themselves quite confused by the many diverging and reconverging channels. Those only familiar with inland rivers will be used to seeing tributaries and feeder creeks merging with a river as it flows downstream and becomes larger. On a flat coastal plain such as that found on the Mississippi Gulf Coast, the rivers spread out as they near the sea, and the result is a maze of meandering waterways. The term "bayou," as used in the Deep South, refers to a smaller waterway that leaves a larger river, as opposed to a "branch" or "creek," which is a tributary flowing into the river. Bayous are plentiful near the coast, and are characteristically sluggish if moving at all. Other bodies of water found within a river delta such as this are dead lakes and sloughs, which are old channels of still water left when the river changed course. Many of these sloughs and bayous can become raging torrents in times of flood, and when waters are high, navigation is even more difficult, as water flows everywhere through trees that all look the same.

This is a land of mysterious cypress and gum forests, where still black waters reflect curtains of Spanish moss that conceal hidden lagoons and passageways. Here, one who is paddling a silent canoe, or drift fishing with the outboard shut off, is likely to hear the eerie call of a barred owl even in daylight hours.

Dense thickets of saw palmettos and canebrakes growing on the muddy, forested banks lend a decidedly tropical atmosphere to this remote wilderness area. In fact, it is so junglelike that a U.S. Navy Seal team that specializes in riverine combat makes their headquarters near here and uses sections of the river and surrounding forest for training. The rounds they fire are blanks, but river travelers unaware of this might be alarmed to hear the sound of heavy machine guns echoing through the swamps.

As unlikely as it might seem to encounter members of the Navy's most elite combat forces in these remote Mississippi wetlands, visitors from other parts will be as surprised to learn that a major NASA manufacturing and testing facility also exists along the river north of Highway 90. This explains all the navigation markers along the river's channel in an area that would seemingly not be used for large-vessel navigation.

THE LOWER PEARL RIVER

The Pearl River emerges out of the jungled forests of the interior and into the scope of our interest where it flows under the bridges of U.S. Highway 90. Most of the marsh and river channels seen when driving across the river here are actually in Louisiana. The East Pearl River channel marks the state line, and this bridge crossing is roughly where the river enters the tidelands and begins to mix with the salt water of the Gulf. The transition here, as in other rivers that empty into the Gulf, is apparent in the vegetation. Trees become sparse, and the few cypress that grow in isolated clumps are small and wind-bent from exposure to Gulf storms.

The navigable section of the lower Pearl River is charted on NOAA chart No. 11367. This chart also covers the extreme western parts of the Mississippi coast as described in the following pages, all the way to Clermont Harbor and Waveland. Chart No. 11372 picks up where 11367 leaves off and shows the remaining section of coastline described in this chapter, as well as much of the rest of the Mississippi coast to Biloxi and beyond.

The East Pearl channel is straightforward and well marked with aids to navigation. If one should venture off into the labyrinth of narrow bayous to the west of this channel, it is a different story. The Louisiana side of this marshland offers many possibilities for long or short loop trips, especially for paddlers of canoes or kayaks. This is one area where open canoes are ideal, since strong winds can only generate limited waves due to the buffer effect of the dense marsh grasses. Canoers have an advantage over kayakers in that they can stand up occasionally and see over the grass in order to check bearings and look for channels. Paddling down the more open waters of the East Pearl itself could be more difficult, as a healthy chop could develop in a sustained wind.

Boaters exploring this waterway won't find many places to land and go ashore, as the shoreline is mostly submerged grass and tidal muck that is less than inviting for walking. Those who do venture onto these banks will surely see signs of the variety of wildlife that thrives here. My canoeing partner Ernest Herndon and I noticed wide paths of beaten-down grass just a few feet in from the bank. We suspected this was the work of alligators, as it was certainly the mark of a large animal. Another quarter mile of paddling revealed that we were wrong. A huge wild hog suddenly crashed off through the grass alongside our canoe. It stayed near the water's edge, fleeing ahead of us along our intended route, so we paddled as fast as we could, trying to get a better glimpse of it. The frightened sow could not move much faster through the waterlogged grass than we could paddle, so she gave up and charged across the bayou directly in front of us and this time finally lost us by heading straight away from the water.

Alligators are certainly present in these waters, but you might spend a lot of time looking before you see one, especially a big one. Other marsh animals include otters, nutria, and raccoons. Those with an interest in birds will certainly find a variety of species here, as will those knowledgeable enough about wildflowers and marsh plants to differentiate the myriad assortment to be found here. At a glance, especially driving by on the highway, the marsh all looks the same, like a monotonous landscape of one kind of plant–grass. Closer inspection will reveal to even the most casual observer that there is far more to the plant life here than grass. When we paddled the area in September, there were dozens of different flowers blooming, and in fact, some of the banks were like a sea of wildflowers of many different colors. Most we couldn't identify, but we could begin to appreciate that there was a diversity of life here that most people never see if they speed by in cars or even travel the waterways in fast powerboats.

After our encounter with the wild hog while exploring a side channel on the Louisiana side, Ernest and I continued paddling down the East Pearl south of the boat ramp where we launched at Highway 90. The marked channel on the East Pearl is easy to follow, though since we were in a canoe we did not have to worry about staying in the deeper waters of the channel. We found no dry place to go ashore until we reached the intersection of another system of bayous and waterways that join the river from the east. Just south of this confluence lies a small island of sand and scrub vegetation.

Port Bienville Industrial Park lies to the east of the river here and is connected to the river by dredged channels in the bayou and the man-made Port Bienville Canal. As we pulled our canoe up on the sand of the little island to stretch our legs, we were surprised to see the *Kopersand*, an oceangoing container ship, steam out of this waterway into the river, outbound to sea. The waterway certainly looks more suited to canoes or bass boats than ocean freighters, but it is obviously deep enough that pleasure boaters will have no trouble navigating it.

Despite the commercial traffic, the waterways leading off to the east at this junction are worth exploring. The canal leads to the other sizeable backwaters such as Cross Bayou and Mulatto Bayou, where cruising boats might find a place to anchor for the night away from the traffic of the main river.

A small freighter, <u>The Kopersand,</u> dwarfs Ernest Herndon and his 17-foot canoe on the Port Bienville Canal.

Those in canoes or other small boats might also be interested in Cowan Bayou, which intersects the Port Bienville canal on the north side, just across from the entrance to Mulatto Bayou on the south. Cowan Bayou roughly parallels the Pearl River from where it crosses Highway 90, but it is much smaller and its twisting course is easily double the distance of the nearly straight river channel.

Although the remaining 4 miles of the East Pearl before its confluence with the Gulf would have been easy paddling, Ernest and I chose to turn back upriver. We explored some canoe-sized side waters on the Louisiana side, hoping to see more marsh wildlife. Paddling upstream to the boat ramp presented no problems in the gentle currents of this lazy river.

A little over a mile south of the island where we stopped, the East Pearl River takes a hard turn to the east and runs in that general direction for a couple of miles before turning south again to empty into the Gulf at Lake Borgne. Mulatto Bayou enters the river from the north about midway in this easterly stretch, offering a shortcut to the Port Bienville Canal. After the river passes under the CSX Railroad Bridge in its final stretch, open water will be clearly visible to the south, and a marked channel leads to the heavily traveled Intracoastal Waterway.

THE GULF INTRACOASTAL WATERWAY

For those who might not already be familiar with it, the Gulf Intracoastal Waterway is a protected navigation route that follows the coastline from Carrabelle, Florida, to Brownsville, Texas. Like its counterpart on the eastern coast of the United States, the Gulf Intracoastal Waterway takes advantage of natural barrier islands and sections of rivers whenever possible to provide an "inside" route for commercial and recreational boat traffic. This route is protected from the exposure of the open Gulf of Mexico and allows travel in conditions that would be impossible offshore. Like the East Coast waterway, there are some sections that are comprised of man-made canals to connect adjacent naturally occurring waterways. On the northern Gulf, many of these canals are found across the Louisiana section, as well as in Alabama and Florida. The Mississippi section of the Intracoastal Waterway is completely natural, however, as here it simply takes advantage of the existing barrier islands and no canals are needed. The waterway consists of a marked channel that runs east and west through the waters of the sound, mostly closer to the barrier islands than to the mainland. In bad weather, it may seem that the Intracoastal Waterway is not sheltered at all, and, indeed, the Mississippi section is the most exposed part of this entire waterway, due to the fact that the islands here are much farther offshore than typical barrier islands. Despite this, the route is more protected than offshore, and even in the worst conditions the barrier islands break up the biggest waves coming in from sea.

The Gulf Intracoastal Waterway is marked with a series of red and green daybeacons and lighted beacons. The buoyage system is set up with red-right returning, if traveling from east to west. Most Gulf Intracoastal Waterway boaters remember this by the phrase "red-right returning-to-Texas." The western end of the Mississippi section of the waterway begins at Lake Borgne, after emerging from the Rigolets and Lake Pontchartrain in Louisiana.

LAKE BORGNE

Lake Borgne is not really a lake at all, being practically as wide open and exposed to wind and consequently rough seas as the Mississippi Sound. It is bounded on the south side by a maze of marsh islands that lie almost seven miles south of the mouth of the Pearl River at their closest point. The dividing line between Lake Borgne and the Mississippi Sound is at St. Joe Pass, three miles east of the river mouth. Here a point of land extends south from the Mississippi coast, and the Intracoastal Waterway passes between this point and Half Moon Island to the south. Half Moon Island and all the marshlands to the south are claimed by Louisiana. The Mississippi coastline on this northern shore of Lake Borgne is mostly undeveloped marsh. At the southwestern tip of the peninsula north of St. Joe Pass, sand beaches can be found for those wishing to go ashore, and traveling kayakers or other beach cruisers might find a spot to bivouac here. There are also beaches on Grassy Island, a small key just to the south of Intracoastal Waterway. Depths around this little island are 4 to 8 feet, so some cruising boats might find a place to anchor here in settled conditions. Only the shallowest draft vessels and kayaks can closely follow the coastline between the mouth of the Pearl River and St. Joe Pass.

Continuing east along the shore past St. Joseph Point, the coastline maintains its wilderness quality, and deeper waters are much closer to shore. Care should be taken when navigating here though, as there are numerous pilings and wrecks shown on the charts.

POINT CLEAR AND BAYOU CADDY

Civilization begins again north of Point Clear, which is at latitude 30 degrees, 14 minutes north. A marked navigation channel leads into Bayou Caddy, just north of this point. Bayou Caddy is a commercial fishing boat harbor with seafood processing facilities on the shore near the docks. There is also a floating casino docked at the entrance to the bayou, as if it is necessary to have one of these at the westernmost developed reaches of the Mississippi coast. This one is a huge mock-up of a paddlewheel riverboat, and it is called the *Northern Belle*.

Beyond the shrimp boat docks, Bayou Caddy continues inland and there is a county marina and public boat ramp on the north side. When I visited this marina, it appeared that all the boats tied up to the docks there were commercial fishing vessels. The boat ramp is wide and there are docks on both sides to make launching easier. Beyond the county marina, there is another marina and boatyard. I discovered this one by road. When driving away from Bayou Caddy on the seawall road that leads northeast to Waveland and the rest of the Mississippi coast, take the first road to the left. After passing a sign that leads to the Bayou Caddy Marina and Boat Launch just described, continue until the road makes a sharp curve and look for the sign that points to Bordages' Marina. Turning left on this side road will lead you across open, piney savannas and marsh country, until the road crosses a cattle gap and you see free-ranging cattle grazing near the road and among several abandoned powerboats scattered in a field. At the end of this road there is a shed that is more barnlike than nautical, and beneath it several small vessels are dry-docked. There is a sort of travel lift that is pulled by an ancient truck. The place is worth a visit for the photo opportunities alone.

Back on the main road, the coastline curves to the northeast from the mouth of Bayou Caddy, and for a mile or so there are no beaches along the shoreline. A concrete seawall meets the waters of the sound here and a two-lane road follows the shore, leading to Waveland and on to Bay St. Louis. Between Bayou Caddy and Waveland, the beaches of mainland Mississippi begin around Clermont Harbor. Two campgrounds with waterfront views and full RV hookups can be found here: Fairview Campground, and Poor John's Campground and RV Park.

WAVELAND TO BAY ST. LOUIS

More camping facilities are to be found further east at Buccaneer State Park. This park offers a large campground with full hookups just across the road from the sound, as well as a water park with a waterslide, and a large sports park with baseball fields, and tennis courts.

Pirate's Alley Nature trail begins across the street from one of the parking areas within the park and offers a nice walk through coastal piney woods. The trail meanders along the edge of a secluded bayou where there are benches to offer rest in the shade of live oaks and tall pines. Some markers are missing on the path and other trails intersect and split off from the main one, but the area is not big and getting lost should not be a problem.

There are picnic areas and shaded pavilions on the main entrance road and then another nice picnic area right across the road from the beach, just east of the main entrance. This area offers grills and tables under the shade of moss-draped live oaks, as well as a playground for children. There is also a large covered pavilion for group activities.

Continuing northeast from Buccaneer State Park, the waterfront road known as South Beach Boulevard leads into the town of Bay St. Louis. Private homes line the waterfront on the west side of the road, but there is plenty of public beach access between the road and the waters of the sound. Approaching the downtown area of the Bay St. Louis waterfront, a public boat ramp and fishing pier will be seen about a half mile south of the railroad bridge. This pier is built out on a long levee. There are two boat ramps, one wide enough for large trailerable multihulls, and docks with cleats are provided on both sides for securing boats during launching and loading. These ramps offer access to the open sound south of the two bridges that span the mouth of St. Louis Bay.

Just across the road from this park is a unique little shop that offers an island atmosphere and a taste of Hawaii. Da Beach House, owned by Todd and Colleen Read, who lived many years in Hawaii, is a combination coffee and sandwich shop/kayak rental and outfitter. You can sit out on the porch next to potted coconut palms and enjoy a view of the sound while having a cup of Kona coffee, or rent a sit-on-top kayak and get out on the water. Da Beach House rents kayaks and also organizes instructional classes and guided trips for beginning paddlers. Trips range from paddling for a few hours along the beach to overnight camping excursions to the barrier islands. Da Beach House also offers yoga seminars and similar opportunities for learning. Bicycles are also available for rent for those who want to explore the quiet, shaded streets of Bay St. Louis.

Though small in area, the waterfront area of Bay St. Louis offers an interesting mix of restaurants, gift shops, and art studios. This is a good place to park the car and get out and spend an afternoon absorbing the local culture or sampling some fresh Gulf seafood.

A short distance north of this central beach area in Bay St. Louis, South Beach Boulevard intersects Highway 90, and immediately to the east this route becomes a long bridge reaching across St. Louis Bay to Henderson Point and the rest of the Mississippi coastline to the east. In the next chapter we will explore the waters of this bay, which is the largest in Mississippi.

NAVIGATOR'S NOTES

The Lower Pearl River
(Use NOAA Chart No. 11367)

To explore this stretch of the Pearl River, pull off of Highway 90 on the Louisiana side of the East Pearl, (this is the first bridge you cross when driving Highway 90 West from Pearlington, Mississippi) and park in the unpaved parking areas near the boat ramp. Those needing the ramp should have no trouble launching small to midsized powerboats here. From this bridge it is a little more than 7 nautical miles to the mouth of the river at Lake Borgne. Minimum depths in the marked channel will be 8 feet, so many cruising-sized boats can venture this far up the river.

From NOAA Chart No. 11367, it can be seen that anchorage areas for cruising boats can be found on the lower river, especially in some of the side channels. The mud bottom offers good holding ground, but one must take into account the current and be sure the hook is well set before retiring for the night.

Those proceeding downriver from Highway 90 will see red daybeacons #38 and #36 on the east side of the channel. Buoyage here is the standard "red-right-returning," meaning that you should keep the red marks on your right returning upriver from sea, or going into a smaller body of water from a larger body. Across the river and just upstream from the lighted green beacon #35, there is a channel that exits to the west. A bar near the entrance limits draft here to 6 or 7 feet, but the rest of this channel holds 15-foot depths until it connects to the East Middle River. These are technically Louisiana waters, but those wishing to explore can connect into a labyrinth of bayous from the East Middle River.

Back on the main river, green daybeacons #33 and #31 lead the way as the river makes an easterly bend and then turns south-southeast. This section of river is seemingly featureless marsh until you notice a small island near the east bank of the river south of lighted red beacon #30.

This island lies just south of the junction of the East Pearl and the dredged Port Bienville Canal. This canal is an industrial waterway used by barges and small container ships. A number of waterways intersect this canal: Cowan Bayou from the north and Cross and Mulatto Bayous from the south.

Because of the commercial traffic, boaters should not consider anchoring in the canal. Anchorage can be found in Cross Bayou, the first channel turning south off this dredged canal, or along Mulatto Bayou, which also turns south off the canal about a half mile east of the river. Cross Bayou reconnects with Mulatto Bayou about a mile to the south. The 2.7-nautical-mile-long Mulatto Bayou rejoins the East Pearl River about 2 miles from the Gulf. This Mulatto Bayou cutoff maintains soundings of 8 to 16 feet, so most pleasure boats can safely navigate this shortcut.

Back on the main river, just a half mile south of this junction of bayous to the east, the mouth of the Old Pearl River enters from the west on the Louisiana side at lighted green beacon #25. Just a little over a mile south of the Old Pearl River mouth, the river takes a major turn to the southeast, then east. At lighted green beacon #19, there is yet another marked waterway leading off to the southwest. This channel also leads into Louisiana waters and connects to the Rigolets and Lake Pontchartrain. Following the Pearl River to the east, the southern terminus of Mulatto Bayou will be seen on the north bank just across from the charted English Lookout, a cluster of fishing camps on the south bank of the river. The river then turns slightly northeast before making its final bend back to the south where it empties into the Gulf at Lake Borgne. In this final bend the river is spanned by the CSX Railroad bridge, which has a closed vertical clearance of 14 feet. This bridge is usually open during daylight hours unless a train is expected.

At the mouth of the river, lighted red beacon #8 leads the way for vessels inbound from sea. A marked channel south of #8 leads vessels needing its depth to the Intracoastal Waterway, 2 miles to the south.

NAVIGATOR'S NOTES

Lake Borgne and the Mississippi Sound,
From the Mouth of the Pearl River to
Bay St. Louis:
(Use NOAA Charts No. 11367 and 11372)

The channel leading south from the mouth of the East Pearl River joins the Gulf Intracoastal Waterway (ICW) just east of the charted mile-marker shown as St. M 40. Eastbound from this point, two floating green can buoys, #7 and #5, lead the way to the Mississippi Sound.

The safest route from the mouth of the East Pearl River to Bay St. Louis is by way of the ICW. This route is far from direct, however, leading far to the southeast, away from land to junction point at ICW St. M 55, from which a long crossing back to the north-northwest is required.

Most recreational vessels can chart their own, more direct route, after traveling west on the ICW from the Pearl River to St. Joe Pass. This pass lies between the mainland at Lighthouse Pt. and Grassy Island and Half Moon Island to the south. West of this pass, Lake Borgne ends and the Mississippi Sound begins, though the transition between these two large bodies of open water will not be readily apparent.

The coastline falls away to the northeast-east of St. Joseph Point, and ample depths of 6 to 9 feet are found within a mile of the land. Just south of latitude 30 degrees, 14 minutes north, off of Point Clear, flashing green beacon #1 marks the entrance to the channel leading into Bayou Caddy. Bayou Caddy is the only well-protected harbor along this section of coast that has reliable entrance depths of at least 5 feet and has a marked channel. A county marina used mostly by commercial fishing vessels is located on the north shore of the bayou.

There are no facilities for cruising-sized boats between Bayou Caddy and the Bay St. Louis waterfront south of the two bridges that span the bay. Depths of 7 feet are charted quite close to the beaches at Waveland and Bay St. Louis, however. With caution and careful attention to Chart No. 11372, it might be possible to anchor off the coast within a short dinghy ride to town. This would only be practical in the most settled weather, of course.

6

BAY ST. LOUIS, THE JOURDAN RIVER, AND THE WOLF RIVER

BAY ST. LOUIS

The large bay that lies north of Highway 90 between the towns of Bay St. Louis and Pass Christian is shown on nautical charts and coastal maps as St. Louis Bay, but like the town, locals call it simply Bay St. Louis. This name seems more appropriate anyway, since the bay was obviously named by the French, and in that language the word for "bay" would appear before the proper noun. In order to avoid confusion and to save readers who might explore these waters from the blank stares of area residents, I will refer to the bay as Bay St. Louis from here throughout this chapter.

Bay St. Louis is the largest bay to be found on the Mississippi Coast, and the bay and the rivers and bayous that empty into it offer a wide variety of places to explore. Most of the bay is extremely shallow, making it off-limits to vessels drawing more than two feet. There are marked navigation channels, however, that carry at least six feet and lead to most of the interesting destinations to be found in the bay.

Navigation into these waters from the Mississippi Sound entails transiting two bridges that span the mouth of the bay. One of these, as mentioned already, is Highway 90, and the other is the CSX Railroad Bridge. Both of these are opening bridges for vessels needing more vertical clearance than 13 feet at the railroad, and 17 feet at Highway 90. There never seems to be a delay getting through the highway drawbridge, but the CSX Railroad can be a different story. Trains are frequent on this railroad, and the bridge tender will not open if one is within a few miles and closing in. In addition, this bridge is a rusty, ancient-looking contraption that swings horizontally rather than opening vertically like most drawbridges. Sometimes it breaks down and cannot be opened at all. As luck would have it, the one time I was out for a Sunday afternoon day sail with family members who had to get back to work on Monday, the bridge broke down and we were delayed until 10:00 P.M. I was keeping my boat at Discovery Bay Marina at the time, so we had to get through this bridge to get to our vehicles. At least we did get in, late as it was. The bridge tender had informed us by VHF radio that it might be the following day before they got the problem fixed. Even when it is working properly, this bridge operates in what seems like slow motion. Please have patience when approaching it and don't make the mistake some do and try to enter the channel before the span has had time to swing open wide enough to permit passage of your vessel. Wind and wave action can put your glossy gelcoat perilously close to the lurking steel girders of the old bridge before you realize what is happening.

There is a navigational hazard present in the waters just to the north of this drawbridge that well illustrates the importance of paying careful attention to even the most minute details shown on navigational charts. Every mark on a chart, no matter how tiny or seemingly insignificant it appears, is there for a reason and should not be overlooked by prudent mariners. If one maintains a course from the Highway 90 drawbridge to the first marker leading into the bay, which is flashing green beacon #1, almost a nautical mile to the north, this hazard would be far enough off to the east not to be a threat. I made the mistake of not paying close attention to the chart here, knowing I was in deep enough water as long as I stayed on this course. Then one day, circling around on the north side waiting for a bridge opening so I could exit the bay, my companion pointed to the water and said there was a "pole" just under the surface. I doubted it, but looked anyway, and sure enough, there was a substantial wooden piling visible, just inches beneath the surface of the muddy bay waters. How could this be? I looked at the chart, and naturally, there it was, a charted "pile," east of the rhumbline between the drawbridge and green beacon #1. That's exactly where we were, drifting around too far east of the rhumbline. Such a piling could hole the hull of a heavy-displacement boat under way at speed. I learned a valuable lesson about charts that day and the importance of always knowing where you are on the chart while navigating.

North of this danger area, there is a junction of three channels that lead into the three main navigable areas of the bay. These channels extend into the lower reaches of the main waterways that drain into the bay: The Jourdan River, the Wolf River, and Bayou Portage. The first channel leads off to the northwest and to the Jourdan River. We will return to that later in this chapter. The channels to the Wolf River and Bayou Portage split at the red and green junction daybeacon "A" that is located to the northeast of the first green marker north of Highway 90. Bayou Portage is reached by taking the channel that leads due east after the split. (Detailed instructions for navigating all these channels are found in the *Navigator's Notes* at the end of this chapter.)

BAYOU PORTAGE AND DISCOVERY BAY

During the three years that I kept my sailboat at Discovery Bay Marina, entering the Bayou Portage channel was like coming home. Even so, negotiating this channel always required caution and my full attention. Wandering outside the dredged cut even with just four feet of draft will quickly put you hard aground. As mentioned above, the Bayou Portage channel splits off to the east from the Wolf River channel at junction marker "A." We will explore this Wolf River channel, but first let's take a long side trip into Bayou Portage and the bizarre ruins and abandoned dreams to be found along its banks.

A straight east-west channel marked by three green beacons, the middle one lighted, leads to the entrance to Bayou Portage. This middle, lighted beacon has a large osprey nest built on top of the piling. Each year as I have sailed in and out past it, I have seen a family of young ospreys reared there.

The old Bayou Portage bridge defined the word "dilapidated." Like a border crossing leading into a Third World country, it stood as an ominous portal and a first glimpse of what to expect in this forgotten backwater known as Bayou Portage. As of this writing, the bridge has been removed and will be replaced in what is estimated to be a two-year project. Previously, the bridge was not manned by a full-time tender, but the tender who was on call could be reached by calling either the Highway 90 bridge tender or Discovery Bay Marina. Reaching Discovery Bay Marina by VHF is always an iffy proposition, depending on whether the bar is open or how loud the jukebox is blasting.

Once inside this bridge crossing you will find yourself in quite protected waters. There are a few residences on the south shore near the bridge, but most of the shore here is marsh and pine trees. Heading straight east past the bridge will take you to a junction of navigation possibilities. A marked channel that leads off to the southeast is used by industrial barges and terminates in a man-made dockage basin where these barges are loaded and unloaded. The other option is to hang a left at the first red navigational marker, which is floating nun buoy #12, and wind your way into the upper reaches of the bayou to Discovery Bay and beyond. This channel is not marked and is surrounded by extremely shallow water. Local advice says to follow the shoreline with it off your port side, staying "about 40 feet from the bank." This has always worked for me, and I have yet to find the bottom here, but you will see soundings of only 5 to 6 feet, even in the deepest part of the channel. This leads you in a northerly direction, and soon the way leads to the entrance of what appears to be a small creek. By now you will see the masts of several sailboats that are docked in the hidden basin; and the ruins of a two-storey building, a few scattered RV's, and some boats on trailers will be visible on the eastern bank of this creek. A no-wake sign is posted at the entrance to the marina, and just inside the narrow passageway, a funky little bar built halfway out over the water on pilings guards the basin. This is the office and watering hole for Discovery Bay Marina, and the place to find perhaps the best cheeseburgers on the entire Gulf coast, if you happen to arrive when Jack Waldrip, the owner, is working behind the bar.

Discovery Bay Marina is not the kind of place you will find to your liking if you are used to posh marinas where you can hook up to all the amenities for the night and enjoy security and convenience to shoreside services.

The bar and docks of Discovery Bay Marina. Photo by Kim Strahan.

This backwoods yacht basin is not convenient to anything, there is no security, and there may or may not be water and electricity at the dock when you arrive. If the electricity does work, don't expect to hook up to it with your normal 30- or 50-amp shorepower cord. You will need an adapter for a regular household three-prong socket to plug in here, and your cord may have to be long enough to try out several of the outlets until you find one that works. The docks themselves are always in need of repair, so before stepping off your deck, be sure you are stepping onto solid wood that is still nailed down. Most of the boats in the basin are badly neglected or even abandoned. More than one sunken vessel will be seen in the slips. The encircling piney woods and abandoned buildings provide protection from strong winds, but these windless conditions frequently enable hordes of marsh mosquitoes and no-see-ums to swarm the marina. These are some of the downsides to the marina. As I said, it may not be to everyone's liking.

If, however, you have traveled in undeveloped countries or done a lot of backcountry exploring, this character-laden marina will appeal to you as it did me. As it turned out, I put up with the inconveniences and kept my sailboat docked there for three years. Most of the time the place is quiet and private. There are freedoms to be had in such a place that you won't find in many marinas. This includes the freedom to build or rebuild your boat right at the dock, or to target practice with your pistol if you prefer. Live-aboards are allowed here, and there are usually at least two or three full-timers living on their boats, as well as others living in RV's parked near the bar.

Despite the lack of other amenities, there is a nice swimming pool near the bar that is kept clean and well maintained. Bathrooms with showers are provided, as well as a commercial washing machine and dryer.

Occasionally there are rowdy parties at the bar, usually when there are football games on TV or during holidays. The marina has also played host to quite a few outdoor parties, live concerts, and even the occasional wedding. These events are few and far between though, and usually the dockage basin is a peaceful environment in which to work on your boat or just lounge on the deck and enjoy the quiet.

Beyond the marina basin, a series of waterways leads even farther into the backcountry. There are a few residents living along these shores, but for the most part the area is heavily wooded. The area surrounding the marina once was part of a 700-acre planned resort community with 1,500 residential lots. The arrival of Hurricane Camille in 1969 put an end to that. No one has been willing or able to invest enough in the property since then to develop a sewage treatment facility, and the county will not permit further construction on the property until this takes place. Six houses were built before 1991, when this restriction was implicated. This explains the presence of the many dilapidated buildings and the poorly maintained road that leads into the area. At the entrance to the property, off Arcadian Road, one can get a feel for the grandiose scale the original developers had in mind. A fountain and brick sign stands at the entrance and rows of tall cabbage palms grow in the median of the broad boulevard that leads to the marina. Perhaps someday someone will invest the necessary money to bring the original plan to life, but until that day, Discovery Bay will retain its unique character.

For those who would like to drive to Discovery Bay for a cheeseburger or just to look at the boats, the easiest route is from Menge Avenue, in Pass Christian. This avenue runs north and south between Highway 90 on the beach and Interstate 10 to the north. Turn west off of Menge onto Arcadian Road, a narrow street that winds through woods and fields and past several homes built up on poles near the edge of the marsh. The entrance to Discovery Bay will be found on the south side of Arcadian Road. The palm-lined boulevard leading in quickly narrows to a roughly paved, pothole-filled road. Follow this across a small bridge, turn left, and then follow the pavement through a series of right turns until it dead-ends into the marina parking lot.

The waterways upstream from the marina can be explored by those in small powerboats, canoes, or kayaks, but cruising-size boats will find nowhere to go other than a few private docks. During hurricanes, quite a few boats are brought into these waterways, and good protection is found from the wind, but the entire area is subject to flooding, and the marina docks have been completely submerged many times by storm surges.

THE SUNKEN SCHOONERS OF BAYOU PORTAGE

Long before Hurricane Camille stopped the completion of the Discovery Bay Resort, Bayou Portage was the scene of another unexpected loss of property. In the early 1930s, when sails began to give way to engines on the commercial fishing vessels, the Dunbar and DuKate Seafood Factory in Pass Christian sailed their old schooners to Bayou Portage. There were 13 or more of these vessels, some as long as 65 feet, docked in the bayou for safekeeping until buyers could be found.

A man was hired to watch over them and perform required maintenance, but after about a year, they all began simultaneously taking on water. They were pumped continuously and the source of the leaking was found to be caused by some type of wood-boring bug. To plug the holes temporarily, dry sawdust was released under the damaged areas so that it would float up inside the holes and swell. This was a common method used to patch holes in wooden hulls until they could be hauled out for more permanent repairs.

Bayou Portage channel. Photo by Kim Strahan.

Despite these efforts, all these schooners sank at their moorings within six more months. The type of organism that caused the damage is still not known for certain. They were not *teredos* (commonly known as shipworms), which are mollusks, but were said to resemble the "roly poly" or pill bug that lives under logs and rocks. These *isopods* have marine relatives, and one of these wood-boring crustaceans is the most likely suspect, but it may never be known for sure which kind of animal sank all these schooners.

THE WOLF RIVER

Back out on the waters of Bay St. Louis, we can now take a look at the other options that larger boats have in this area. As mentioned before, it is possible to enter the Wolf River from the bay, if one turns north at the green and red junction marker found at the entrance to the Bayou Portage channel. NOAA Chart No. 11372 shows the entrance channel to the Wolf River to carry 3-foot depths to a width of 100 feet, as of February 2000. According to Claiborne Young's *Cruising Guide to the Northern Gulf*, "The entrance channel is only sparsely marked and carries low-tide soundings of only 5 to 5½ feet in several places. There are also several unmarked, tricky sections that call for extra caution." Young says that the river is only appropriate for boats that draw less than 4½ feet and are no longer than 36 feet. This makes it really questionable for any vessels drawing more than 4 feet, but for those who can find their way into the river, the extra caution required will be worth the effort. Most of the area is still natural, though a few homes over-look the river in places. Anchorage can be found in the lower reaches of the river, once inside the tricky entrance, but boats needing more than 28 feet of vertical clearance will have to turn back at the first bridge, which is a fixed span. The area above this bridge is popular with kayakers, and outfit-ter Joe Feil of Wolf River Canoe and Kayak can provide rentals as well as shuttle service and guided tours. The upper reaches of the Wolf River pro-vide excellent wilderness canoe tripping opportunities. Detailed information about this part of the river can be found in the guidebook *Canoeing Mississippi* by Ernest Herndon.

All of the lower river and surrounding marsh country is accessible to sea kayakers, and it is a beautiful area well worth taking the trouble to explore. The shallow reaches of the river and northern side of the bay that are such a nuisance to deep-draft vessels are a haven for paddlers looking to escape the marine traffic of more navigable waters. Many were the times that I longed for the simplicity of a kayak while motoring down the dredged channel of Bayou Portage in my deep-keeled sailboat. At such times I wondered what caused me to make the transition from the utter freedom and simplicity of kayaking to all the headaches and worries of sailing a larger vessel. I'm still not sure what the answer to that is, but I suppose life is all about learning, and I was attracted to the intricacies of sailing.

THE JOURDAN RIVER

One other major navigation route exists in Bay St. Louis, and this is the chan-nel that leads into the Jourdan River. This channel begins back out in the open bay north of the Highway 90 drawbridge at flashing green beacon #1.

Like the rest of the bay, much of the water outside this marked channel is quite thin, so care must be taken to maintain a straight course between the widely spaced markers leading to the river. At the mouth of the river, the channel passes close to the shoreline to the south, and the route becomes much more obvious.

A well-protected basin on this southern shore was once the sight of Bay Cove Marina, which many say was the most picturesque marina in Mississippi. Now Casino Magic, a huge gambling resort, occupies this southern shoreline of the river, and much of the marina is gone, except for a small dockage basin on the eastern side of the marina property.

There is also an RV campground on the casino property and a boat ramp, which might prove useful to some who are arriving by road with a trailerable boat to begin their explorations of the Jourdan River and Bay St. Louis.

West of the old Bay Cove entrance channel, the river broadens and depths are good, with soundings of 18 to 21 feet in places. By staying in the middle parts of the stream you can proceed here without worry about finding the bottom. The banks become more sparsely developed, and opportunities for anchorage are abundant. This part of the Jourdan River is a beautiful cruising ground, and once you have reached this section, you will be glad you made the long side trip from the Mississippi Sound to explore it. Good protected anchorage in bad weather can be found by continuing upstream to the point where the river turns to the north. There is a fixed double bridge several miles upstream with an estimated clearance of 40 feet. Vessels able to slip under this can find excellent anchorage in 8 to 16 feet of water on the north side of this bridge. Those in smaller boats will find many more side channels to explore, and the upper Jourdan River, like the Wolf, is popular with canoers. The wide open reaches and good depths of this river also make the area popular for water-skiers and personal watercraft operating at high speed, so paddlers should be alert and be prepared to take evasive action. The best strategy for quiet paddling, as in so many other waterways of coastal Mississippi, is to go on weekdays or off-season weekends when other boaters are not out in force.

NAVIGATOR'S NOTES

Entering Bay St. Louis from the ICW
(Use NOAA Chart No. 11372)

For those transiting this coastline by way of the Intracoastal Waterway and wishing to make a side trip to the bay, the distance north to the entrance of the bay is almost 8 nautical miles. Use NOAA chart No. 11372 for navigation to and within the bay. On the ICW, at the east end of Grand Island Channel, and one nautical mile to the southwest of charted ICW mile-marker St. M 55, flashing green beacon #1 makes a good jumping off point to detour to Bay St. Louis. From this ICW marker, one should lay a course to the flashing red beacon #2 that lies just west of the charted Square Handkerchief Shoal and just over 2 nautical miles south of the CSX Railroad Bridge. This course is a run of 5.5 nautical miles. Much of the time you might be out of sight of any landmarks, but it is necessary to maintain a course that takes you west of the Square Handkerchief and its shallow waters. Passing this red #2 marker on your starboard side will ensure that you are well clear of the shoals, and from here you can lay a course directly for the opening span of the railroad bridge. The vertical clearance at this bridge is 13 feet. The bridge swings horizontally, and the navigation channel is on the west side of the center pivot and operator's station. Commercial barge traffic occasionally transits this bridge, and many of these vessels require the entire horizontal clearance of the swinging span. This is something skippers should always be mindful of when approaching any bridge, as right of way must be given to larger and less maneuverable vessels.

Once inside the CSX Railroad Bridge, it is a mere half mile to the drawbridge on Highway 90. Closed vertical clearance at this span is 17 feet. This drawbridge opens on demand and the bridge tender is usually quick to respond to VHF requests for an opening.

Heading into the bay from the Highway 90 drawbridge, set a course for flashing green daybeacon #1, almost 1 nautical mile to the north. Pay close attention to sideways drift between the bridge and this marker, and this course will keep you well to the west of the charted piling that stands barely submerged just north of the bridge.

Most of the bay is extremely shallow. Vessels drawing 2 feet or less can explore most areas except the mud flats near shore, but deep-draft vessels will have little choice of routes within the estuary. These routes all begin with this first flashing green daybeacon. One exception is the channel that leads into the Bay-Waveland Yacht Club, located on the western shore of the bay north of the Highway 90 bridge terminus.

Private aids to navigation lead the way into the channel to this harbor. All other vessels not heading to this private dockage facility will have two choices once abeam of green beacon #1: the route northeast into the Bayou Portage/Wolf River channel or northwest to the Jourdan River.

NAVIGATOR'S NOTES

Bayou Portage
(Use NOAA Chart No. 11372)

To enter this channel from green beacon #1, you must lay a course to come abeam of unlighted daybeacon "A" on its easterly side. Daybeacon "A" lies half a nautical mile to the northeast of green #1. This rectangular marker shows both red and green, and the junction it signifies is the split the channel makes here, with the northeasterly fork leading to Bayou Portage and the northern channel leading into the Wolf River.

To enter Bayou Portage from junction marker "A," head for red daybeacon #2, keeping it to starboard, as this is a standard "red-right-returning" channel. You will see another red daybeacon, #4, and at this point the channel turns directly east and makes a straight run to a county road drawbridge spanning the bayou. There are three green daybeacons leading the way to the bridge crossing; the second one, #7, is lighted. It is important to keep your course in a straight line passing just to the south of these three markers. Strong crosswinds can make this difficult if you don't occasionally look astern to check for sideways drift. Again, the penalty for getting out of the dredged channel is a solid grounding.

As of this writing, the old Bayou Portage drawbridge has been removed and the new one is under construction. Barges with construction equipment may at times obstruct the entrance channel, and the channel may be marked with temporary floating aids to navigation until this project is completed. All boaters are urged to use caution in this area.

Once past the bridge area, continue east to floating red nun buoy #12. At this point, a marked channel leads off to the southeast to an industrial dockage basin.

To enter Discovery Bay, turn north at #12 and follow the shoreline to your port side, keeping off approximately 40 feet. Depths will be as shallow as 5 to 6 feet in places. From here you will enter what appears to be a small creek. Stay to the center until past the dirt boat ramp and the building to your starboard side, and you will reach a basin with 3 separate docks with boat slips on each side. Depths are more than adequate at all the slips near the ends of the docks.

NAVIGATOR'S NOTES

The Wolf River

(Use NOAA Chart No. 11372)

The Wolf River is accessed by the channel that begins in the bay at the red and green junction marker "A" where the Bayou Portage channel splits off. The Wolf River channel runs almost due north to flashing green beacon #3, then turns northeast to green #5. This entrance channel is charted as only 3 feet deep for a width of 100 feet. Because of this, the Wolf River should be approached with caution by larger vessels.

Once inside the mouth of the river, depths run 7 to 10 feet, but a fixed bridge with a vertical clearance of 28 feet spans the river just a little over one nautical mile upstream. Skippers of vessels that can pass under this bridge will find several more miles of navigable waters upstream.

NAVIGATOR'S NOTES

Jourdan River

(Use NOAA Chart No. 11372)

The Jourdan River channel begins at the first navigation marker in Bay St. Louis found north of the Highway 90 drawbridge. This is flashing green beacon #1. The Jourdan River channel diverges off to the northwest from the Wolf River/Bayou Portage channels at #1.

Entering the bay from the south, put this green marker abeam off your port side and turn northwest. The channel is charted as 5½ feet deep for a width of 100 feet. 1.3 nautical miles northwest of #1, green daybeacon #3 leads the way in to the Jourdan River channel. Keep these markers lined up as you proceed, paying careful attention to sideways drift. The course continues on the same heading to the next marker, flashing green beacon #5. Put this marker abeam to port also, and then you will spot unlighted green daybeacon #7, which lies to the west-southwest. Pass to the north of this marker and you will see one final green daybeacon, #9, also on this west-southwest heading. Once past this marker on its northerly side, you are entering into the natural mouth of the river, and the charted soundings show anywhere from 7 to 19 feet in this reach. There are two additional markers west of #9—#1 and #2—leading into the Bay Cove Marina dockage basin.

The Jourdan River channel west of this point is deep and wide, making for easy navigation for several miles, in which the river turns north. A fixed double bridge spans the river at this point, with an estimated vertical clearance of 40 feet.

7

PASS CHRISTIAN TO BILOXI, INCLUDING DEER ISLAND

East of Bay St. Louis, the mainland shore closely parallels Highway 90, a busy four-lane that serves as a major east-west corridor along this most heavily developed section of the Mississippi coast. Driving this highway from Pass Christian to Biloxi, one will see a continuous beach of white sand between the seawall just south of the roadway and the waters of the Mississippi Sound. This wide expanse of sand is not natural. It was created by dredging sand from the sound and is said to be the "longest man-made beach in the world." Man-made or not, these beaches are as pretty as any and are widely enjoyed by residents and visitors alike as the most accessible beaches the state has to offer. Casino development has all but buried some stretches of this coastline under hotels and parking lots, but, on the other hand, much money has been spent improving the public beaches that are not built on and some sections have been planted in sea oats and reserved for bird nesting only. Natural-looking dunes are being slowly built up in these areas so that they are beginning to resemble the outer beaches found on the Gulf side of the barrier islands.

Because of the proximity of Highway 90 and all of its attendant residential and commercial development, those exploring the coast looking for solitude and quiet won't find it here, except on Deer Island, at the easternmost end of this section. What this shoreline does have to offer is easy access to the water, with regularly spaced launching ramps, marinas, and 29 miles of beach access for those with kayaks or other lightweight boats that can be carried across the sand. This coastline also offers the most opportunities for those who do not own boats to get out on the water on rental craft or commercially operated ferry and charter boats.

The 29 miles of coastline from the mouth of Bay St. Louis at Henderson Point to Point Cadet on the eastern end of the Biloxi peninsula is the longest stretch covered in this book that is not interrupted by marshes or estuaries. This, of course, is the reason that this entire area is easily accessible by road. Since most readers will likely first reach this coastline from shoreside rather than by boat, we will navigate eastward by road as well as by sea.

BAY ST. LOUIS TO PASS CHRISTIAN

Leaving the protection of Bay St. Louis, bound for the open sound or Gulf beyond, boaters will pass under two bridges, Highway 90 and the CSX railroad, described in the previous chapter. On the east side of the bay, there is a dry storage marina located between Highway 90 and the railroad. This is Pelican Cove Marina, and the facilities include a ship's store, fuel dock, and a launch ramp. To reach this marina by road, after crossing the Highway 90 bridge from Bay St. Louis, turn right onto Bayview Drive and follow it straight to the launch ramp. A series of quiet residential streets roughly follows the shoreline of Henderson Point east of the marina, until the beach and Highway 90 merge to begin their long parallel reach to Biloxi.

The near-shore waters around Henderson Point are shallow, so caution is needed transiting this area in any vessel drawing more than 2 feet. Pay close attention to NOAA Chart No. 11372 and stay in the deeper water a half mile south of the beaches. Beware of the treacherous shoals found 2 miles south of Henderson Point, however. This is an area of extensive oyster reefs known as the Square Handkerchief Shoal.

Drawing four feet, three inches on my sailboat *Intensity*, I managed to run aground in this area one day while preoccupied with good conversation and flying along on a fine beam reach. Luckily, I was able to heel the boat

Brian Nobles carries his ultralight mahogany sea kayak across the beach to launch near Pass Christian.

with the sails to lift the keel enough to plow my way back to deeper water with the engine.

Pass Christian municipal harbor is relatively easy to approach from the west, so long as you stay in the deep water between the mainland and the outlying shoals. The entrance to the breakwater that protects the harbor is well marked with aids to navigation.

Those traveling Highway 90 will see the Pass Christian harbor just two and a half miles east of Henderson Point. There are two boat ramps, restroom facilities, and a large parking lot available to the public. The Pass Christian Yacht Club is also located in this basin. The Pass Christian area is one of the nicest areas remaining along the Highway 90 beaches. So far, there are no casinos or high-rise hotels in this area, but instead, facing seaward from the low bluffs on the north side of the highway, are dozens of fine old mansions and beach houses surrounded by landscaped gardens of subtropical vegetation. I have often enjoyed paddling my kayak along this shore as it offers nice scenery and a relatively peaceful setting for those times when I only could go out for an hour or two. It is only necessary to paddle out a quarter of a mile or so to escape the noise of the busy highway and put yourself in another world from all those shorebound folks in their mad rush. From this vantage point, you can watch the distant traffic in a detached way, while listening to the crying of gulls and the lapping of waves against your hull.

PASS CHRISTIAN TO GULFPORT

Continuing east on Highway 90, past 6 miles of public beaches, the next town east of Pass Christian is Long Beach. There is a municipal marina here as well, and as at Pass Christian, the Long Beach Yacht Club is located in the harbor. Three public boat ramps are available, as well as restrooms and a large parking area.

For those with trailerable boats or sea kayaks, the Long Beach area is a good place to launch for a passage to Cat Island. This is the westernmost of the barrier islands, and the crossing from Long Beach is one of the shortest passages to the islands. There is less commercial traffic in this part of the sound than in other areas farther east, so this might be a good start for less experienced boaters who want to begin exploring the islands. In good weather the island is clearly visible on the horizon, seven miles south of Long Beach.

Farther east, casinos and high-rise hotels south of Highway 90 mark the Gulfport area of the mainland beach, and on a clear day, these can be seen from the waters off Bay St. Louis. These are the first of many new beach-side developments that we will come to as we travel east to Biloxi.

Gulfport is one of the most important commercial shipping ports of the Gulf of Mexico. Freighters from all over the world visit these docks. As of this writing, Carnival Cruise lines has recently begun operating a major Caribbean cruise ship out of Gulfport.

East of the commercial harbor, Gulfport Small Craft Harbor includes a large marina, a Coast Guard station, and the Gulfport Yacht Club. There are also fish bait vendors located at the harbor and four extra-wide launching ramps with ample parking areas.

Those who do not own boats can experience one of Mississippi's barrier islands by boarding one of the Ship Island Excursion boats docked in the central part of the harbor just north of the Coast Guard station. The Skrmetta family has operated this ferry service to West Ship Island for over seventy years. The company operates three excursion vessels, the *Captain Pete* and the *Gulf Islander*, both of which are fast, modern aluminum cruisers, and the *Pan American Clipper*, a locally built wooden vessel. There are several departure times per day during the season, which runs from March through October. Passengers have the option of spending a few hours or a whole day on the island. These excursion boats offer open decks and air-conditioned cabins, as well as snack bars with food and cold drinks. The boats run seven days per week during the season, but all trips are subject to cancellation due to bad weather. For more information on these trips, call (228) 864-1014 or 1-800-388-3290. West Ship Island will be described in detail in chapter 13 of this book. Because of these excursion boats, this island receives far more visitors per season than any of the other barrier islands. The whole operation is run under the strict guidelines of the National Park Service, though, so despite this heavy use, West Ship Island remains relatively pristine compared to the mainland.

Just to the south of the excursion boat docks is the Marine Life Oceanarium, which is one of the oldest such facilities in the country, having been founded in 1956. Marine Life is one of Mississippi's largest family attractions and is dedicated to providing education and up-close personal experiences with marine mammals such as the Atlantic bottlenose dolphin and the California sea lion. The dolphins displayed are the same species as the ones commonly encountered by boaters in the Mississippi Sound. The Oceanarium is open year around, with up to seven shows daily. Shows include divers interacting with dolphins and sea turtles and displays of trained dolphins and seals performing stunts. A trip to Marine Life is great fun for the entire family and a special treat to children of all ages.

Much of the land just north of Gulfport Small Craft Harbor is incorporated in the public Bert Jones Park. This park provides picnic tables and a playground, and is often the site of special events and outdoor concerts throughout the year.

GULFPORT TO BILOXI

East of Gulfport, along the public beaches, there are several seasonal concessions that rent personal watercraft such as Waverunners, the ubiquitous Hobie Cat catamarans, and assorted other water toys such as sailboards and pedal-powered boats with huge floating wheels. These rental boats are generally limited to the close inshore area in the vicinity of the vendors, but they can still offer a fun time on the water for those not inclined to ride a crowded passenger ferry.

Navigation along this section of the coast by boat is straightforward. All that is really necessary is to stay at least a half mile off the beaches, where the water depths begin to slope from less than 4 feet to 7 to 9 feet.

Even this close to the bustle and congestion of Highway 90, those boaters with cruising accommodations might find a pleasant anchorage for a night or two along this stretch of coast. When I returned to my home waters of Mississippi after a nine-day cruise back from south Florida on my sailboat, I dropped the hook in this area to spend one more night out before heading for my slip in Discovery Bay Marina. It had been a rough passage most of the way, and this night anchored off Gulfport was the first time I could really relax and know I had made it. I was home, within the sights and sounds and smells of this familiar place, yet still self-contained in my little floating world and not yet ready to go ashore. I cooked a good meal on board and then sat in the darkness watching the lights of the cars go by less than a mile away. The following day I knew I would tie up to the dock and go back to my familiar life of work and friends and family, but that night I was still in the world of a sailor. I enjoyed a beer and smoked a good cigar and thought about those scary but exhilarating nights out on the open Gulf. I might have missed that experience of anchoring there so close to the city if not for that longer cruise, since my usual destination for an overnight trip had always been one of the barrier islands.

The Broadwater Beach Resort is the next marina located on the coast east of the Gulfport Small Craft Harbor. This marina can accommodate few sailboats, as most of the slips are covered. It is mainly a powerboater's marina and is one of the best full-service, luxurious marinas between Mobile and New Orleans. There is an on-site marina restaurant with a dining area overlooking the dockage basin. The restaurant features a Polynesian theme and fresh seafood and steaks. Showers, bathrooms, and laundry facilities are available for guests, and on the docks there are 30- and 50-amp power connections and water connections. There is also a small ship's and variety store, fuel dock, and waste pump-out station.

Many of the powerboats docked here are charter sportfishing boats, so this is a good place for those interested in offshore fishing to find a boat for hire. The President Casino is also located at the south end of this harbor, along with a large parking area for casino visitors. There are no boat ramps at this marina.

This marina is within walking distance of the Beauvoir Mansion, located on the north side of Highway 90 just a short distance to the west. This was the beachfront home of Jefferson Davis, the first and only president of the Confederate States of America. It is now a museum with many interesting exhibits open for public viewing.

The next "landmark" one will encounter traveling east from the Broadwater is a huge and horrendously ugly rendition of a square-rigged pirate ship called Treasure Bay Casino. This marks the beginning of a long strip of bars, restaurants, and beach stores that crowd the Biloxi coast on both sides of Highway 90.

BILOXI HARBOR AND POINT CADET

Three miles east of the Broadwater channel lies the entrance to Biloxi Channel, the long, narrow passage between the mainland and Deer Island. This marked channel begins two miles offshore to lead deep-draft vessels in through an area of shoals and spoil banks. A detailed guide to navigating this channel is given in the *Navigator's Notes* section at the end of this chapter. A long-standing landmark found on the shore north of this inbound channel is the old Biloxi Lighthouse. It stands in the middle of the Highway 90 median, and has weathered hurricanes and other storms since it was first lit in 1824. The lighthouse is built of brick surrounded by a cast iron shell.

Times have changed, and the Biloxi Lighthouse, a relic of the past, is no longer used for navigation into Biloxi harbor. Now the most prominent landmark here is the Beau Rivage Casino and Resort, which is probably the most extravagant of all the casinos in Mississippi. It stands just east of the I-110 spur that loops out over the waters of the sound before merging with Highway 90. One has to wonder about the purpose or practicality of this bit of highway engineering. Was building an exit loop on piers out over the beach and beyond the only way they could find to route traffic from I-110 to Highway 90, or was this simply a designer's statement, an opportunity to build something unique?

The Beau Rivage hotel and casino is visible from as far out as the barrier islands on a clear day. The presence of this and other large buildings on "Casino Row" has forever altered the way the Biloxi waterfront appears to mariners approaching from seaward.

Beau Rivage includes a marina, so cruisers who might be inclined to stop here and try their luck can tie up to the docks and step right into the casino. Once past the entrance to the Beau Rivage Marina, boaters will find themselves in a narrow passageway with the cliff-like walls of the resort to the north and rock jetties and sandy islets to the south. These islets are detached from Deer Island, which begins about a mile further east. There are channels between them that might be tempting as shortcuts, but these are too shallow for anything but lightweight boats such as kayaks, and even in these you might have to get out and drag over the shoals at low tide.

On the north side of the channel east of Beau Rivage lies the entrance to Biloxi Small Craft Harbor, which is protected by a high concrete breakwater. This harbor is as busy as Gulfport, so caution is needed when entering as well as when passing the entrance in the channel. The harbor is crowded with commercial and recreational craft, and there is a boat ramp and a Travel-lift available. There is a fuel dock and bait shop in the harbor, as well as a seafood restaurant and bar. A parasail boat also operates out of this harbor, for those wanting to get a gull's eye view of the Mississippi Sound. There is

The western end of Deer Island, seen from a parking garage on the Biloxi mainland

also a tour boat called the *Sailfish* that takes passengers on a "shrimp tour" with a trawl net set to show how commercial fishing is done and to introduce guests to some of the varieties of marine life found in the sound.

East of the harbor lies another breakwater, which protects the docks of Pelican Cay. These docks are affiliated with the Pelican Cay Condominiums across Highway 90 on the mainland and offer no facilities for transient yachts. The next set of docks beyond Pelican Cay belongs to the Biloxi Yacht Club, and the clubhouse and parking lot is located adjacent to it on the north side of Highway 90.

There is a popular public launching ramp just east of the yacht club at Kuhn Street. This public park offers a wide concrete ramp protected by wooden breakwaters and a long pier with a covered area at the end. There is a parking lot for vehicles with trailers, but it is small and can get crowded on weekends. This ramp is heavily used because of its convenient location in the channel with the protection of Deer Island just under half a mile away. This is a great place to launch a small boat or kayak for a quick trip to Deer Island or beyond.

The Biloxi Channel continues east between Deer Island and the next row of casinos, which begins with the Biloxi Grand Casino. There is another public launch ramp at Oak Street, but driving by on Highway 90 it is easily missed as this side street turns south between the casino and a multilevel parking garage.

The last marina on this stretch of the coast is at Point Cadet, where the Biloxi peninsula ends and the Highway 90 bridge to Ocean Springs begins. This is a large marina with several commercial charter vessels operating from its docks. Perhaps the most notable of these are the two replica Biloxi schooners, the *Mike Sekul* and the *Glen L. Sweatman*. Both of these wooden vessels were built locally to the same lines and specifications as the original working schooners that sailed the Mississippi Sound before powered fishing vessels came into use. These schooners depart daily from the docks at Point Cadet for short sails in the sound and sometimes special charter trips to the barrier islands. The schooners are maintained and operated by the Biloxi Maritime and Seafood Industry Museum located at 115 1st Street in Biloxi. For information on sailing schedules, contact the museum at (228) 435-6320.

This museum is located on the point just north of the beginning of the Highway 90 bridge that crosses to Ocean Springs. The museum, open to the public for a small entry fee, contains many interesting displays on the maritime history of the Biloxi area, beginning with the Biloxi Indians. There are artifacts from this long extinct culture, as well as early artists' depictions of the way their villages appeared at the time of the French colonization.

Other exhibits illustrate the early methods of fishing in the Mississippi Sound in the grand days of sail, and lots of old black and white photos of heavy-laden Biloxi schooners adorn the walls of the museum. In one room a full-sized model of the ribs of a schooner shows the way these traditional boats were constructed. There are also nets and other related fishing equipment on display.

Part of the museum is dedicated to the history of Gulf coast hurricanes, with dates and statistics for dozens of major storms since the time they were first recorded. Hurricane Camille, of course, occupies a sizable part of this section. For those at all interested in the history of boating on the Mississippi Gulf Coast, a visit to the museum is a must.

Also located at Point Cadet, on the south side of Highway 90 and just north of the marina, is the J. L. Scott Marine Education Center and Aquarium. Opened in 1984, this 33,000-square-foot facility accommodates students and visitors interested in learning more about the coastal environment. The center contains 47 aquariums, which showcase native fish and other creatures of the ocean, bayous, bays and rivers. The centerpiece is the 42,000-gallon Gulf of Mexico Tank, which is home to sharks, eels, redfish, striped bass, and other large fish. An adjacent vivarium features turtles and alligators. The center also features a collection of more than 900 seashells from around the world, an interactive laboratory, changing art exhibits, and a 313-seat auditorium with continuous documentary videos. A gift shop offers resource books, educational materials, and jewelry and novelty items.

In addition to the two Biloxi schooners, another large and unique sailing vessel operating out of Point Cadet is *Yellow Bird*, a 48-by-28-foot charter catamaran that accommodates up to 45 passengers. This catamaran offers regularly scheduled trips to the barrier islands and private charter trips. Because of its shallow draft, the catamaran can sail right up to the barrier islands and drop a boarding ladder, which allows passengers to step off practically on the beach.

Point Cadet Marina is one of the few marinas on the Mississippi coast that has a large population of live-aboard boaters. Many marinas on this coast do not permit live-aboards, but at Point Cadet it is not at all discouraged. There are metered electrical hookups at each dock, as well as water and optional telephone and cable TV connections. The bathrooms are well maintained and climate-controlled and offer three shower stalls in each. A laundry room is provided in a convenient location between the men's and women's restrooms. The harbormaster's office is located on the top floor of the building that houses the restrooms, and the second floor is occupied by Gorenflo's Bait and Tackle Shop. A fuel dock is located on the end of the pier south of this building, and parking for marina residents is provided just north of the docks. The entire harbor is surrounded by a modern breakwater, but it is still somewhat exposed to strong southeasterly winds. At the time of this writing, I have been living aboard my sailboat, *Intensity*, for three months at Point Cadet, having left Discovery Bay to find a harbor not land-locked by bridges.

Beyond Point Cadet is the entrance to Back Bay of Biloxi and the bridge to Ocean Springs on the other side of the bay. Back Bay and its many water-ways and places of interest will be explored fully in the next chapter.

DEER ISLAND

Deer Island is the last area to explore along this section of the coast and is certainly one of the more interesting areas. This island is not a barrier island, as it lies within the protection of the chain of islands much farther offshore. It has many similarities to the barrier islands, though, and offers relatively secluded beaches that are easily reached from the mainland. The island is still undeveloped and heavily wooded, despite the fact that it was privately owned until recently and not under any government protection. There was much recent discussion of plans for developing this island, and the casino companies were eager to get their hands on it to build an island resort linked to the mainland by a causeway. They talked of high-rise resort hotels on the beach and Florida-style condominiums. There was strong opposition by local residents and environmentalists. For a long time the fate of the island seemed quite uncertain, but the amount of money the casinos devel-opers could pay seemed to make saving the island unlikely. The owners of the island said that they did not wish to sell it to greedy developers who would forever alter the character of a pristine island. The owners and local residents alike wanted the state to step in and purchase the island outright for the people of Mississippi, to be developed as a state park or just left alone. At last this has happened, and Deer Island has been purchased by the state, after a long period of uncertainty and debate. At the time of this writ-ing the plan is simply to leave the island as it is, although there has been talk of a state park with some low-impact visitor facilities, such as a boat dock and boardwalks.

The easiest access to Deer Island is from the Kuhn Street public boat ramp already mentioned. At this point the island's western end lies within a half mile of the mainland. The rest of the four-mile-long island angles away from the mainland to the southeast, though it is still within two miles of the Ocean Springs side of the bay. At the western tip, there are nice beaches and sparse open woods where the island is not too difficult to walk across. Boaters often use this end of the island for picnicking and camping, since the insects are not as bad as in the dense thickets and marshes of most of the island. Shallow-draft boats can get right up to the beaches on this end of the island. Extremely shoal waters with many hidden tree stumps and oyster reefs surround most of Deer Island, so owners of deep-draft vessels will have to anchor far from the beaches and dinghy ashore. I have often run aground even in my kayak while paddling around Deer Island, as the water is usually murky and the bottom obscured.

Because of its proximity to the mainland, Deer Island makes an excellent destination for beginning sea kayakers who might not be ready for a passage to the barrier islands. Experienced paddlers might even cross to Deer Island in open canoes, since the crossing is sheltered in all but the worst weather, and powerboat wakes are usually the biggest waves to contend with. For sea kayakers looking for a workout, a 9-mile circumnavigation of this island offers convenience and a chance to make a loop trip with new scenery all the way. Even at the closest point to the mainland, almost in the shadow of the Grand Casino, one can feel the seclusion and separation from the rest of the world that only an island can provide. Because of the dense woodlands covering the island, wildlife is abundant, including raccoons, alligators, and nesting ospreys.

Pines are the predominant tree species in these island forests, but along the more sheltered beaches on the north side of the island you will find many ancient, gnarled live oaks like those found in quiet neighborhoods on the mainland coast. These oaks are often hung with Spanish moss and in many areas the undergrowth of the island consists of subtropical palmettos that grow in dense thickets and conceal the rattlesnakes and cottonmouths that are also abundant on the island. Keep a sharp eye out for snakes when walking through the underbrush. On a recent visit to Deer Island, I followed a path through the woods to the south-side beaches, and just ten minutes later, returning on the same path, almost stepped on a 3-foot cottonmouth.

The island widens as you travel southeast away from the narrow western tip. The main body of the island is between 400 and 500 yards wide, but even this short distance can be difficult to traverse due to briar and palmetto thickets that are full of biting deer flies and deep blackwater lagoons inhabited by alligators. Walking along the perimeter beaches is not all that hard, other than a few places where you might have to scramble over deadfall trees and exposed roots. These beaches offer excellent hiking, especially on weekdays when you are likely to have them all to yourself. It's not possible to walk around the entire island with dry feet, however, as there is one fairly wide opening in the beach that connects a deep, winding slough with the waters of the sound. This entrance is located on the north side of the island about two miles from the western tip. Kayakers can easily enter here at high tide and paddle a twisting route through the marsh grass into the interior of the island. Because of the marshes, this part of Deer Island is mostly open, with a few scraggly pines standing on the dunes near the beaches. East of this slough, the island remains grassy and mostly open. Much of the water around the eastern tip is less than a foot deep, with 1- or 2-foot depths extending over a mile out in places. Near this eastern tip of the island is an area of recent development in the form of a rock retaining wall that has been built to help prevent erosion of the island's beaches. The beaches on the north shore are constantly being washed away, and this long jetty will help break up the prevailing swell coming in from the southeast.

The south shore of Deer Island feels much more remote than the north shore, as the island forest blocks the mainland from sight and the empty beaches front the wide expanse of the Mississippi Sound. In clear weather, East Ship Island and Horn Island can be seen from these beaches. The opportunities for solitude and recreation on an island so near the busiest part of Mississippi's mainland make Deer Island a special treasure for those lucky enough to discover it. This unspoiled island in its natural state is surely worth more to the people of Mississippi than another resort with more

A winding creek leading across the interior of Deer Island

high-rise hotels and parking lots. This is one more treasure that state residents and visitors alike can be thankful for.

In a world where places like Deer Island are becoming increasingly scarce, we have not only this one but all the other barrier islands to enjoy and pass on to future generations.

NAVIGATOR'S NOTES

Bay St. Louis to Pass Christian Harbor
(Use NOAA Chart No. 11372)

For those in shallow-draft vessels, navigating this stretch of coastline is as simple as keeping the land to your left and watching out for other marine traffic. Those drawing 2 feet or more will have to be more careful. Within a half mile of the shoreline, depths are 5 feet or less, with numerous shoals. Farther out, beginning about 2 miles south of Henderson Point, an extensive oyster reef known as the Square Handkerchief Shoal can present problems for deep-draft vessels, with some areas as shallow as 2 feet.

The safest route for east-bound vessels between Bay St. Louis and Pass Christian is through the area of 10- to 12-foot depths that lie approximately one nautical mile south of the mainland.

Just south of the Pass Christian municipal harbor, the chart shows a long finger of shoal water extending south from the mainland, with some areas as shallow as three feet. There is a channel through this area and into the harbor, with lighted buoys marking the entrance for vessels approaching from the west or the east. Deep-draft vessels proceeding east along our route to Biloxi will need to follow this channel in as if entering Pass Christian harbor from the west, and then exit back out into the sound via the eastern entrance. The marina offers transient slips for cruising boats wishing to stop over here, as well as a fuel dock. The Pass Christian Yacht Club is also located on the eastern side of this harbor.

NAVIGATOR'S NOTES

Pass Christian Harbor to Gulfport Small Craft Harbor
(Use NOAA Chart No. 11372)

East of Pass Christian, it is 5½ nautical miles to the next harbor at Long Beach. Deep-draft vessels should stay at least a mile off this section of coast, as there are many areas of 4 feet or less closer in. A clearly marked channel leads into the straightforward entrance to Longbeach Harbor, which offers similar facilities as Pass Christian. There is a municipal marina, and as at Pass Christian, the Long Beach Yacht Club is located in the harbor.

To continue east in the sound to Gulfport and beyond, boaters will have to travel a mile and a half off the beaches to skirt around the commercial ship docks at the Port of Gulfport. The channel leading into the port is a busy area and all mariners should exercise caution and give freighters and other ships plenty of room. The captains of these ships will announce their intentions when entering or leaving the harbor, so boaters who continuously monitor VHF channel 16 will have a better idea of what to expect.

The entrance to the Gulfport Small Craft Harbor is found just to the east of the ship channel.

This is a busy channel as well, and not all the vessels using it are small, when compared to most recreational boats. There is a Coast Guard station in this harbor, as well as Ship Island excursion boats, and numerous large charter vessels and big yachts. Boaters should proceed into this harbor at slow speeds and with plenty of caution.

NAVIGATOR'S NOTES

Gulfport to Point Cadet
(Use NOAA Chart No. 11372)

Those piloting their own vessels east of Gulfport can generally navigate safely within a half mile of shore, where the bottom begins to slope off from 4- to 5-foot depths to 7 to 9 feet. Shallow draft power boats should stay this far off anyway as much of the area closer in beyond a row of pilings stretching east to west is a designated swimming area and is off limits.

The next harbor encountered along this coast after leaving Gulfport Small Craft Harbor is Broadwater Beach Resort in Biloxi, 6 nautical miles to the east. There is a marked channel beginning one and a half nautical miles out in the sound and leading directly north into the harbor. The channel averages 10 to 12 feet deep, and the same depths can be found at the docks.

Those approaching Biloxi from the west can enter the natural harbor area between the peninsula and Deer Island, by means of a well–marked channel. From the ICW, just east of the charted mile marker St M 80, and north of East Ship Island, flashing daybeacon "S" will be seen on the north side of the channel. From this marker "S," take a northerly heading for approximately 4½ nautical miles to reach the first two markers of the West Biloxi Channel, flashing red beacon #2 and unlighted green day-beacon #1. From these two outer markers, the channel can be easily followed to the north. Good depths are found in the sound until you come adjacent of green marker #5. Skippers following the shoreline from Gulfport can enter the channel here, rather than going all the way out to the entrance at markers #1 and #2. North of #5, however, there are several charted areas that show less than 4 feet.

From #5, the old Biloxi lighthouse, the I-110 exit loop, and the Beau Rivage will be clearly visible on the mainland. Following the channel toward these unmistakable landmarks is easy and straightforward. Closer to shore, another set of double markers, flashing red #10 and green daybeacon #9 mark the beginning of the channel's turn to the east. From these two, follow the reds—#12, #14, and #16—as they lead you inside the harbor, past the rock jetties that extend out from Deer Island's western tip.

The channel runs due east here, within the protection of the jetties and a small sandy islet that is separate from the main part of Deer Island. The distance from the entrance at the jetties to the end of the peninsula at Point Cadet is 2 nautical miles. Several harbors on the mainland side offer docking facilities, beginning with the Beau Rivage Marina, the Biloxi Small Craft Harbor, the Biloxi Yacht Club, and finally Point

Cadet Marina, near the eastern end of the channel. One potential overnight anchorage area with 4- to 5-foot depths inshore and 8 feet closer to the channel can be found north of the channel between flashing red beacon #18 and unlighted red daybeacon #22. Transient cruisers passing through the area often anchor here for a night or two.

Deer Island, though attractive and inviting, should be approached with caution by all skippers of larger vessels. All of the surrounding waters are extremely shallow, and the island is best visited by dinghy after anchoring or docking on the north side of the channel.

8

BACK BAY AND ADJOINING WATERWAYS

Back Bay is the second largest estuary on the Mississippi coast, and while smaller in area than Bay St. Louis, it contains many miles of deep, navigable water. This bay has always been of major importance to those who settled on the Biloxi peninsula, from the first natives to the Europeans who arrived later. Protected on the north by the mainland and on the south by the peninsula and Deer Island, the waters within this estuary provide shelter from all but the worst storms.

Back Bay offers numerous opportunities for side trips into its adjoining waters, which are even more sheltered than the main bay. Many of these waterways are deep and wide enough to accommodate cruising-sized vessels. Good anchorages can be found in these side waters, and when hurricanes threaten the Mississippi coast, the side waters of Back Bay fill with thousands of vessels fleeing the exposed "out front" marinas.

Several full-service boatyards also provide haul-out facilities and yacht repair services in Back Bay. Cruisers transiting the area who need repairs or maintenance will find the yards here friendly and laid-back, less crowded, and less expensive than those found in other Gulf coast states.

ENTERING BACK BAY

Like so many other areas of the Mississippi coast, the approach to Back Bay is not completely straightforward, and there are shoal waters everywhere. Most of the waters around Deer Island are extremely shallow, and Back Bay can only be reached from the sound by passing near this island. There are two approaches to the bay, one to the east of the island, in the channel that passes between Deer Island and the mainland at Ocean Springs, and the other to the west of the island, in the narrow natural harbor between Deer Island and the Biloxi peninsula. These two routes to Biloxi and Back Bay, as well as all charted waters within the bay, are found on NOAA Chart No. 11372.

The approach to Biloxi harbor from the west has been described in the previous chapter. Back Bay is reached from this natural harbor by continuing along the marked channel to the east, past Point Cadet Marina. This channel intersects with the channel that approaches Back Bay from the eastern side of Deer Island. At this junction there is also a channel leading off to the northeast. This is the entrance to Davis Bayou, in Ocean Springs, and will be described in the next chapter. For now we will focus on entering Back Bay and what lies in store for those willing to make this long side trip off of the ICW. Detailed instructions for navigating into Back Bay are found in the back of this chapter in the *Navigator's Notes*.

From the junction of channels it is one nautical mile northwest to the first obstacle encountered by those wishing to enter Back Bay. This is the Highway 90 bridge that spans the bay between Biloxi and Ocean Springs. At a low-tide height of 40 feet at center, it is much higher than the Highway 90 bridge at Bay St. Louis, and many vessels will be able to pass under this one without requesting an opening. The drawbridge is manned full-time by an operator who monitors VHF channel 13, so those needing more clearance can get an opening without delay. Just inside the Highway 90 drawbridge lies an older, abandoned bridge with the middle span permanently removed. On the north side of this old span, the entrance to a side channel will be apparent to your west, and the channel continuing into Back Bay will be blocked by yet another bridge, the CSX Railroad. This railroad swing bridge looks exactly like the one at Bay St. Louis and operates with about the same lack of speed and efficiency. One plus here is that the Back Bay channel is a lot busier with commercial navigation, so the bridge tender usually keeps the bridge open instead of closed, unless a train is expected. The vertical clearance on this bridge is 14 feet, for those vessels low enough to pass without an opening.

OTT BAYOU

The side channel leading west-southwest between the Highway 90 bridge and the CSX Railroad Bridge is known as Ott Bayou. There are two full-service boatyards located on this waterway's northern banks. The first is Bay Marine Boatworks, which is equipped with a 60-ton Travelift, and then Rebel Boat Works, which has a 35-ton Travelift.

On the south shore of the bayou, which is property dominated by the Palace Casino, there is a new marina owned by the casino that offers transient and permanent dockage. Beyond this point, navigable water ends. If you are not in need of boatyard services or do not wish to dock at the Palace Casino, then there is little reason to take a side trip into Ott Bayou.

OLD FORT BAYOU

Back on the north side of the CSX Railroad, where we left off after passing through this last obstacle to entering Back Bay, there is one more side trip option available before continuing westward into the main bay channel. Old Fort Bayou enters the bay from the north just west of the charted point of land shown as Old Fort Point. This is a tricky channel to approach because of all the shoal water outside the dredged cut. Detailed instructions for entering this channel from the mouth of the bay at the railroad bridge are given in the *Navigator's Notes* at the back of this chapter.

The Old Fort Bayou channel passes close to shore near Fort Point. From there it begins to turn to the east and then southeast, with markers more frequent and easily followed. It is the initial departure from the main channel at the railroad bridge that is daunting, and from NOAA chart No. 11372 it looks as if there is no way to avoid passing through waters of only 1 to 2 feet. I would not have considered taking my sailboat with her 4-foot, 3-inch draft into this channel had I not been assured by someone with local knowledge that it was quite possible. As it turned out, I'm glad I had the opportunity to explore the bayou, even though the circumstances were more of an emergency in nature rather than a pleasure cruise.

My boat had been dry-docked at Covacevich Yacht and Sail, a nearby boatyard to be described later in this chapter, when not one, but two hurricanes threatened the Mississippi coast. Rather than take the chance that 100 mph-plus winds would blow the boat off the jackstands in the yard, I had her relaunched, when Isidore, the first storm approached, so I could flee to more protected waters to ride it out on my anchors. I chose the upper Biloxi River as a refuge in that storm and escaped with no damage, but as soon as I returned to the yard, Hurricane Lili was in the southern Gulf of Mexico and headed north.

John Whitfield, another sailor at the yard in a much larger boat told me that he had found a good "hurricane hole" in Old Fort Bayou and that he was going there again if Lili continued on her projected path. He said I was welcome to follow, and he assured me that my draft would not be a problem. I had been stuck on the upper Biloxi for days after Isidore passed, because I was north of the Interstate 10 fixed bridge and the river flooded due to the torrential rains associated with the storm. The higher river level made it impossible for me to pass under the bridge with my mast, so I had to wait for the waters to recede. In light of this, Old Fort Bayou sounded like a good alternative. I refilled my water and fuel tanks and restocked my groceries, preparing for at least another week of being stuck in some remote place unable to leave or buy anything. The storm was still coming, so I set off in company with the skipper of the larger boat and followed him out to the floating red marker #2 at the railroad bridge and then across the reach of shallow waters to Fort Point and the mouth of the bayou. Far fewer fleeing vessels were taking this route, and I was glad we were going

A sailboat secured with storm anchors in Old Fort Bayou, in
anticipation of advancing Hurricane Lili

this way as I watched the mad exodus of huge powerboats barreling to the
west up the main Back Bay channel in what was anything but an orderly
evacuation.

Once we were north of Fort Point, I could see that navigation in the
bayou was much easier. As the channel starts to turn southeast at red daybeacon #14, depths are better and it is easy to see the route. As we passed
through this open section, several large sailboats were already securely
moored in the side waters off the channel. There are quite a few little
pockets of water off the channel that are deep enough for this, but we

continued on, in search of even more protected waters where we could not only put down anchors but, we hoped, tie off to nearby trees on the shore as well.

From Fort Point, the channel runs southeast for approximately a nautical mile before turning more to the east at red daybeacon #30. Just east of #30 a drawbridge crosses the bayou, with only 25 feet of vertical clearance at center. We were able to get an opening here without delay, but in hurricane evacuations, it is important to transit drawbridges as early as possible, as they will be ordered to shut down and stay closed when winds exceed gale force and the storm is eminent.

Beyond this drawbridge, the shores of the bayou become a mix of woods and marsh, and of light residential development and natural, unspoiled areas. Surprisingly, depths increase, with soundings of 15 feet common and up to 30 feet found in places. There are no further official aids to navigation in place, but the bayou channel is naturally well defined and easy to follow. By keeping to the middle reaches you will have no problems.

Being new to the area on this trip, I trusted John's familiarity with the bayou and followed him to what he thought was the best spot to ride out the hurricane. En route, we passed still more sailboats and a few large powerboats that had been secured in corners and side waters of the bayou, many with multiple storm anchors deployed. Our destination turned out to be a small side channel that turned off the main bayou to the east, at a place where the bayou itself bends away to the north. A couple of houses were nearby on the south bank, but other than that, there were few obstructions, and a high, forested ridge to the south seemed to offer some protection from the brunt of anything coming in from the Gulf. I let the skipper of the bigger boat take his pick of where to set his anchors in the channel, and he went in about three hundred feet and proceeded to lay a web of anchors and lines in all directions from where he stopped the boat midstream. I chose not to raft alongside, but rather to place my boat closer to the mouth of this stream and a bit off to one side. I was glad I did so later when three other large yachts with obviously ill-prepared skippers came barreling into the channel in a panic at the last minute to raft up with John.

It turned out they were all drinking buddies from a local yacht club. I was glad to be away from them, feeling that my smaller boat would come out of a storm much better if there was less chance of getting crushed by a larger vessel. A strong-looking pine tree provided one anchor point, and I put my main 22-pound Delta with a combination nylon and chain rode off the bow upstream toward the rafted boats. A smaller CQR was laid out on a different angle upstream, and then two large Danforths were angled out into the waters of the main bayou astern. My 9-foot sit-on-top kayak was used to position the anchors, and it would be my last-ditch escape vehicle if something bad happened and I felt I had to abandon the sailboat. All that afternoon more boats began to pass our position, headed even farther up the bayou. Most of these were commercial fishing boats. Apparently they had a favorite spot somewhere even farther inland.

According to forecasters, Hurricane Lili was on a fast track across the Gulf of Mexico and was gaining tremendous strength. I received cell phone calls from worried family members telling me that the storm was forecast to be of Category 4 intensity by the time it made landfall. They thought I should abandon the boat and head for safety, but I knew I would wait and see. There would be time to escape if need be, but I felt sure the track would pass well to the west of the Mississippi coast, just like Isidore had done the previous week. John and his friends that were rafted up with him were not worried. From the forecast, it seemed that the area west of Grand Isle, Louisiana, would get the direct impact. I listened to an AM radio station broadcasting from New Orleans. People in the path of the storm were getting worried. It did reach Category 4 status with winds in excess of 140 MPH. It was still tracking straight, but there was always a possibility of a northeast turn that would bring it over the Mississippi coast. I plotted the coordinates of the storm on my nautical charts each time an updated position was given. It was a long and nerve-wracking night as strong wind gusts howled across the bayou and shook the rigging of my anchored vessel. But the storm stayed on its course and with each position putting it farther north and west, I began to relax a bit in the hours before daylight. Forecasters were predicting major destruction in Louisiana and expected landfall by dawn. Everyone was amazed and relieved when this monster hurricane suddenly began to lose strength as it neared land and ended up striking the coast as only a minor, Category 1 hurricane that rapidly diminished to a tropical storm. No lives were lost anywhere, and our preparations in Old Fort Bayou thankfully turned out to be a drill. I was certain that this was a good spot to ride out a storm in a boat though. I waited there an extra day and night after the threat passed to let all the commotion die down. It seemed wise to stay out of the way of the impatient boaters who were seemingly in just as big of a panic on the way out as they were on the way in.

I hope that readers who are interested in exploring Old Fort Bayou on their own can do so in a more leisurely fashion, rather than in a time of such urgent need for refuge. I would likely seek shelter there again if I was in the area and a hurricane threatened, but the bayou would also make an interesting destination for a quiet weekend cruise. Those who favor smaller boats, and especially kayaks, can of course explore much farther up the bayou. Depths are not charted more than about a mile upstream of the drawbridge, but locals say that the stream carries ample water for many miles past that point.

BACK BAY CHANNEL

Back out on the main entrance to Back Bay, if you choose not to take the side trip into Old Fort Bayou after passing inside the railroad bridge, the route west is easy to follow. Simply pass to the south side of floating red nun buoy #2, and keep the series of green daybeacons and lighted beacons to port as the channel takes you near the north side of the Biloxi peninsula. Commercial fishing docks occupy much of the waterfront along the bay's south shore, and extremely shallow water lies outside the channel to the north and around marshy Big Island.

An excellent haul-out facility is also found on this south shore, nestled in among the commercial fishing docks. Covacevich Yacht and Sail can be identified from the water by the large steel shed just up the hill from the shore and the concrete piers surrounding two slipways. A 35-ton Travelift is available, and the yard can handle a variety of repairs or they will allow

Sunrise at the shrimpboat docks of Back Bay, Biloxi

owners to do their own maintenance. This is a family-owned business, and it began a hundred years ago as a shipbuilding facility where many working and pleasure vessels were built in the traditional methods of wooden boat construction. As mentioned before, this is the yard where I had my sailboat dry-docked when Hurricane Isidore threatened. Unlike boatyards in other locations, the folks at Covacevich did not use this as an opportunity to make money, but rather relaunched my vessel and many others that were there at the time and then hauled us back out with no extra charge when the storm had passed. Working conditions are pleasant in the yard, and Biloxi Hardware, a store that stocks many boat-maintenance items, is conveniently located just across the street.

Just to the west of the Covacevich yard, the channel takes a turn to the northwest in the direction of the high twin spans of the Interstate 110 drawbridge. This bridge has a closed vertical clearance of 60 feet, so most pleasure boats will not need an opening, but if you are the skipper of a tall-masted vessel, be aware that six hours notice is required to open this bridge.

A cruising sailboat being "hauled-out" on the Travelift at Covacevich Shipyard, Biloxi

A small dockage basin on the north side just beneath the bridge is home to several boats, and on the shore just east of that, which is known as Shipyard Point, lies the boatyard of wooden boat builder Bill Holland.

Holland grew up on Back Bay in a time when the waterfront was alive with the sound of wooden boats being built in the time-honored way-by hand. Holland builds everything from Lafitte skiffs to Biloxi schooners, using the local yellow pine, red cypress, and juniper that was traditionally used by Mississippi boatbuilders before the age of mass-produced fiberglass and metal boats. He has built more than a dozen large vessels at his boatyard there and repaired or rebuilt many more. He is perhaps best known in the Biloxi area for the *Glen L. Swetman* (mentioned in the section on Point Cadet in the previous chapter). This wooden sailing vessel is a 68-foot, full-size replica of the traditional Biloxi schooners that were used in the local shrimp and oyster fisheries in the days of working sailing vessels. This schooner was built for the Biloxi Maritime and Seafood Industry Museum in 1989 and is used for educational purposes and day charter.

West of the Interstate 110 drawbridge, the character of the bay changes a bit from the busy scene of working shrimp boats and shipyards to a more tranquil environment of wooded shorelines interspersed with light residential development. The channel continues to the northwest for about a half mile, favoring the northern shoreline of the bay and passing to the north of Goat Island, which is a marshy wildland with some pine forest and lots of shallow mudflats surrounding it. West of Goat Island, the channel meanders to the west-southwest and on the southern shore of the bay the grounds of Keesler Air Force Base can be seen, along with a private marina used by base personnel. North of the channel here there are wide expanses of bay waters that are suitable for exploration if your draft is shallow, but in most places depths are 4 feet or less. The main channel here carries 14 to 20 feet of water and is well marked and well maintained due to heavy commercial traffic transiting the area en route to the Industrial Seaway farther to the west. All mariners in Back Bay should always be alert for commercial barge traffic when following or crossing the channel.

It is 4½ nautical miles from the Interstate 110 bridge to the next drawbridge, at Popp's Ferry Road. This bridge has a vertical clearance of 25 feet when closed but opens on demand anytime but on weekdays during the rush hours between 6 A.M. and 8 A.M. and 4 P.M. to 6 P.M.

BIG LAKE AND THE BILOXI RIVER

The large expanse of open water just west of the Popp's Ferry drawbridge is known as Big Lake. Since most of the lake is extremely shallow, with depths of 1 to 4 feet, most of this water will be off limits to cruising vessels. There are two alternate routes here that deep draft vessels can take, however. One is the Biloxi River channel, to the north, and the other is the Bernard Bayou/Industrial Seaway channel that continues on to the west. First we will explore the Biloxi River route.

To enter the river, all you have to do after clearing the Popp's Ferry bridge is turn north, following the shoreline in the charted 14- to 23-foot depths that are found quite close in. You will pass a single green daybeacon,

#1, a short distance north of the bridge. Keep this to port and the bank to starboard, and depth will be no problem. Charted depths are shown only a short distance north of this daybeacon, but the river remains plenty deep and the channel is not too hard to guess at if you have any experience at all in reading a river. When Hurricane Isidore set her course for the Mississippi coast and I had to seek shelter in a place that was both deep enough and protected, I choose the Biloxi River, not knowing at the time about conditions on Old Fort Bayou. As luck would have it, at about the same time I was motoring up the river channel past the last area of charted depths, a commercial tow and barge overtook me and continued upriver. I had no doubts when following this vessel that there was ample water beneath my keel, so I proceeded with confidence as the channel passed through expanses of open marsh and was intersected with various side channels. One of these channels is another coastal river that joins the Biloxi from the northeast. This river is called the Tchoutacabouffa. (This apparently unpronounceable word is pronounced: "shoota ka-buff". It is supposedly an ancient Native American name meaning "broken pots.")

No soundings are shown on chart No. 11372 for the Tchoutacabouffa, but it certainly carries sufficient depth midstream for cruising boats to at least explore the lower reaches of it. Just proceed with caution and be careful of mud banks that might extend far out in some of the bends. All of these waters are better suited for small boats and kayaks, as well as canoes at times when the wind is not too strong.

The barge I followed up the Biloxi River continued west past the mouth of the Tchoutacabouffa and past a bend shown on the charts as Devil's Elbow. West of here the river turns sharply to the north again, and several houses line the shores of the eastern bank. North of these houses, the river splits into three branches, the westernmost branch appearing to be a man-made canal. A large power plant is clearly visible to the west here, and it was this dredged cut that the tow and barge took to flee Isidore. My goal was to get as far inland as possible, so I stayed with what appeared to be the main channel, which continued to the north. There is also a middle channel here that offers anchorage possibilities.

Going farther north up what was now clearly the main river, I began to notice that I was pushing against a current, but there were still readings of 6 to 7 feet showing on my depth sounder at midriver. I continued until the river made a bend to the west again, and from there I could see the fixed twin bridges of Interstate 10. The river bends north again and passes under the bridges. A gauge showed 37 feet of vertical clearance and depth was still good, so I proceeded slowly, wishing to get north of the interstate to find my hurricane hole. My mast height is 35 feet, so I was able to clear the bridges without even scraping my VHF antenna. A passing fisherman in a flat-bottomed boat warned me that there were sand bars at the next river bend, so I went only a short distance north of the interstate and anchored near the eastern shore in a long straight stretch of the river.

The depth was nearly 12 feet right up to within a boat length of the bank, so I picked a spot close enough to a stout-looking cypress tree so that I could back up my anchors with a line to the shore. I then put my main Delta anchor and a large Danforth anchor out at angles upstream on long rodes, and a CQR and Danforth on angles downstream. A line to the cypress tree completed my preparations, and the boat was suspended between the heavy nylon rodes like a spider in the middle of a web. I stripped the mainsail from the mast and folded and secured the bimini in an effort to reduce windage as much as possible. I felt that I would be safe here even in a direct hit, especially since Isidore was forecast to be only a Category 1 storm. The river here was small enough that no large waves could be generated, and the surrounding forest would be a buffer against the wind. I knew the waters would rise with storm surge, but by staying aboard, I could adjust my anchor lines and keep my boat away from the shore. I would not have stayed aboard if I had thought there was real risk to my life, but I wanted to do everything within reason to save my boat from destruction or damage. When I had made all the preparations I knew to do, I settled in and watched the progression of ominous dark clouds streaming overhead from the east and prepared for a long night.

Isidore's track passed well to the west of my position, but torrential rains inundated the area and wind gusts of gale force rocked my boat all throughout the stormy night. All my anchors held as the vessel was slung in one direction and then another in brief but furious gusts of howling wind. Sheets of rain raced horizontally across the surface of the river, and the current increased as the river swelled to flood stage.

When the direct danger from the storm had passed the next day, my main concern was with all the floating debris that was rushing down the river. A small tree scraped my newly painted hull, and I used a boat hook to fend off an abandoned bass boat that came careening down the river later in the afternoon. No real damage was sustained though, and my paint job was not finished anyway, as I had been in the boatyard at Covacevich to completely change the color of the boat and dename her in the proper tradition so I could rechristen her *Intensity*. It turned out to be an apt name. Little did I know when I sanded off the old name that she would be christened by two hurricanes, Isidore and Lili, before she would be relaunched as *Intensity*.

Getting out of the Biloxi River proved to be a much bigger problem than getting in. The river rose so much that there was less than 30 feet of vertical clearance showing on gauge at the interstate bridge. I waited three days for the water levels to drop sufficiently so I could get under again, and then I had to wait an extra day for the raging current to subside before I could break out the four anchors that were deeply lodged in the riverbed mud. When at last I was able to leave, the job of retrieving the anchors took two hours.

BERNARD BAYOU, INDUSTRIAL SEAWAY

Now if we backtrack to the waters of Big Lake, just to the west of the Popp's Ferry drawbridge, we can look at the other waterway that leads to the west where we took off to the north up the Biloxi River. This route, which includes Bernard Bayou and the man-made Industrial Seaway canal, is where the vast majority of the boaters I saw fleeing both hurricanes were headed. There are deep places to anchor, and there is ample room for hundreds of vessels. My way of thinking is that the greatest threat to a boat during a hurricane is the possibility of other larger, and possibly poorly secured, boats breaking loose to become missiles that could hole and sink anything in the vicinity. Most people seek safety in numbers, though, so I am sure that this route will always be the most popular spot on Back Bay during times of hurricanes.

It is also an interesting route to explore for other reasons, and might be worth the side trip for those who like cruising in well-protected waterways. Care should be taken crossing Big Lake by way of the marked channel near the south shore, especially if you draw more than 4 feet. The passage begins at the red and green junction daybeacon west of the drawbridge. Pass to the south of it, and then keep the subsequent red daybeacons to starboard as well. On the western side of the lake the marked channel turns to the northwest into the man-made cut that is called the Industrial Seaway. If you wish to follow the natural channel that is Bernard Bayou, turn west at red daybeacon #3 and stay to the middle of the stream. Stay well off from the lighted green beacon #1 that stands out from the marshy shore on the north side of the entrance. I made the mistake of cutting too close to this marker and buried my keel deep in the mud, and only got ungrounded with great difficulty. Once past this entrance point, the Bernard Bayou channel is straightforward and deep. Like the rest of the waters of Back Bay, the shoreline is a mix of natural woodland, marsh, and light residential development. About one mile west of the lake you will pass a public park on the south shore of the bayou. This park is owned by the city of Gulfport and is called James Hill Park. There is a long boardwalk out over the marsh, as well as pavilions and picnic tables. Many park visitors fish from the piers and boardwalks, and there are two wide boat ramps provided at the small side creek that enters the bayou from the south.

For those who do not arrive by boat on the bayou, the park is off the north side of Switzer Road in Gulfport, just behind the Handsboro Community Center.

West of this park, also on the south shore of the bayou, lies yet another excellent haul-out and boat repair facility, known as Kremer Marine. As well as a boatyard, Kremer has a dockage basin with several wet slips and a dry-storage yard for boats on trailers. Transient slips are not available in the basin though, so a haul-out is the main reason visiting yachts might find their way to Kremer. Sufficient room to anchor can be found in the bayou, however, if one is inclined to spend the evening there.

West of Kremer Marine there is another bridge crossing at Cowan Road, this one fixed at a vertical height of just 28 feet. This will force most sailcraft to turn back, but those who can get under this bridge can continue for several miles to where Bernard Bayou rejoins the Industrial Seaway, making a long loop trip back to Big Lake possible. If you are fortunate enough to be piloting a craft low enough to slip beneath this bridge, you are in for a treat if you stop at the docks of the restaurant located on the south side of the bayou. This local eatery is called the Blowfly Inn, and a trademark that comes on whatever you choose to order from their extensive seafood menu is a little black plastic "blowfly." Whether you care for a "fly" on your food or not, everything I've ordered there has been good and the atmosphere is great. You can tie a small boat up to the docks and order your meal from one of the tables on the spacious, shaded deck, or sit inside behind the extensive windows and enjoy a view of the bayou. My brother, Jeff, and I once created quite a stir when we paddled up in a pair of sleek wooden kayaks that I built. We ordered Coronas on the deck and met several other patrons who were interested in our unusual varnished mahogany watercraft.

Those who can't get under the bridge at Cowan Road can still reach the waters of the western section of Bernard Bayou by backtracking to Big Lake and taking the canal route on the Seaway. There is a drawbridge where Cowan Road crosses this canal—a newly built twin-span with 30 feet of closed vertical clearance. It is possible to cruise west on the Industrial Seaway almost to U.S. Highway 49. Pleasure craft will find little reason to go beyond the Bernard Bayou loop, though, as this waterway is heavily used by barges and much of the shoreline consists of industrial development.

NAVIGATOR'S NOTES

Approaches to Back Bay
(Use NOAA Chart No. 11372)

Western Approach to Back Bay:
To continue on to the entrance to Back Bay from Biloxi Harbor, you must transit the harbor until you pass Point Cadet Marina to your port side, as well as flashing green

marker #27, which leads westbound boaters in to Point Cadet. Once past #27, a channel defined by all red markers leads to the east. Keep all these to your starboard side, following the usual red-right-returning buoyage system. At flashing red #30, the channel turns to the east-northeast and red daybeacon #32 and flashing red beacon #34 lead to the junction of this channel with the Biloxi Bay channel that comes in from the eastern side of Deer Island. Though this channel from Point Cadet to the junction is well marked, be aware that it is charted as 8½ feet deep for a width of only 150 feet. Waters outside the channel are 3 feet or less, and strong southeasterly or northerly winds can easily push an unwary skipper out of line with the markers and lead to a quick grounding.

Green daybeacon #35 on the west side and flashing red beacon #26 on the east side mark this junction of channels. A side channel heading off to the northeast leads to Ocean Springs. The route to Back Bay is the channel leading northwest towards the two bridges that span the mouth of the bay.

From this junction of the eastern and western Biloxi channels, one can turn north and enter Back Bay. Before we go on to Back Bay, the following instructions should guide boaters who are approaching the area from the east and wish to use the eastern channel to come in from the ICW and Mississippi Sound.

Eastern Approach to Back Bay:
From the ICW, the entrance to this channel lies almost directly north of the western tip of Horn Island and Dog Keys Pass. Westbound on the ICW, this point will be just over two miles west of the charted mile marker, St M 90. Flashing red beacon #8 will be the last ICW marker that you pass to the south of before reaching the turning point. The first two markers are an unlighted green daybeacon, #1, adjacent to a flashing red beacon labeled #2. This entrance lies just three-quarters of a nautical mile north of the ICW channel.

The northbound channel from #1 and #2 is well marked by a series of closely spaced red and green lighted and unlighted beacons, leading 7 nautical miles to the junction with the above-described western approach channel. Navigators should have no trouble following this inbound channel. There are two gradual turns to the northwest, the first at green daybeacon #9 and the second at green daybeacon #13. Other than that, the channel is arrow-straight.

As described above, the junction between these two major channels lies at flashing red beacon #26 and green daybeacon #35.

NAVIGATOR'S NOTES

Entering Back Bay
(Use NOAA Chart No. 11372)

From the junction of the east and west approach channels, it is one nautical mile northwest to the Highway 90 bridge span that crosses the mouth of the bay. Closed vertical clearance for this bridge is 40 feet. The bridge opens on demand and the tender monitors VHF channel 13. Just inside this drawbridge and south of the CSX Railroad bridge lies an abandoned highway bridge with the center span removed.

Between the abandoned bridge and the CSX Railroad bridge, a side channel leads off to the southwest. This Ott Bayou channel is marked by a series of green daybeacons beginning with #1 and carries a depth of 7 feet. The channel leads to a basin west of green daybeacon #7. Two full-service boatyards occupy the north shore of this basin, and the marina at the Palace Casino is located on the south shore.

Northeast of this Ott Bayou side channel, the CSX Railroad crosses the mouth of the bay, with a horizontally pivoting center span that has a closed vertical clearance of 14 feet. The span is kept open when trains are not expected.

NAVIGATOR'S NOTES

Old Fort Bayou
(Use NOAA Chart No. 11372)

Just to the north of the CSX Railroad bridge floating red nun buoy #2 lies at the junction between the channel into the bay and the optional side trip to the north into the waters of Old Fort Bayou. Looking northward beyond floating nun #2, the next pair of daybeacons visible are green #5 and red #4. To reach the Old Fort Bayou channel, pass east of #2 and lay a course to pass between these next two markers. Very shoal water lies outside this channel, which itself only carries 4½ to 5 feet in places. Red daybeacon #8 is located off the western end of Fort Point and marks the way around this point and into the mouth of the bayou. The next daybeacons are green #9 and red #10. From this point, the channel bends to the east, then southeast, and is well marked by closely spaced daybeacons leading up to red #30, beyond which a drawbridge spanning the bayou will be seen. This bridge has a closed vertical clearance of 25 feet and opens on demand.

Upstream of the drawbridge, the Old Fort Bayou channel is not marked with aids to navigation. Depths are charted for another mile, however, ranging from 10 to 30 feet at midstream. By staying well off the banks, most vessels can travel at least 2 miles upstream from the bridge.

NAVIGATOR'S NOTES

Back Bay Channel
(Use NOAA Chart No. 11372)

The route west into Back Bay begins at floating red nun buoy #2 and green daybeacon #3, located approximately one quarter of a nautical mile north-northwest of the CSX Railroad bridge. From these entrance markers, the channel runs slightly north of due west, marked by a line of green daybeacons and flashing beacons on the south side and intermittent red daybeacons on the north side. Depths in this channel are a minimum of 10 feet.

The channel runs straight for almost 1½ nautical miles to the point where it passes south of the marshy island shown on the chart as Big Island. At this point, the channel turns to the northwest and runs one nautical mile on this heading to the high I-110 drawbridge that spans the entire bay from the Biloxi peninsula on the south side to D'Iberville on the north shore. At the approach to this bridge there is a row of large pilings on the south side of the channel that are used as moorings for barges. Use caution transiting this area, due to heavy commercial traffic.

The I-110 drawbridge has a closed vertical clearance of 60 feet. Few recreational vessels will need an opening to clear this bridge. For those with tall masts that do require an opening, be aware that opening this interstate bridge requires a 6-hour notice.

West of the interstate bridge, the channel favors the north shore of the bay, with a series of red daybeacons, beginning with #12, defining the northern limits of deep water. These red daybeacons continue as the channel meanders back to the south side of the gradually narrowing bay.

Another much smaller drawbridge spans the narrow bay 4½ miles to the west. This is the Popp's Ferry drawbridge, which has a closed vertical clearance of 25 feet. This bridge opens on demand except during weekday rush hours of 6 A.M. to 8 A.M. and 4 P.M. to 6 P.M.

NAVIGATOR'S NOTES

Big Lake, Biloxi River, and Bernard Bayou
(Use NOAA Chart No. 11372)

The large body of open water just east of the Popp's Ferry drawbridge, shown on the chart as Big Lake, is extremely shallow and out of the question for navigation except for two channels.

The first of these channels skirts around the eastern and northern shores of the lake and leads into the lower Biloxi River. To enter the Biloxi River after clearing the Popp's Ferry drawbridge, stay in the charted deep water as you turn north and closely follow the shoreline off your starboard side. Depths here are 14 to 23 feet. A single green daybeacon, #1, will be seen as you follow this northerly course. Stay between this marker and the shoreline to your starboard side to avoid the extreme shallows just to the west of this marker.

Charted soundings end just north of this green daybeacon, and the river bends to the northwest and passes through an area of open marsh at the confluence of the Tchoutacabouffa River, which empties here from the northeast. Good depths continue in the Biloxi River all the way to the Interstate 10 bridge crossing, but those without local knowledge of the channel should proceed slowly and use caution due to the lack of charted information.

The other channel across Big Lake continues west of the Popp's Ferry drawbridge and crosses near the southern shore of this shallow body of water. This channel is marked with a series of red and green daybeacons. On the west side of the lake, at flashing green beacon #1, this channel splits. Staying to the south side of #1, keeping well off the mud flats around the marker, you can enter the natural channel of Bernard Bayou. The other option is to keep #1 to port and enter the straight, man-made canal of the Industrial Seaway.

Good depths are found in the entire length of Bernard Bayou, which loops back to the north and rejoins the Industrial Seaway. A fixed bridge span with a vertical clearance of 28 spans the bayou just west of the Kremer Marine boatyard and marina. This same road crosses the Industrial Seaway, but at this crossing there is a new draw-bridge with 30 feet of closed vertical clearance.

9

OCEAN SPRINGS, DAVIS BAYOU, AND BELLEFONTAINE POINT

On the eastern side of the Highway 90 bridge that spans Back Bay from Biloxi lies the quieter town of Ocean Springs. Crossing this bridge, for now at least, one leaves behind the high-rise glitter of casinos and their associated hotels and enters an artist's community of character-laden old wooden houses and oak-shaded side streets. Immediately upon reaching the eastern side of the highway bridge, one can turn south onto the beachfront road, which is appropriately named Beach Drive, and for the first time since leaving the Bay St. Louis waterfront, drive along a shore fronted by only a quiet, two-lane road. Here the water's edge is much closer than it is to Highway 90, and ample parking spots along the way invite one to get out and take a walk on the beach.

This part of the Mississippi coast has many attractions that are available to those traveling by road as well as by boat, so we will visit attractions on the shore as well as the waterfront.

OCEAN SPRINGS BEACHES AND OCEAN SPRINGS HARBOR

Right at the foot of the Highway 90 bridge, just as you turn south onto the beachfront road, you will notice a waterfront building and a fleet of catamarans beached on the sand nearby. This is the Ocean Springs Yacht Club. There is no yacht basin here, but the building is the clubhouse and the catamarans belong to members who daysail out of this ideal location. Deer Island lies just across Biloxi Bay from this beach, and most of the water outside the channel is shallow and therefore ideal for catamarans.

Just past the yacht club beach, there are designated parking areas all along the road where kayakers and others with lightweight watercraft can stop and launch from a narrow beach. From this beach one can cruise north under the bridge and into Back Bay, make the crossing to Deer Island, or follow the shore on to the south to the entrance to Davis Bayou. This is also a good jumping-off place for kayakers wishing to make a longer crossing to Horn or East Ship Islands. I have often made the trip to the barrier islands from here, sometimes stopping on the southeast tip of Deer Island to regroup and prepare for the open-water leg of the trip.

Beach Drive continues to the southeast, closely following the water's edge and passing under bluffs with several grand mansions overlooking. A small nature preserve and a replica fort built of huge square logs and surrounded by a log palisade also overlooks the beach from one of these bluffs. This is a replica of Fort Maurepas, the first settlement founded by the French explorers in 1699. Fort Maurepas was the capital of Louisiana until 1702, and then again from 1719 to 1720. The grounds surrounding the fort are a nice place to walk and take in the view of Biloxi Bay and Deer Island.

The beach road forks beyond this fort, and if you bear to the right you can continue following the waterfront until you reach the point where the road makes an abrupt 90-degree turn to the left. The road turns here at the entrance to Ocean Springs harbor, where a marked channel leads into the inlet. There is a large parking area at this inlet, as well as additional parking along the side of the beach road. A fishing pier follows the jetties out to the entrance of the channel and ends in a large covered deck with benches.

There are four extra-wide boat-launching ramps at the entrance to this harbor as well. These ramps have docks along both sides, and because of their width I often launched my 11-foot-wide catamaran here. There is ample parking for vehicles with trailers, but on nice weekends these ramps can get quite busy and you might have to wait in line to launch.

The outer part of the harbor just east of the boat ramps is occupied by commercial fishing boats. The dockage basin for recreational boats in the inner part of the harbor is tranquil and beautiful. This basin is surrounded by high banks that offer excellent shelter. The scene is of a peaceful harbor in the midst of quiet residences and huge old oak trees. A road crosses over the waterway that continues on to the northwest. Beyond this low bridge span, there are additional docks for the low clearance vessels that can squeeze under the bridge. This is called the Inner Harbor, and there is an Ocean Springs city park occupying the land on the east side of it. This park features tennis courts, a pavilion, boardwalks along the water's edge, and several picnic tables in the shade of tall pines.

WALTER INGLIS ANDERSON

To continue by road around the harbor and to this bridge that spans the creek, you must make a series of right turns through a residential area and then take another right on Pershing Avenue. This becomes Shearwater Drive after crossing the corner of the harbor on the bridge just described. Shearwater Drive continues southeast, and from here you will see the signs that lead to Shearwater Pottery. An unpaved road leads through a jungle of live oaks and palmettos to the old wood-framed building that was late Ocean Springs artist Walter Inglis Anderson's pottery. Anderson ran this pottery near the banks of Davis Bayou as a way to make a living while he devoted the rest of his time to his art. Shearwater Pottery is open to tourists and includes a store that sells replicas of the pottery produced, as well as prints of the artist's work.

To see the actual artwork of Walter Inglis Anderson, a visit to the fantastic museum devoted to his work should be on every Gulf Coast visitor's itinerary. This museum, located, at 510 Washington Avenue in downtown Ocean Springs, was opened in 1991.

Anderson, who died at the age of 62 in 1965, like many artists did not live to see his work gain widespread recognition and appreciation. Born in

1903 in New Orleans, Anderson was strongly influenced by his mother's love of art, music, and literature. He was educated at a private boarding school and attended the Parsons Institute of Design in New York and the Pennsylvania Academy of Fine Arts. He later traveled throughout Europe and was especially influenced by the primitive cave art he saw at Les Eyzies in France. The unique style he later developed reflected his fascination with aboriginal artistic expressions.

When Anderson returned to the Gulf Coast, he married Agnes Grinstead of Ocean Springs and went into business creating molds and decorating earthenware at Shearwater Pottery, which was founded by his brother Peter. He felt that an artist should be able to create affordable work that could bring pleasure to others, and in return, the artist should be able to pursue his artistic passions. In the 1930s, he worked on regional Works Progress Administration mural projects and began to view his role in art as a muralist.

Anderson was later diagnosed with severe depression and spent three years in and out of hospitals. In 1947, with the understanding of his family, he left his wife and children and embarked on a private and solitary existence. He lived alone in a cottage near the Shearwater Pottery, and increased his solo visits to Horn Island. He spent long periods of time on this uninhabited island during the last 18 years of his life, living in primitive conditions with only minimum necessities and his art supplies. More details of his trips to the island in a small rowboat are given in chapter 12 of this book, in which Horn Island is described in detail.

Anderson's most famous works are the hundreds of watercolors, drawings, and sculptures he created depicting the vegetation, animals, birds, and marine life of his private island paradise. His works are intense and evocative, conveying a sense of his obsession to be one with the natural world.

Walter Anderson died in a New Orleans hospital of lung cancer. Much of his work was discovered later by chance, and those treasures today await the visitor to the museum dedicated to this talented local artist.

The museum's skylit interior of southern yellow pine includes a main galleria and two additional galleries, which echo the natural beauty and simplicity of the displayed works. Adjacent to the museum is the Ocean Springs Community Center, home of Walter Anderson's largest mural.

DAVIS BAYOU BEYOND THE TURNOFF TO SHEARWATER POTTERY

Shearwater Drive continues to the southeast and parallels the shore for a short distance along the entrance to Davis Bayou. The road ends at the Gulf Coast Research Laboratory. Beyond this facility, the shoreline is owned by the National Park Service, and here is found the headquarters of the Mississippi section of the Gulf Islands National Seashore. The park can be accessed from Hanley Road, at the western entrance, but the easiest way for those not familiar with the area is to turn into the main entrance to the park off of Highway 90, about 4 miles east of the Ocean Springs bridge. A well-marked paved road leads into the park, and at the end of this road are several parking areas and a visitor center with a mini-museum that contains natural history displays depicting the barrier islands. There are nature trails around the visitor center, complete with boardwalks out over the marsh and signs describing the various tree species found in the surrounding woodlands. A large picnic area in the shade of live oaks is located near the edge of Davis Bayou, and just beyond this is a public fishing pier, as well as docks for park service patrol boats.

A side road that turns right off of the main access road before you get to the visitor center leads to the large campground that is available in the park. Campsites include full hookups, and showers and restrooms are conveniently located in the middle of the area. These quiet paved roads winding through the park woodlands are popular with bicyclists, joggers, and walkers who come here to exercise in the serenity. A series of boat ramps are also provided in this area, along with ample parking for vehicles with trailers. There are covered docks near the ramps and plenty of places to fish in the bayou from shore for those who do not have boats. This ramp area is also a good place to launch kayaks or canoes, and Davis Bayou offers many miles of quiet, protected waters for those who do not want to venture out into Biloxi Bay or the open sound.

A Tiki 26 catamaran at Harbor Point Marina, Davis Bayou

A privately marked channel leads to the upper reaches of Davis Bayou and terminates at Harbor Point Apartments, where there is a marina. This marina basin is surrounded by the buildings of the apartment complex, so a more protected dockage could hardly be found. There are some fairly large vessels docked at this marina, which is more than two miles inland from the entrance to this channel. The harbormaster there told me, however, that many of them can only leave on a high tide. At any rate, without specific local knowledge, you must enter Davis Bayou with suspicion if you draw much over two feet.

For those exploring by kayak or canoe, Davis Bayou offers many more options besides these main channels. There are several small side creeks that lead far into the marsh and coastal woodlands. Along the shore of the main bayou one can also discover perfect little hidden beaches. I once spent an entire day relaxing in the shade of giant live oak whose branches hung so low over the water that they concealed the sand of a little pocket beach and hid both me and my kayak from the eyes of powerboaters speeding by. This little hidden beach area was like a mystical world unto itself, with knarled roots growing out of the sand and wispy beards of Spanish moss draped from the branches. Tall palmettos crowded out other undergrowth and lent a tropical atmosphere to the surroundings. It is the discovery of quiet little hideaways like this that make paddling a small boat so appealing. There are many such places tucked away along the bayous of the Mississippi coast, just waiting to be explored.

BELLEFONTAINE POINT

East of the entrance to Davis Bayou, the coverage of NOAA Chart No. 11372 ends and NOAA Chart No. 11374 begins. The section of coastline east of Davis Bayou all the way to the West Pascagoula River is best explored by small boat, as shallows extend well out from shore. The mainland coast here angles off to the southeast for about 4 nautical miles to form Belle-fontaine Point, which is the closest point on the mainland to any of the barrier islands. Horn Island lies just over 5 nautical miles to the south of this point. A prominent abandoned lighthouse stands on this southernmost point of the mainland and is so large that it is visible from Horn Island on a clear day. A small area of public beach near the lighthouse makes a good jumping-off point for sea kayakers wanting to make a crossing to Horn Island with the least possible exposure to open water.

Kayakers and other small boat enthusiasts can also closely follow the coastline from Davis Bayou to Bellefontaine Point and continue on to the mouth of the West Pascagoula River. Between this point and this major river mouth, another stream called Graveline Bayou opens up into the sound and offers further opportunities for inland exploration. Graveline Bayou is deep in many places, but the waters near its mouth are extremely shallow, mostly 1 to 2 feet or even less. The bayou winds its way to the west-northwest from the sound and ends at the large but shallow Graveline Lake. Much of this area is still undeveloped wetlands and forests, but areas of new subdivisions are also springing up on both the western and eastern sides of this bayou.

Nonresidents traveling along Highway 90 between Ocean Springs and Gautier will see little evidence of all the beautiful hideaways that lie to the south at Bellefontaine Point and areas to the east of it. There are no signs on this highway pointing the way to public beaches or other attractions, but instead only strip malls and other businesses interspersed with piney woods and undeveloped commercial property. The area south of Highway 90 in this part of Jackson County is perhaps one of the best-kept secrets on the Mississippi coast, and the lucky few who live there have good reason for wanting to keep it that way. Still, there are public roads leading to these places, and anyone with a county map who cares to do a little exploring can see some areas of the coast that are far different than the busy beaches that front Highway 90 from Biloxi to Pass Christian.

Fountainbleau Road is the main route that leads to Bellefontaine Point. The road reaches the coastline near the lighthouse mentioned above, and here is found the only public beach in the area. The road leading west is a narrow paved street that continues another 2 miles or so. This road is bordered by undeveloped marsh and woods to the north and perhaps the most beautiful beaches on the sound to the south. These beaches are natural and are much narrower than the broad, man-made beaches elsewhere on the coast. There is a continuous line of houses along this beachfront, but many of these are designed in a way to fit into the landscape without destroying the charm of this shoreline. Large, moss-draped live oaks overhang the roadway and shade the houses, and many palm trees and other exotic plants lend a decidedly Caribbean atmosphere to the scene. Every resident has a splendid view of the sound and Horn Island on the south side. The island with its heavy cloak of forest is plainly visible just over 5 miles away. This is clearly a style of beach living that is laid-back and quiet, in a place that has the serenity of ocean on one side and unspoiled woods and marsh on the other. The road dead-ends to the west where the beach runs out and the marsh meets the sound directly, leaving no room for further expansion of this idyllic community. Certainly the fortunate few who own property here must be thankful for this.

There are additional beachfront homes in a similar setting on the road that runs east of the Bellefontaine lighthouse. This road does not go as far as the western road before it dead-ends. The area just to the north of the lighthouse is occupied by the sprawling grounds of the St. Andrews Golf Course and a large residential area that reaches from the beach to Graveline Bay.

Graveline Bayou and its surrounding marshes separate this area from the community of Gautier, which begins on the eastern side of this estuary.

Also to the north and west of Graveline Bayou and Bellefontaine Point, a large area of the Mississippi Sandhill Crane National Wildlife Refuge is located on both sides of Highway 90. The biggest portion of this refuge is located farther north, on the north side of Interstate 10. The refuge consists of more than 19,000 acres in four separate units. It was established in 1975 to safeguard the endangered Mississippi sandhill crane and its unique habitat. Most of this refuge is closed to the public, since both the wet pine savanna and the cranes are sensitive to disturbance. There is a visitor center located about a half mile north of Interstate 10 at Exit 61, off the Gautier-Vancleave Road. A three-quarter mile nature trail adjacent to the visitor center winds through the pine savanna and tidal marsh. In January and February, conditions permitting, the refuge offers scheduled tours to blinds overlooking crane feeding areas.

The city of Gautier occupies the western bank of the West Pascagoula River, which will be discussed in detail in the following chapter. Between this river and Graveline Bayou, however, the mainland coast is still geographically part of Bellefontaine Point, so I will describe it here. There are more waterfront homes on this section of the coast, and like those described above, many are in hidden beach areas at the end of discreet roads that are not advertised to passersby on Highway 90. One such route that leads south to the coast from the highway is Dolphin Drive. Another is Ladner Road. The beach communities found in this area are off the beaten path and not on the way to anywhere else.

There is one large area of public land to be found in this region, though it is not on the shoreline and has no access directly to the Gulf. This is Shepard State Park. Signs on Highway 90 point the way to this park, which provides numerous opportunities for outdoor recreation.

A shady picnic area in a forest of giant live oaks and tall pines offers tables and grills in a beautiful natural setting. The picnic area is located on a long peninsula of high, wooded ground surrounded by marsh. The picnic area also includes a large pavilion that can be reserved by groups and a playground for children.

There are two campgrounds in the park, one for primitive camping, and the other developed for RVs. The primitive camping area offers 10 tent sites with picnic tables and grills. There are 28 sites with water and electricity in the developed campground.

In addition to camping and picnicking, Shepard State Park offers 5 miles of hiking trails and an 18-hole disc golf course. A boat ramp was available, but at the time of my visit, the access road to the ramp was closed due to storm damage.

NAVIGATOR'S NOTES

Entering Ocean Springs Harbor
(Use NOAA Chart No. 11372)

NOAA Chart No. 11372 covers the entrance to Ocean Springs Harbor and Davis Bayou. Mariners who wish to enter this harbor from the Mississippi Sound can approach from the Biloxi Bay Channel described in the previous chapter. There is a 4-way junction at green daybeacon #35 and flashing red beacon #26. This is where the West Biloxi Harbor Channel intersects the East Biloxi Bay Channel. From this 4-way junction, you can go west to Point Cadet, north to Back Bay, southeast to open sea, or northeast to Ocean Springs Harbor. The Ocean Springs Harbor channel is straightforward from this junction. Pass to the north of flashing red #26 and then flashing red #2 as well. Closer in, a series of small daybeacons leads past the jetties and into the harbor, which is L-shaped and turns 90 degrees to the northwest beyond a row of commercial fishing boat docks. Beyond these docks will be found the marina basin for recreational vessels.

NAVIGATOR'S NOTES

Davis Bayou
(Use NOAA Charts No. 11372 and No. 11374)

There is a marked channel leading into Davis Bayou from the Biloxi Bay channel. This channel entrance is about a half mile south of the 4-way junction that marks the beginning of the Ocean Springs Harbor channel. From red daybeacon #24, which is the first one south of the junction on the main channel, you will see a series of closely spaced red daybeacons leading off to the east. The entrance to the bayou can be seen from here, as there is a long point of land on the outside of the entrance that is shown as Marsh Point on NOAA Chart No. 11372. There are low sandy beaches on this point, as well as marsh grass.

To enter the Davis Bayou channel, leave Biloxi Bay channel at #24 and cross an area of charted 4-foot depths to the first of these red markers, which is #4. The chart does not give the controlling depth for this channel. There is supposed to be 5 feet minimum, with soundings averaging 6 feet or more all the way to the National Park Service docks. Outside the channel depths are 1 to 2 feet or even less. Beyond the park headquarters, a privately marked channel continues inland, but with less reliable depths. Locals say it carries 3 feet all the way to Harbor Point Apartments, where there is a marina.

NOAA Chart No. 11374 picks up where No. 11372 leaves off, and shows the upper reaches of Davis Bayou, as well as the mainland coast east to Pascagoula.

NAVIGATOR'S NOTES

Davis Bayou to the West Pascagoula River
(Use NOAA Chart No. 11374)

This section of the mainland, which is dominated by Bellefontaine Point, is unsuitable for close inshore navigation. Depths of 1 to 3 feet extend out more than half a mile from the shore in this area, which offers no deep-water harbors or anchorage areas. Deep draft vessels traveling from the Ocean Spring area to Pascagoula should follow the ICW or carefully plot a course closer in to the coast in the areas of 5- to 7-foot depths shown on the chart.

10

THE PASCAGOULA RIVER, ROUND ISLAND, AND GRAND BAY

Like the Pearl River on the western boundary of the state, the Pascagoula River is a major river, and its drainage basin is the second largest in the state. The Pascagoula itself is relatively short, flowing some 81 miles from where it begins at the confluence of the Leaf and Chickasawhay Rivers to the Gulf of Mexico. Many of the state's important streams make up this river system, including the Okatoma, Bowie River, Chunky River, Tallahala Creek, Black Creek, Red Creek, and the Escatawpa River. The Pascagoula River system is unique in being among the last free-flowing major river systems in the lower 48 states. This means there are no dams on the river or any of its main tributaries, though there are some small ones on the upper reaches of some of the feeder creeks, such as Little Black Creek Water Park, Lake Bogue Homa, and Okatibbee Lake. No other rivers in North America, outside of Alaska and Canada remain this unchanged. This river and many of its tributaries have a wild character that is almost impossible to find today, especially in the Deep South. Most of the river is bordered by the 37,124-acre Pascagoula Wildlife Management Area and the 9,494-acre Ward Bayou Wildlife Management Area. In addition to this, there is the 501,000-acre Desoto National Forest to the west, and the 19,273-acre Mississippi Sandhill Crane National Wildlife Refuge to the southwest. Recent additions to the protected lands in this region are the 18,500-acre Grand Bay Reserve and the 7,000-acre Grand Bay National Wildlife Refuge.

The swampy wilderness surrounding the Pascagoula River is rich in legend. The name comes from the Native American people who inhabited the region and appears to be derived from *pasca* for bread and *okla* for people. The legend that lends mystery to this river is the other name by which the waterway is known: The Singing River. This legend has been so persistent for such a long period of time that even modern buildings such as the Singing River Mall and the Singing River Hospital refer to it. For centuries, reports of a "singing" noise heard on the river have kept the legend alive. The explanation offered by the legends is that the native Pascagoula people, realizing that they faced extinction from war and disease because of the invasion of white settlers, decided to commit mass suicide. They waded into the water holding hands and singing, and were never seen again. Now their singing can still be heard on rare occasions from the dark waters of the big river at night, according to those who have experienced it. My canoeing partner Ernest Herndon claims to have heard it, but he says that in his case it was not Indian spirits but the "singing" of thousands of mosquitoes swarming about his tent. Having spent quite a few nights camped along the river myself, I can say with confidence that you too, if you decide to go, will hear this kind of music produced by the whir of tiny wings. As for mysterious noises in the night, nothing can quite compare to the weird and maniacal screaming and laughter of the barred owl, which can be heard emanating from the black forests most any night.

Like the Pearl River, the higher reaches of the Pascagoula flow through magnificent stands of old-growth hardwood and cypress forests. These forests are as junglelike as any you'll find in North America, replete with abundant venomous snakes, alligators, wild hogs, and, according to plenty of local witnesses, elusive and secretive panthers. For canoeing and camping, these upper reaches offer solitude and wide beaches of white sand upon which to pitch a tent. The smaller tributaries, such as Black Creek, offer perhaps the best canoeing to be found in the southeastern United States. For a complete description of the Pascagoula's many tributaries and canoe routes, refer to Ernest Herndon's excellent guidebook *Canoeing Mississippi*.

THE LOWER PASCAGOULA RIVER

For our purposes here, we will consider the parts of the Pascagoula that are south of the Interstate 10 bridge crossing to be part of the marine waters of the state. Driving across this long causeway over the marsh, one can begin to grasp the immensity of this swampy wilderness. To the north of the interstate, the hardwood forests are visible on the horizon. To the south, trees are much less a part of the landscape, which is mainly a sea of marsh grass cut with winding backwater channels. Several miles north of the interstate, the river splits into two main channels, which become the West Pascagoula River and the East Pascagoula River. At the point where the bridge crosses, these two channels are widely separated, about three miles apart, which is the reason such a long bridge was needed. In between are winding bayous and connecting waterways that split off and then rejoin the main river. All of these bayous and both river branches offer fine opportunities for exploring or fishing if you are traveling in a small, shoal draft boat. The West Pascagoula River is not marked or charted for navigation by larger vessels, mainly because there is no access to the open sound because of the low fixed bridges that span this branch of the river. Highway 90 crosses the West Pascagoula near its mouth with a fixed vertical clearance of 12 feet. Less than half a mile to the south, the CSX Railroad bridge crosses with a fixed vertical clearance of just 7 feet. About 4 miles north of the Highway 90 crossing, the Interstate 10 span also crosses the West Pascagoula with a low vertical clearance.

Taller vessels do enter the West Pascagoula, however, by way of connecting channels from the more navigable East Pascagoula. Since the East Pascagoula is the gateway to this labyrinth of waterways, we will begin our exploration of the river by describing the entrance to the East Pascagoula. NOAA Chart No. 11374 covers all the navigation areas in this chapter, from Bellefontaine Point to Grand Bay, as well as approaches from Round Island and the ICW. Before we get to the details of the East Pascagoula itself, it would be helpful to look at the approach to the Pascagoula River area from the ICW, and the small, uninhabited island found nearby off the coast.

ROUND ISLAND

Only boaters traveling in kayaks or other extremely shoal draft boats should consider approaching the Pascagoula area from Gautier and points west by closely following the shore. As mentioned in the preceding chapter, shoals abound near shore off of Graveline Bayou and Bellefontaine Point.

The Intracoastal Waterway, which passes through the sound 3½ miles south of Bellefontaine Point and more than 4½ miles south of the mouth of the West Pascagoula, is the safest way to approach Pascagoula from the west. The ICW makes a sharp turn to the southeast to avoid the shoals that lie to the south of a small isolated island located in the sound about midway between the mainland and the barrier islands.

Round Island is not part of the National Seashore, nor is it a barrier island. Like Deer Island, it is uninhabited and undeveloped. A distinctive abandoned lighthouse, the only man-made feature on the island, once stood on the southern tip, but in 1998 it was destroyed by Hurricane Georges. Narrow

Abandoned lighthouse at Round Island

beaches ring the entire perimeter of the island, which is heavily wooded, mostly in pine forest and dense undergrowth.

The island does get visitors, mainly boaters who come to picnic and some who camp on the beach. Because of its midway location, Round Island is an excellent stopover for kayakers headed to Horn Island from the Pascagoula area. On many trips from the West Pascagoula River to Horn Island, I have stopped to camp for a night on the beaches of Round Island.

DEEP TROUBLE IN A SEA KAYAK

One of these trips, in particular, was memorable because it nearly ended in disaster. My canoeing buddy, Ernest Herndon, and I had spent the previous week paddling to the coast from the upper reaches of Black Creek, south of Hattiesburg. We arrived at Gautier a day early, so for our final night of the trip, I suggested that we continue on out to Round Island to give him a taste of island camping.

This trip had been Ernest's first experience in a sea kayak. He had years of canoeing experience, and now after a week in the kayak on the river, I didn't think twice about him having problems kayaking in open water. He expressed some doubts when we stopped near the railroad bridge at the mouth of the river and looked out across the choppy waters of the sound at Round Island, which appeared as a hazy hump of blue 5 miles to the south. I assured him that we would have no problems reaching the island in the seaworthy kayaks, and besides the Mississippi Sound is protected by the string of barrier islands lying farther offshore. The waves would not be big enough to threaten us.

After this brief discussion, we sealed ourselves back into the kayaks and set out through the outlying marshes at the river mouth. Ernest had never learned any kayak self-rescue techniques and had never experienced a "wet exit," which is the kayaker's term for getting out of an upside down boat without panicking. I didn't think he would need any of this knowledge, but an hour later, I was to find out how wrong I was.

We passed Singing River Island, which is the last land near shore and the site of the Pascagoula Naval Station, and entered the more exposed waters of the open sound. The wind was out of the south, so we were punching through a chop of 1- to 2-foot breaking waves. Ernest thought it was great. He pulled far ahead while I fell into a rhythmic stroke and contemplated the long journey ahead. Ernest would be going home tomorrow after our night on the island. I was continuing onward, heading east and south along the Florida coast on the first leg of a long-awaited kayak expedition to the Caribbean. My expectations were high, and I rejoiced in at last being free of the river and free of the land, heading out to sea with the open horizon before me.

When we reached a point about a mile from Round Island, we found ourselves in much nastier chop. The waves were steep, 3 to 4 feet high, and breaking into plunging white crests. My kayak was heavily laden for my long voyage, and was under the water most of the time in these sea conditions. Paddling seemed to get harder, and the kayak seemed to be riding lower in the water than normal. Then a pool of water formed inside the cockpit and grew deeper until it was almost around my waist. The stern of my boat was awash, and now I realized the entire compartment behind my seat was flooded. This was a problem! I yelled for Ernest, but he was probably 200 yards upwind of me, blissfully paddling into the breaking waves and oblivious of my predicament. All well-equipped sea kayakers carry a hand-operated bilge pump. I reached for mine and began pumping out the cockpit, as more angry waves broke over my decks. I carried a loud Coast Guard approved signal whistle lashed to my life vest. I remembered this and blew sharp blasts on it as I pumped. Whether Ernest heard the whistle or just looked back to see where I was, I don't know, but when he looked, I waved frantically and motioned for him to come to me.

As he slowly made his way back to my position, I pumped as fast as I could in an effort to stay afloat. Since the stern compartment was crammed completely full of gear, which although heavy, was still lighter than water, the kayak did not take on enough water to sink.

Ernest was having a tough time negotiating the breaking waves. Thanks to me, here he was more than a mile from the nearest land in rough conditions with no prior knowledge of bracing strokes or kayak handling. And the only person who could help him was in a sinking boat. I watched him struggle as I pumped, and then a particularly large wave caught him broadside as he tried to maneuver close to me. The next thing I saw was the upturned yellow hull of his kayak. It seemed like forever before he finally broke the surface, coughing and spitting seawater, hanging on to the inverted kayak with one hand and his paddle with the other.

Reentering a capsized and flooded kayak requires a precise and practiced technique even in calm conditions. Ernest didn't know where to start, and he was being pummeled by breaking waves and had lost his glasses in the capsize.

I managed to maneuver my half-sunken kayak alongside him and instructed him to roll his upright. I then handed him the pump, and he began pumping his cockpit out while treading water and nervously wondering what might be swimming around beneath him in the murky, choppy, waters of the sound. When he had most of the water out, I held his boat tightly alongside mine, and by climbing up on the stern of mine, he was able to slide back into his seat without capsizing.

We stayed close together, and despite my waterlogged, overweight boat and his nervous, newly formed respect for the breaking chop, we at last made it to the beaches of Round Island. Ernest was seasick from all the motion and swallowing seawater. I was exhausted, but immediately emptied all the wet gear out of my boat and began inspecting the hull to see what damage there was. As it turned out, it was a manufacturing flaw. The hull was too flexible to withstand rough seas when so heavily laden. The flexing had caused the rear bulkhead to break loose and lose its watertight integrity. I realized then and there that this was not the kayak for my long journey. The trip would have to be postponed until I could get a more seaworthy model. We spent the night on Round Island that night, and the next morning the sea calmed to a mirror-smooth surface, so we were able to paddle back to the Pascagoula River.

THE PASCAGOULA SHIP CHANNEL

Although it might be possible to anchor off the southwest coast of Round Island after a careful approach to avoid the shoals, most skippers of cruising-sized vessels will want to bypass this island and stay in the ICW until its intersection with the Pascagoula Ship Channel. This intersection lies about 4 nautical miles east of Round Island, and just north of the western tip of Petit Bois Island. Approaching from the east it is easily identified as a long string of closely spaced channel markers running in a north-south line. This well-marked ship channel is deep and easy to follow. It is used by vessels as large as United States Navy battleships.

The channel splits 2 miles to the north of the ICW. The left fork bearing off to the northwest leads into the East Pascagoula and the right fork leads to Bayou Casotte. Bayou Casotte is heavily used by industrial marine traffic and is not recommended for pleasure craft. The Pascagoula Channel also sees a lot of industrial traffic, but the quiet waters upstream of the shipyards and commercial docks make it a worthwhile side trip. It is a 4-nautical-mile run from the Bayou Casotte split to the entrance to the East Pascagoula.

One side trip that cruising yachtsmen might want to make is a visit to the Singing River Yacht Club, which is located near the entrance to a small channel called Bayou Chico. The entrance and dockside depths are only 4 to 4½ feet, but for cruisers who can handle these shallows, the club welcomes members of other yacht clubs with reciprocal privileges. Instructions for this detour are included in the *Navigator's Notes* for the East Pascagoula at the end of this chapter.

SINGING RIVER ISLAND

For those continuing on the ship channel to inland waters, the route turns north again, just off Singing River Island. Singing River Island is Mississippi's newest island, and it is entirely man-made, created by dredge material from the Pascagoula River channel. The island began to be built up in the 1960s and reached its present size in the 1970s. The island is approximately 480 acres in size and was originally known as "Mud Lump." In 1985, the secretary of the Navy announced that a new naval station would be built on the island, and construction began in 1988. A causeway was built and the naval station was completed in 1992. More than 2,000 personnel are assigned to the station, which occupies 187 acres of the island on the northeast corner. The remainder of the island has been left in a natural state and is a haven to wildlife, including, rabbits, nutria, and snakes. Bobcats have been introduced to help control the rabbits and nutria. An elevated nature trail and fishing pier have been built along the eastern shore, and part of the island is open to the public.

THE EAST PASCAGOULA RIVER

Beyond Singing River Island, boaters will encounter depths in the lower industrial section of the river of 20 feet or more from bank to bank. On the east side of the river mouth, a marked channel leads into Lake Yazoo, where there are anchorage opportunities and public boat ramps. These boat ramps can be reached by road by driving to the western end of Pascacoula's Beach Boulevard. The western banks of the East Pascagoula are occupied by Ingalls Shipyard and a U.S. Coast Guard base. Large U.S. Navy ships are often seen alongside the docks at Ingalls. The first bridge crossing encountered on the river is the CSX Railroad, which has a vertical clearance of only 7 feet. It is usually left open unless a train is expected.

Just to the north of the railroad bridge, the river is also spanned by Highway 90. At the time of the this writing, Highway 90 is a drawbridge with 31 feet of closed vertical clearance, and a restrictive opening schedule. A new much higher fixed bridge is under construction, however, and should be open by the time this book is in print.

Just north of the bridge the public Pascagoula River Park occupies the west bank. This park features a fishing pier, picnic tables, playground, and a boat ramp. There is also a unique exhibit called the Scranton Museum. This museum is unusual in that it is an old commercial shrimp boat that has been permanently grounded after being salvaged in the wake of Hurricane Camille. A flight of steps leads up to the deck, where nets and other fishing gear are still in place. Visitors can tour the interior of the vessel and see the pilothouse and captain's quarters the way they were once used. The lower part of the vessel that was once the hold is now filled with coastal natural history exhibits.

Upstream of this park, the river bends to the northwest. The first of two possible routes for cruising boats headed for the West Pascagoula River begins just north of the park. This route is Marsh Lake Channel, an arrow-straight cut that carries minimum depths of 6 feet.

THE WEST PASCAGOULA RIVER AND MARY WALKER BAYOU

Where this dredged channel crosses Marsh Lake, it is important to stay lined up with the canal openings in front of and behind you, as the lake waters to the north and south are very shallow. West of this lake, the canal runs another mile before opening up into the West Pascagoula River.

Across from this entrance into the river, another significant channel enters the river from the west. This stream is called Mary Walker Bayou, and along its banks are found the best facilities for visiting pleasure craft in the Pascagoula area. Boaters entering the West Pascagoula River at this point, by way of the Marsh Lake channel from the East Pascagoula River, are probably doing so because they could not clear the low Highway 90 and railroad bridges that span the west river. Therefore, going downriver is not an option, as Highway 90 crosses just below the point where the Marsh Lake channel and Mary Walker Bayou enter the river.

The first development found on the bayou is just north of the Highway 90 bridge, on the south shore of the bayou. This is a marina, bait shop, and campground called Tucei's Fishing Camp. There are several slips on the waterfront here, but dockside depths are only 4 feet. For those who can negotiate these depths, a gasoline pump is also located on the dock. Two boat ramps are provided, and a building on stilts offers lodging for overnight guests. There is also a parking area with hookups for recreational vehicles.

Immediately upstream of Tucei's is another dockage area called Braly's Point Loma Marina. This marina appears to be well kept and offers covered slips in a well-protected basin off the main waterway. Adjacent to the marina is The Porch Restaurant and Lounge.

The major marina on this bayou is Mary Walker Marina, a large facility with approximately 200 slips, including dockage for transient vessels. Power and water connections are available, as well as gasoline and diesel. Mary Walker Marina also offers haul-out and repair service, and has a lift that can handle boats as large as 32 feet. A restaurant called the Tiki Room is located near the docks, as well as a small general store.

Just past Mary Walker Marina, also on the south side of the bayou, Pitalo's Marine offers a Travelift and full-service boatyard, as well as a marine supply and hardware store.

For those traveling by road rather than on the river, these marine facilities on Mary Walker Bayou can be reached by following the signs and turning north off of Highway 90 just west of the river in Gautier. Another worthwhile place to stop, especially for those who are driving, is the new Gautier City Park that is located on the bayou just west of Pitalo's Marine. This park features a long boardwalk pier out over the marsh, with a view of a pretty hardwood hammock a short distance from the end. These hammocks are typical in big riverine marshes like the lower reaches of the Pascagoula. They are actually islands of higher ground, densely forested in live oaks and other hardwood trees, cutoff from the outside world by the surrounding marshes.

Two boat ramps with adjacent docks are also provided at this city park, as well as a covered pavilion, a playground, and a building used as a Senior Citizens Center.

Boaters cruising the bayou in all but the smallest craft will not want to go much past Pitalo's Marine. The bayou forks west of there, and depths become much less reliable.

Back on the main West Pascagoula, good depths are found all the way to the Interstate 10 bridge. This river channel is broad and deep, but there is a current and not much protection for anchorage. There are several abundant opportunities for those in smaller boats, however. On one small cutoff channel called Swift Bayou, I had the good fortune to see up close a wild alligator that was surely at the upper limit of the species' size potential. My buddy Jeff Hudson and I were on the last day of an 8-day canoe journey from Hattiesburg to the Gulf Coast, by way of the Leaf and Pascagoula Rivers. North of the Interstate 10 bridge, we took a shortcut I had discovered on a previous trip and were paddling down the winding, narrow waters of Swift Bayou. This waterway is bordered almost exclusively by marsh grass and mud banks, offering no good place for landing unless you are prepared to wallow up to your hips in stinking swamp mud. We rounded one sharp 90-degree bend after another, and upon one such turn, something piled up on the right bank ahead of us caught my eye. It looked like a bunch of old car tires strewn upon the bank in the grass. We kept paddling, and as we got closer, I focused on the object in disbelief. It was an alligator, but way out of proportion to any such river reptile I had ever seen before. This creature was more like a dinosaur. Its entire body was out of the water, stretched upon the mud bank, which was barely 6 inches above water level. The prehistoric-looking scales of its back and tail were draped with some kind of greenish-black river-bottom weed. The one huge eye we could see was open, but unblinking, and the creature did not move. Was it alive or dead? It seemed as if it could not be real. It was so big I at first thought it had to be some plastic version of an alligator created for a movie set. Jeff had never seen an alligator of any size up close and in the wild. We spoke in low whispers as we drifted ever closer. Our route would take us right past this monstrous reptile, if we chose to continue. The only other option to reach Gautier, our destination, would be to backtrack all the way back to the beginning of this bayou and then head down the main branch of the West Pascagoula. That would add miles to our trip, and we were ready to go home.

We decided to sneak on past the big 'gator, as it seemed to be asleep. We were in my hand-built 20-foot decked canoe, a real speed machine, but I still felt vulnerable having to paddle within 20 feet or so of such an animal. I now realized that of all the time I'd spent camping on low mud banks and swimming in swampy rivers, there could have been alligators like this one around. I could see no difference in a 'gator this size and a man-eating crocodile. I told Jeff that if this guy wanted us, he could get us. Despite all this, once we were just a little past the closest point we would have to come to the sleeping giant, I could not resist slapping the water loudly with the paddle to see if I could get a response. I wasn't even sure if this thing was alive. The splash assured me that it was, however, and I felt a chill run down my spine when it raised its head, which looked to be 3 feet long by itself, and looked at us with jaws agape. We dug in with paddles and got out of there fast. The alligator remained on the bank, indignant about being awakened but not interested in giving chase.

Jeff Hudson on a canoe trip on the lower reaches of the Pascagoula River

A couple of years later, there was a photo in the newspaper of a 13-foot alligator some trapper had caught on the lower Pascagoula near Gautier. It looked huge in the photo, but I am sure this was not the one we saw, as it had to be bigger than 13 feet. Though most people familiar with alligators these days would not believe it, the largest American alligator on record measured 19 feet, 4 inches long. When the Deep South was still wild, huge 'gators were not at all uncommon, according to the journals of early explorers. When the animals began to be hunted out for their valuable hides, the largest ones were the first to disappear. Continued pressure from human contact and illegal hunting makes it extremely unlikely for alligators in the wild to survive long enough to reach such extraordinary sizes.

Since I could not convince Jeff to get out of the canoe and stand near the alligator for a photo, I have no way of proving how big it was. Whatever length this great reptile would have measured, I hope it is still out there somewhere in the marshes of this watery wilderness. But whether it is or not, my days of swimming in such places are over.

EAST PASCAGOULA RIVER TO THE ESCATAWPA RIVER

For those not exploring the marsh by canoe or other small boat, Bayou Chemise enters the West Pascagoula just north of the Marsh Lake Channel, and offers another option for larger vessels returning to the East Pascagoula. This is a much more roundabout route, as the bayou runs north and then bends to the southeast and back to northeast before joining the east river. If entering this bayou from the south, stick to the easterly channel around the charted oblong island that bisects the mouth of the bayou. Charted depths here are 28 to 30 feet. North of this island, depths of 9 to 14 feet are found in the midwidth of the stream. Stick to the main channel by favoring the southern bank to your starboard. Several intersecting waterways come in from the north but are not suitable for navigation. Bayou Chemise splits from the East Pascagoula River a little less than 2 nautical miles upstream from where we left the river to head west on Marsh Lake Channel.

In the stretch of river between these two routes to the West Pascagoula, the East Pascagoula is well marked and easy to navigate. Midway in this stretch, about a mile north of the Highway 90 bridge crossing on the East Pascagoula, yet another waterway opens up to the east, adding more choices in the labyrinth of avenues to explore. This is McInnis Bayou. It is too shallow for deep draft vessels, but for those who can handle areas of 2- to 3-foot depths, it offers a long, winding side trip along the shore at the town of Moss Point. McInnis Bayou diverges from the East Pascagoula about a mile north of where Bayou Chemise splits off to the west.

Driving along the waterfront north of Highway 90 on the east side of the East Pascagoula, one can follow the signs to Old Spanish Fort, a museum housed in what is advertised as the "oldest standing outpost in the Mississippi valley." This fort was established in 1718. East of the fort, along the waterfront, O'Sullivan's marina offers a bait and tackle shop and a few docks along the shore that were all occupied by commercial fishing boats when I visited. Just north of this is a small boatyard with a Travelift, located at the intersection of Cedar Street and Lake.

North of this area, River Road loosely follows the waterfront to the town of Moss Point. Along the way, Choctaw Marina offers two boat ramps as well as a bar and dockage for smaller cruising boats. For those navigating the river who wish to continue upstream, the East Pascagoula offers the opportunity for further inland exploration.

Upstream of the McInnis Bayou split, the Escatawpa River merges with the East Pascagoula channel. Those traveling upstream will find that navigation markers continue to east, in the right-hand fork, which is the Escatawpa River. The Pascagoula River is the left-hand fork, which turns sharply to the north. This route is shoal and not charted, and should therefore be attempted only by those in smaller vessels. The Escatawpa, however, is navigable for many more miles. The first bridge crossing this stream is a fixed bridge with 77 feet of vertical clearance. East of this bridge, the channel splits again, with the marked route continuing eastward and an alternate channel turning off to the southeast. This alternate route is deep, and soundings are charted on the Pascagoula River Extension inset found on NOAA Chart No. 11374. The channel leads south along the shores of the community of Moss Point and offers several possibilities for anchorage in sheltered side waters such as O'Leary Lake and McInnis Lake. After making this loop to the south, this channel rejoins the main Escatawpa River, and good depths continue on to the east, where the river passes under another high fixed bridge with a vertical clearance of 73 feet. East of this bridge a low railroad swing bridge spans the river, but it is usually left open unless a train is due. Large commercial fishing vessels are seen even this far upriver, attesting to the good depths still to be found. The channel soon splits again, however, about a half mile east of this railroad bridge. There are good places to anchor in either fork, but beyond this point depths are uncharted and further exploration is best left to shallow-draft boats. The upper Escatawpa River, like so many of the other streams that make up the Pascagoula River system, offers excellent wilderness canoeing. It flows through some of the wildest bottomland forests remaining in Mississippi before reaching these industrialized areas of navigable waters near the coast.

GRAND BAY

There is one other large area of undeveloped coastline and marshes, as well as wild interior forests on the Mississippi Gulf Coast. This vast area is called Grand Bay. It consists of a maze of bayous, small bays, marsh islands, and mudflats extending east of the Pascagoula area to include portions of the Alabama coastline west of Mobile Bay. The most undeveloped stretch of this coastline lies between Bayou Casotte, an industrial waterway east of Pascagoula, and Bayou La Batre, in Alabama. The waters near the coast in this part of the Mississippi Sound are extremely shallow, with depths of only half a foot in places and 1 to 2 feet in many others. The area is not suitable for navigation in anything but small skiffs and perhaps kayaks.

Much of this area is now included in the Grand Bay National Wildlife Refuge, which was established in 1992. This refuge protects thousands of acres of tidal marsh and pine savanna. The main purpose of the refuge is to protect wildlife habitat and endangered species such as the gopher tortoise and bald eagle.

The refuge is open to the public, but there are no facilities for visitors and the main activities available are wildlife observation, photography, and boating in the marsh. The emphasis here is on habitat protection rather than recreation, but everyone interested in preserving what is left of the natural Gulf coast should be glad that this is one more area that is safe from development and change.

NAVIGATOR'S NOTES

Approaches to Pascagoula from the ICW, and Round Island
(Use NOAA Chart No. 11374)

The Intracoastal Waterway passes well to the south of the mainland between Biloxi and Pascagoula. The route transits the Mississippi Sound in an area of 12- to 15-foot depths 3½ miles south of Bellefontaine Point and more than 4½ miles south of the mouth of the West Pascagoula. Mariners traveling the ICW from west to east will see a small, isolated island shown on the chart as Round Island. The channel makes a sharp turn to the southeast at flashing green beacon #5A to avoid the extensive shoals that extend to the south of this island. Those who want to explore the island can do so by departing the ICW at this turn and heading northeast to the single flashing yellow beacon #8 that is located less than a half mile from the western shore of the island. The charted line of 7-foot depths between this beacon and the beach is a suitable place for anchorage in settled weather, and close enough to go ashore in a dinghy.

Eastbound boaters traveling the ICW who do not wish to stop at Round Island before turning north to the East Pascagoula, should turn southeast at flashing green #5A and set a course for the next ICW marker in line, flashing green #3. The ICW then runs slightly north of due east on a course of 88 degrees for a distance of 5 nautical miles. At this point the Pascagoula Ship Channel crosses the ICW at a point ¾ of a nautical mile west of ICW charted mile marker St M 105. From its junction with the ICW, the channel's entrance from seaward between the western tip of Petit Bois and the man-made spoil island west of Petit Bois is clearly visible.

Westbound mariners traveling the ICW from Dauphin Island, Alabama and points east will spot this junction of the Pascagoula Ship Channel as they pass north of Petit Bois Island.

NAVIGATOR'S NOTES

Entering the East Pascagoula River via the Pascagoula Ship Channel
(Use NOAA Chart No. 11374)

Lighted beacons green #23 and red #24 are the first pair of channel markers located north of the intersection of the ICW and the Pascagoula Ship Channel. A series of red and green markers lead in a straight line slightly west of due north from these markers. Two miles to the north of the ICW, at flashing red beacon #30, the channel splits. The channel that continues almost due north is the Bayou Casotte Channel. The Pascagoula Channel bears off to the northwest at this split.

The Bayou Casotte Channel is a heavily used industrial waterway with little attraction to recreational boaters. From the Bayou Casotte split the Pascagoula Ship Channel runs 4 more nautical miles to the entrance to the East Pascagoula River. One possible side trip off this route is a visit to the Singing River Yacht Club, located at the mouth of Bayou Chico. This bayou empties into the sound a little over 2 nautical miles east of the mouth of the East Pascagoula. To make this detour, turn east-northeast off the ship channel at flashing red beacon #42 and head for flashing yellow daybeacon "E," which leads the way into the privately marked channel.

For those continuing on the ship channel, the route turns north again at flashing green beacon #43, just off Singing River Island. A side channel leading into Lake Yazoo cuts to the northeast at flashing red beacon #46. To enter this canal, follow the two red daybeacons #2 and #4, keeping them to starboard. Depths are only about 4½ feet at this entrance. Staying in the middle, follow the canal to the lake, passing a series of 4 public boat ramps and fishing piers. The depths in the canal are 5 to 5½ feet, and decrease to 4½ feet in Lake Yazoo. There are several sailboats on permanent moorings in the middle of the lake and many more boats docked around the eastern shore at Pascagoula Street. For boats that can anchor in these shallow waters, the lake offers sheltered waters for dropping the hook.

From the river mouth, the East Pascagoula runs straight north past heavily industrialized banks to the first bridge crossing the river, the CSX Railroad swing bridge. This bridge has a closed vertical clearance of 7 feet. Just to the north, Highway 90 crosses the river. A new bridge is under construction. The present bridge is a drawbridge with 31 feet of closed vertical clearance.

Upstream of this bridge, the river bends to the northwest. At unlighted red daybeacon #4, cruisers have the option of turning south into a well-protected anchorage shown on the chart as a dead-end pocket of 7-foot depths that extends almost back to Highway 90.

NAVIGATOR'S NOTES

The West Pascagoula River and Mary Walker Bayou
(Use NOAA Chart No. 11374)

The first of two routes from the East Pascagoula to the West Pascagoula also begins adjacent to red daybeacon #4. Marsh Lake Channel is the most direct route for those bound to the West Pascagoula from the ICW. Enter the channel by turning northwest into the dredged canal just south of #4. Depths in this cut are at least 6 feet. The canal crosses Marsh Lake and continues on the same course for another nautical mile, where it opens into the West Pascagoula River.

Travel downstream on the West Pascagoula River is restricted by two low, fixed bridges, Highway 90 with 12 feet of vertical clearance, and the CSX Railroad, with just 7 feet.

Directly across the river from where the Marsh Lake channel enters, the navigable Mary Walker Bayou enters from the west. To enter Mary Walker Bayou, favor the south bank to avoid the area of charted 4-foot depths extending from the north side at the mouth. Other than this shallow area, the rest of the bayou holds 7-foot depths at midwidth. The bayou is navigable for most vessels at least to Pitalo's Marine haul-out facility. Beyond this point, about a mile upstream of the West Pascagoula, Lang Bayou enters from the north and depths become questionable beyond this junction.

The main body of the West Pascagoula River itself is wide and quite deep and can be explored to the north at least to the point where Interstate 10 crosses it with a low fixed bridge.

Just to the north of where Mary Walker Bayou enters the west river from the west, another large bayou enters the east bank from the northeast. This is Bayou Chemise, which provides another deepwater route between the East Pascagoula River and the West Pascagoula River.

To enter Bayou Chemise from the West Pascagoula, stay near the east bank just north of the mouth of the Marsh Lake Channel. Keep the charted oblong island that bisects the mouth of Bayou Chemise to your port side, and you will find depths of 28 to 30 feet midstream. North of the island, depths decrease to 9 to 14 feet. Favor the south bank as the bayou winds its way generally northeastward for almost 2 nautical miles. Bayou Chemise rejoins the East Pascagoula just past green daybeacon #1, which will be passed off your starboard beam as you enter the river. Beyond this marker, red daybeacon #10 is part of the East Pascagoula channel.

NAVIGATOR'S NOTES

East Pascagoula River to Lower Escatawpa River
(Use NOAA Chart No. 11374)

Those heading up the East Pascagoula River from the Highway 90 bridge crossing will bypass the Marsh Lake Channel at red daybeacon #4 and follow the river north-northeast to red daybeacon #6, where it then makes a 90-degree bend to the west-northwest. At #6, McInnis Bayou enters the river channel from the east. This bayou is navigable, but only for those vessels drawing no more than 2 feet.

The main east river channel runs northwest to the point where Bayou Chemise splits off to the southwest at red daybeacon #10. From here the route is north again, until the river winds back around to the northeast. Two nautical miles upstream from the Bayou Chemise split lies the junction of the East Pascagoula River and the Escatawpa River. North of this point, navigation on the Pascagoula River becomes questionable and soundings are uncharted.

The marked channel into the Escatawpa River continues on to the east-northeast and passes through a series of lakes. Two fixed bridges span the river in the region of these lakes, the first with a generous vertical clearance of 77 feet, and the second with a 73-foot clearance. Anchorage opportunities abound in the charted deep side waters south of the channel. Soundings are charted for at least another mile upstream, past a railroad swing bridge with 5 feet of vertical clearance.

NAVIGATOR'S NOTES

Pascagoula River to Alabama State Line
(Use NOAA Chart No. 11374)

This easternmost part of the Mississippi coast includes the Grand Bay area mentioned in the text. Inshore navigation here is limited to shoal draft vessels for the most part. NOAA Chart No. 11374 shows no marked channels in this region, but soundings are given that would allow adventurous skippers to edge into some of the interesting areas.

Point Aux Chenes Bay has a large area of 4- to 5-foot depths that could serve as an anchorage area and allow further exploration of the coastal bayous and swamps by dinghy.

Part 3

MISSISSIPPI'S BARRIER ISLANDS

11

PETIT BOIS
ISLAND

The barrier islands that lie like thin slivers of hazy blue on the horizon to the south are a world apart from the mainland. These long narrow islands are called barrier islands because they guard the mainland shores from the wind-driven waves of the open Gulf of Mexico and create the lagoonlike body of water in between, known as the Mississippi Sound. Barrier islands such as these are found along many coastlines throughout the world, but one thing that makes Mississippi's barrier islands unique is that they are unusually distant from the mainland they protect.

These islands were built up between 3,500 and 6,000 years ago from sand deposited by wave action. Longshore currents set up by prevailing southeasterly waves in the Gulf carry the sand from the delta south of Mobile Bay toward the west. It has been recorded since the 1700s that the islands are in a constant state of movement and rebuilding, as they gradually creep towards the west. The western ends of the islands build up as the eastern ends erode away. Some of the islands have moved as much as a mile in one hundred years. All barrier islands are in a continual state of change like this, and this pounding and erosion they take from the sea protects the mainland from similar damage.

Mississippi's barrier islands create a sound about eighty miles long, and this body of protected water averages about ten feet deep. Several rivers empty into the sound, including the Pearl and the Pascagoula, and the influx of fresh water results in a salinity level only about half that of the open Gulf. These rivers also bring sediments that cloud the waters of the sound and cover most of the bottom with mud deposits.

This chain of barrier islands actually begins in Alabama, with Dauphin Island. Petit Bois was once part of Dauphin Island, until the late 1700s when it was separated by a storm in the same way that Ship Island was cut in two by Hurricane Camille in 1969.

We will begin our exploration of each of these unique islands with Petit Bois, and like the gradual movement of the barrier islands themselves, slowly work our way to the west where the chain ends with Cat Island.

Petis Bois means "little wood" in French. The name came perhaps from the small stand of pine trees located near the eastern end of an otherwise treeless expanse of marsh and sand dunes. When seen from a boat a mile or more offshore, Petit Bois Island appears to offer little of interest. It is in fact a fascinating place to explore on foot, as I had ample opportunity to do so on my first trip there, many years ago.

WEATHER-BOUND ON AN UNINHABITED ISLAND

Since the island is actually closer to Dauphin Island, Alabama, than any point on the Mississippi mainland, I decided to drive there to launch my kayak for an overnight trip to Petit Bois. This was a winter trip, in early February, so I expected harsh conditions and hoped to find solitude. I parked near a commercial fishing dock on Dauphin Island, loaded my gear, and spent the first afternoon paddling along the shore the 11 miles to the west end of that island. There I found a secluded spot among the grassy dunes to pitch my tent so I could be rested for the 5-mile crossing to Petit Bois early the next morning. From this point I could see the hazy blue hump that was the "little woods" on Petit Bois. The rest of the island was too low to appear on the horizon from that distance.

When morning came I was surprised to find a dense fog had moved in over the Gulf waters and I could no longer see either Petit Bois or the mainland to the north. I broke camp and launched the kayak anyway, confidently following my deck-mounted compass on a course of 250 degrees, where I knew Petit Bois had to be. This was among my first few open water crossings in a kayak, and the first in fog. Handheld GPS receivers were not yet heard of. After Dauphin Island had disappeared in the mist behind me, I could see nothing all around but gray water and gray sky. There was little if any wind, so the surface of the sea was smooth, yet it moved under my hull in great undulating swells from the open Gulf. Throughout the crossing I heard the weird, laughing calls of loons, coming from somewhere nearby but out of sight in the fog. I began to doubt my compass. Though I was following the course I knew to be correct from the charts and from my visual sighting of Petit Bois the night before, it just didn't seem right. It felt more like I was paddling a great, curving arc of a circle rather than a straight-line compass course. I stopped paddling after an hour to drift and eat a high-energy snack for paddling fuel. As I drifted, I debated whether I should continue on blindly in the fog or turn back for Dauphin Island before it was too late. My greatest fear was that I was not really headed for Petit Bois but was instead somehow on course for the open sea, being pulled south of the pass between the two islands. I dug out my chart and checked the compass bearing again to be sure. Despite the nagging doubts and some instinctive distrust of the compass in these conditions, I knew that a magnetic compass could not lie, and I knew I would have to have faith and believe in it to reach my destination. I started paddling west again, determined to stay on course, and after another hour the fog began to lift and I could see the pine trees and white sand dunes of a deserted island dead ahead.

I landed on a desolate stretch of beach and walked around, noting the absence of any human footprints other than my own. It was obvious that no one had been there lately, probably because of the time of year. I found a good place to set up camp and spent the rest of the day walking the island and looking around. I had planned to spend one night on Petit Bois and return the next day to my car, so I had brought just enough food for that length of time.

I learned a valuable lesson about paddling to remote islands from this trip, when I awoke the next morning to discover that a raging cold front had moved into the area and the wind was blowing out of the north at 25 to 30 knots. I had not gotten a marine forecast before the trip and did not foresee any conditions that would prevent me from returning on schedule. Now the Mississippi Sound was a boiling cauldron of breaking whitecaps, and freezing temperatures combined with the north wind made the prospect of paddling anywhere seem ludicrous. I ate the last two packets of instant oatmeal I had for breakfast and began to wonder what I would eat while waiting for this weather to change. And how long would it be before it did change? I had little experience on the islands at that time, and I had no idea.

At least I had found the solitude I was seeking. There was no sign of human life anywhere. No boats of any kind were visible on the horizon, just endless lines of churning whitecaps as far as I could see. I resigned myself to a longer stay on the island than I had planned. There was nothing else to do but explore my surroundings, so I set out on foot to see what I could find. The forest of pine trees drew my attention first, so I hiked over there and found dense thickets of small pines growing on the rolling sand dunes. Clumps of prickly pear cactus gave the island a desert feeling and reminded me of the pine- and cactus-covered hills of New Mexico. Away from the shore among the trees, the sound of crashing waves was diminished, and the interior of the island was much more peaceful than the shoreline.

Areas of marsh with deep standing water forced me to make long detours, but I was able to walk over every part of the island in a day. There was nothing else to do. I looked over the debris and man-made junk that had washed ashore from the sea. There was nothing that I could find a use for in a few short days, but there was enough good lumber for a modern-day Robinson Crusoe to build a fine house, if he had a mind to stay a while.

I had no fishing gear, so that means of getting food was not an option. There were lots of ducks and rabbits on the island, but likewise, I had no way of catching one. I turned my attention instead to wild plant food. Two species that I knew I could eat were abundant-the fruit of the prickly pear

Driftwood and cast-off mooring rope on trackless beach on Petit Bois Island

cactus and the tender young shoots of cattails, which grew thick in the marshes. The prickly pears required some careful work to peel without getting fingers full of tiny spines, but the fruit was good. To get the cattail shoots, I waded into the mud and pulled them up near the base. With the green exterior peeled away, these yielded succulent white inner stems that are quite good even eaten raw.

I also worried about my water supply, as I had not brought enough for an extended stay. I had remembered reading about beach wells in a survival manual, so I started digging about twenty feet back from the water's edge on the sound side of the island. I used my cooking pot to scoop out the sand, and soon had a hole about three feet deep. At this depth, it began to fill with water. The first scoops of this were brackish, and then to my surprise and delight, the water filling the hole tasted fresh and completely drinkable. Apparently sandy islands like this hold a supply of rainwater that has a accumulated over time and sits on top of the underlying brackish water. At least my water worries were over, and there was something to eat, even if it wasn't everything I wanted.

The next day the wind and waves had not abated at all. There was no way I was going to be leaving the island. This was starting to be inconvenient. I had a meeting I was supposed to attend that night, and other people would be wondering where I was. This was years before the advent of cell phones, so I had no way to contact anyone and let them know why I was overdue. I was starting to realize that travel by small boat on the sea could not be done on a schedule, and that commitments on land meant little out here.

With nothing else to do, I set out walking again and retraced my steps of the previous day. I looked through the flotsam and jetsam for anything new, and spent time just staring out to sea on the sound side at the walls of breakers rolling in to the beach.

By that afternoon the wind seemed to decrease somewhat, and throughout the night it gradually tapered off. When I crawled out of the tent on my third morning on Petit Bois, there was still a good chop in the sound, but the waves were smaller and less menacing. I knew the kayak could handle these conditions, though it would be a cold and wet ride. My planned stay of one night on Petit Bois Island had turned into three, and it was time to leave. The crossing back to Dauphin Island was uneventful. I had discovered a wilderness island close to home and had even gotten a taste of what it's like to be marooned. I knew from that moment on that I would never again paddle to a remote island without extra supplies and a flexible schedule that allowed for nature's unexpected whims.

A SECOND LOOK

When I left Petit Bois Island that morning, I fully expected to return within a few months, with more supplies and more careful preparation, of course. I was enchanted by the island's sense of remoteness, and I envisioned spending a lot more time there on subsequent kayak journeys.

Life takes a lot of unexpected twists, however, and though I made numerous kayak journeys to the other barrier islands over the years, I never returned to Petit Bois by kayak, and it was nearly 15 years later before I went ashore on the island again.

This time I arrived by sailboat, dropping the anchor off those still desolate shores en route home from a weeklong cruise of north Florida. My companions and I had caught the conditions on Mobile Bay just right and were able to cross this wide body of water on an exhilarating reach, making the 39 miles from the Alabama canal in just a few hours and without running the engine at all.

We dropped the hook just before sunset off the north shore of Petit Bois Island, near the western tip, one of the few places where the chart showed that I could approach within easy dinghy rowing range with my 4-foot, 3-inch draft. Since the wind was still blowing 10 to 15 knots, I decided to dive on the anchor and check the set. Being this close to shore could result in a beaching if the anchor was to drag even a short distance. The water was amazingly clear for the Mississippi Sound, perhaps more so than I had ever seen it. We had expected to do a lot of snorkeling in Florida, but the water had been churned up by a passing storm. The visibility here was much better than what we encountered in north Florida or in Alabama waters.

Later that night, while washing up the evening dinner dishes, I noticed sparkling in the water and discovered that the surrounding water was full of phosphorescent plankton. There is almost always some of this evident in the sea at night, but on rare occasions it appears in high density and anything moving through it, such as a fish or a boat oar, leaves a fiery trail of brilliant sparks. It is a beautiful phenomenon, and my companions were in awe, as they had never seen this before. We got into the dinghy and rowed ashore, marveling at the light glowing in the swirls left by the oars. Walking the beach that night in company, it seemed I had come a long way from the lonely isolation of those days I spent on Petit Bois during my first visit. But I had changed, not the island. The little clump of pine trees was still there, as I remembered. And I knew that if it were needed, the cattail marshes and clumps of prickly pear cactus scattered among the dunes would provide food. It was good to be back in Mississippi waters and comforting to know that there are at least some things that don't change. The mainland had been transformed by casinos and other development in those years between my visits to the island, but these lonely shores and the natural communities they harbor remained the same.

NATIONAL PARK SERVICE PROTECTION

Petit Bois's isolation from the mainland in terms of distance has contributed much to its remaining unchanged, but without the protection of the National Park Service, even distance would not have been enough to protect it. There was much controversy over the island years ago when a Mississippi politician fought relentlessly to develop the island, Florida-style, with a proposed causeway connecting it to the mainland and condominiums and hotels on the Gulf-side beaches. Despite the fact that the island was already a part of the Gulf Islands National Seashore, many people were in favor of this, citing economic development and tourism as justification for forever changing this wild island. Thankfully, conservationists and more far-sighted individuals saw the greater value in preserving the island in its natural state. Now Petit Bois and Horn Island are not only part of the Gulf Islands National Seashore but also federally designated wilderness areas. This means that no development can take place whatsoever, and these islands will be left alone for future generations to enjoy just as they are.

The wilderness status of these two islands serves the primary purpose of preserving them unchanged in a natural state and providing a habitat for the native wildlife populations that live there. The islands are also open to the public for recreational purposes, provided that these uses do not in any way alter the wild character of the landscape and surrounding waters. Visitors are allowed to go to the islands either by private boat or chartered vessels, but no commercial ferry service like that on West Ship Island is permitted.

In April of 2002, the park service banned the use of personal watercraft from the waters within one mile of all the beaches in the national seashore. This ban has been challenged in several watercraft industry lawsuits, and the outcome awaits environmental impact evaluations by the park service. There may be some limited use allowed after these studies are completed. For current information on this issue, readers should call the Gulf Islands National Seashore headquarters at 228-875-9057. The term "personal watercraft" or "PWC," as defined by the park service, refers to "a vessel usually less than 16 feet in length which uses an inboard, internal combustion engine

powering a water jet pump as a primary source of propulsion and is operated by a person or persons sitting, standing, or kneeling on the vessel
rather than in the confines of the hull."

Personal watercraft are now banned in almost all national parks, and the
purpose of this ban is to "protect the natural resources including air, water,
animals, and natural quiet." Boat owners are permitted to tow their PWCs
in park waters, so long as they do not use them within the boundaries. The
waters within 1 mile of the islands are also closed to commercial fishing of any
kind, but sport fishing is permitted and regulated according to state fishing
laws. Hunting and possession of firearms is not permitted on the islands.

Camping is permitted on Petit Bois Island, year-round, as well as on Horn
Island and East Ship Island. Certain sections of the islands may be temporarily closed by rangers to protect shorebirds during nesting season. Campers
should also avoid pitching tents close to trees containing osprey nests, as this
can drive the parent birds away from their young.

Campers may build fires, but only on the beach below the high tide line
where the debris will be carried away by the waves. Driftwood is abundant
on all the islands, so cutting firewood is prohibited.

Whether visiting Petit Bois and the other islands for a day trip or an
overnight camping trip, boaters should remember that it is their responsibility
to be self-sufficient. This means having a seaworthy vessel in good working
order and all the fuel, drinking water, and food that is needed for the trip. It is
not the responsibility of park rangers to provide services that boaters might
require because of poor preparation. The rangers are not allowed to tow private boats, nor can they sell or give gasoline to those who might have run out.
If you find your vessel disabled or aground off one of the islands, you will need
to call a friend or a commercial towing service. For information on such towing companies, see the listings in the back of this book under Marine Services.

BOATING TO PETIT BOIS ISLAND

Boaters planning trips to Petit Bois Island will need NOAA chart No. 11374.
This covers the island in detail, as well as approaches from the mainland and

from neighboring Horn and Dauphin Islands. As mentioned earlier in this chapter, Petit Bois Island is not quite as convenient to boaters as the other barrier islands. There are three basic approaches to the island. The first is from the east, crossing over from Dauphin Island, Alabama, the way I did on my first kayak trip. A causeway connects Dauphin Island to the mainland west of Mobile, and those with kayaks or trailerable boats can launch there for an expedition to Petit Bois. Dauphin Island is, however, a long island, and the distance from the causeway, which connects to the eastern end of the island, to the western tip, is 11 miles. Most likely you will have to launch and park near the eastern end, as the rest of the island is residential in nature or undeveloped. From the western tip of Dauphin Island, it is a 4½-nautical-mile paddle on a course of 250 degrees to the eastern end of Petit Bois Island.

Petit Bois Island can be reached from mainland Mississippi by way of the well-marked Pascagoula ship channel, which leads out of the East Pascagoula River. The excellent marine facilities in the Pascagoula area are convenient to the island, and this area is the nearest point on the mainland to offer fuel, dockage, and other basics.

Sunday boaters anchored in the cove of the man-made spoil island near Petit Bois

The third approach to Petit Bois Island is from the west, crossing directly from Horn Island's eastern tip in kayaks or other shoal draft boats, or transiting the Mississippi Sound via the ICW from Biloxi or other ports farther west. The island's location at the far eastern edge of Mississippi's marine waters makes it less convenient than the other islands for the majority of state boaters.

Although it might require a little more time to get there by paddle or sail, or more fuel if traveling by powerboat, the trip to Petit Bois is highly recommended and worth the inconvenience. Visit this island if at all possible, but if you can only make it to one island in this national seashore, then read the next chapter before making your choice.

NAVIGATOR'S NOTES

Approaches to Petit Bois Island
(Use NOAA Chart No. 11374)

NOAA Chart No. 11374 covers the western half of Dauphin Island, Alabama. Mariners approaching the Mississippi Sound from points east on the ICW will enter the coverage area of this chart west of the Dauphin Island Parkway bridge. West of charted mile marker St M 120, at flashing red beacon #40, the closely spaced markers leading the way along the south shore of Dauphin Island end, and the ICW strikes out across open water on a course of 268 degrees. ICW charted mile marker St M 115 lies in a line due north of Dauphin Island's western tip. Five miles to the west, mile marker 110 of the ICW is located 2 miles north of Petit Bois Island's eastern tip. Boaters bound for the anchorage areas of Petit Bois Island can set a course that passes about a mile south of the ICW but should not venture into the area directly between the two islands.

Numerous shoals of 2 to 4 feet are scattered in the pass between Dauphin and Petit Bois Islands. There is a marked channel leading out to sea around the west end of Dauphin Island, but the safest pass is the one to the west of Petit Bois Island, the Horn Island Pass channel that is the standard route from the Gulf to the Pascagoula Ship Channel.

From the chart it can be seen that the best area for anchorage off the north shore of Petit Bois Island is the area of 14- to 18-foot depths that reach quite close inshore in about the center of the island. This area is west of the small patch of pine forest that is located on the eastern third of the island.

For those approaching Petit Bois Island from the mainland at Pascagoula, it is a simple matter of following the ship channel out of the East Pascagoula River. Leaving the mouth of the river, this channel bears southeast at Singing River Island and runs for 4½ nautical miles in this direction until it merges with the Bayou Casotte Channel and turns almost due south to a heading of 170 degrees. From this junction, it is another 4½ nautical miles to the western tip of Petit Bois Island. The marked channel then turns seaward on a southwest heading at flashing red beacon #14 and flashing green beacon #15 and leads past the western tip of the island through the Horn Island Pass channel.

West of this marked channel, about a half-mile to the northwest of Petit Bois's western tip, a high sandy island with no charted name is visible. This island is known as "Sand Island" or "Spoil Island" and is a man-made spoil island built up by years of dredging in the channel. The island lies within waters managed by the national park service, so the same rules and regulations apply as to the other islands. Camping is allowed, and there is a good anchorage for small boats in the horseshoe-shaped cove on the north side of the island. Vegetation has taken hold, and someday the island will probably be forested and will continue to expand in size and drift to the west like all the others.

The best approach to Petit Bois Island from the west is to follow the ICW channel through the tricky area between Horn Island and the shoals that spread northward of Round Island. Just east of charted mile marker St M 100, the ICW passes about 1½ nautical miles north of the eastern tip of Horn Island.

Although the distance between Horn Island and Petit Bois is less than 3 nautical miles, on a course of 100 degrees, the direct rhumbline crosses shoal areas, like those common in all the barrier island passes. The best route is to stay on the ICW to pass well to the north of the above-mentioned spoil island, and then change course to the south at the intersection of the ICW and the Pascagoula Ship Channel to reach Petit Bois Island. This intersection is located just to the south of the ship channel markers green #23 and red #24, and three-quarters of a mile west of charted ICW mile marker St M 105.

12

HORN ISLAND

In the middle of a chain of beautiful pristine barrier islands that make up the Gulf Islands National Seashore, Horn Island stands out as the largest, most diverse, and perhaps most beautiful.

This island, like Petit Bois, is a federally designated wilderness area, and, like Petit Bois, its distance from the mainland has limited public access and helped preserve its wild qualities. At 13 miles long and up to three-quarters of a mile wide in some places, Horn Island is much larger than Petit Bois or East Ship Island, its closest neighbors. A walk around the perimeter of this island would entail 27 miles of beach hiking, all of it empty save for the occasional visitors who sometimes set up camp for a night or two on the shore. Horn Island consists of many ecosystems and varied topography, from high, windswept dunes to broad salt marshes, and dense pine forests. These habitats support large populations of wildlife, including many reptiles such as alligators, lizards, snakes and turtles, and mammals such as otters, rats, rabbits, raccoons, and nutria. Bird species seen on the island at various times number over 250 and include osprey, pelicans, bald eagles, and many types of shorebirds. Visitors to the island at any time other than cold, windy winter days will also become well acquainted with the abundant insect populations of Horn Island, which include voracious salt marsh mosquitoes, biting gnats called "no-see-ums" or sand fleas, and a variety of deerflies and horseflies.

Brackish lagoons like this one are found throughout the interior of Horn Island.

HORN ISLAND RANGER STATION

Although Horn Island is a designated wilderness area, there is one human habitation in the center of the island in the form of a park ranger station and research area. This station is jokingly referred to as the "Horn Island Hilton" by the rangers who have spent time there. This place is certainly no luxury resort, but rather a small, prefabricated building that serves as both an office and bunkhouse for the rangers who study and protect the Mississippi portion of the Gulf Islands National Seashore.

Around 37,000 visitors make their way to Horn Island each year by either private or chartered boats, but few of them ever see the Horn Island Hilton. There are no facilities there for visitors, and consequently no reason to seek it out unless there is an urgent need to see the ranger, as in an emergency.

Ben Moore, a Pascagoula native, is a park ranger who has been based on Horn Island for ten years. His duties include patrolling the island and surrounding waters to enforce Park Service rules as well as assisting other law enforcement agencies when needed. Other duties include assisting the U.S. Coast Guard with rescue operations and assisting with firefighting operations if needed. Moore and other rangers patrol the surrounding waters with fast Boston-whaler skiffs and use four-wheeler ATVs for patrolling the island itself. The most common violations of park rules are improper beach fires and improper disposal of trash. The islands are plagued by trash from visitors and from boaters who use the sea as a big trash can. All the rangers stress the importance of "bringing everything you need to the islands and taking away everything you bring."

The Park Service in Mississippi patrols 6,434 acres on the islands and another mile of water around each of them, totaling 63,880 acres. The staff numbers 30 to 35, depending on the time of year, many of whom work on much more heavily visited West Ship Island and at the Davis Bayou portion of the park on the mainland.

Life on Horn Island is one of isolation for the ranger who is stationed there. A supply boat brings equipment and basic necessities to the island. The nearest store is a 12-mile boat ride away. Electricity for the house is supplied by a generator and solar panels, and water is supplied by a well. Amenities are basic, with heat, light, air-conditioning, and, perhaps most important, screens to escape the insect hordes. One ranger lived on the island for eight years with his family, but it is a difficult life for a family. Now Moore is the main resident at the Hilton. For him the inconveniences are worth it, and he intends to stay as long as he is physically able to do his job.

The island is so large and heavily wooded that the ranger's presence will hardly be noticeable to most visitors. The only sign of this station visible from the beach is the dock on the north side of the island, where the ranger's patrol boat is suspended by davits above the tides. Two radio towers that reach above the pines mark the spot where the house and compound is located. Visitors hiking the island will probably see the tracks from the four-wheeler, but the impact is minimal as no one else is allowed to use such equipment on the island.

THE RED WOLVES OF HORN ISLAND

This island has been the sight of many wildlife research programs, including a captive breeding program for the endangered southern red wolf. Because of its remote location and suitable habitat, it was decided that Horn Island would be an ideal location to try and breed red wolves as part of a program to reestablish this predator in the southeastern United States. The first pair of wolves was brought to the island in 1989 by the U.S. Fish and Wildlife Service. The pair bred successfully, and the pups were transferred to a refuge in North Carolina. The wolves at one time had free run of the island, with rabbits and other small animals available as prey. On a kayak camping trip during this period, I saw their tracks almost everywhere I hiked, but I never saw one of the elusive, nocturnal hunters.

WALTER INGLIS ANDERSON'S ISLAND LIFE

With the fairly recent widespread recognition of the late Gulf coast artist Walter Inglis Anderson, (see chapter 9) Horn Island has become well known as the retreat of this reclusive naturalist who used it as a second home and studio. Anderson studied art in New York and Paris, becoming fascinated with the primitive rock art found in French caves, and later returned to Ocean Springs where he developed his own semi-primitive style of depicting nature, mostly working in watercolor. His work was not accepted on the Mississippi coast at that time, in the 1950s and early 1960s, so he made a modest living as a potter, working out of his Shearwater Pottery studio on Davis Bayou. During this time in Ocean Springs, he traveled widely in search of subject matter for his art but always returned to Horn Island as he found it a pure and elemental place where "one image succeeds another with surprising regularity." He began to spend more time on the island than the mainland, rowing out in a small open boat for stays of up to two months. Obsessed with his work, Anderson was impervious to swarms of insects and slept unprotected under his overturned boat on the beach.

Walter Anderson spent whole days in these Horn Island lagoons, stalking the subjects of his paintings.

He spent hours neck-deep in the marshes or crawling through the mud to stalk the subjects of his paintings, which were most often birds. On one occasion, he was bitten by a poisonous cottonmouth snake but remained on the island and recovered. He rode out the fury of Hurricane Betsy by lashing himself to a large pine tree in the middle of the island. During this period he logged 82 visits to Horn Island and some of the other islands and is thought to have made many more unrecorded trips. These logs are now published in the Horn Island Logs of Walter Inglis Anderson and make interesting reading for anyone contemplating a trip to Horn Island.

EXPLORING HORN ISLAND

If you do visit the island, you may, like Anderson, find yourself "in a constant state of applause." The images that inspired him are still there. They may remind you of other places you've been or be like nothing else you've ever experienced. Walking along the Gulf beaches of Horn Island once in

November, I found coconuts washed ashore that transported me back to the islands of the Caribbean where I spent many months sea kayaking. Later the same day, the laughter of a loon from out on the water reminded me of a journey through Canada's north woods. You may find the island different each time you visit, depending on the time of year. In summer, blistering sun and warm, clear waters make it a deserted tropical cay, but in a winter cold front with gale-force northerly winds and temperatures in the 20s, you may feel you are on a mountain expedition.

Visiting in the winter is the surest way to find solitude, and maybe freedom from the insect hordes, but even in the summer there are few people around on weekdays.

Because of its length stretching from east to west, Horn Island can be reached from many points on the mainland between Biloxi and Pascagoula. As a general guide to those in small, shoal-draft boats or sea kayaks, I will outline the various routes to the island here. Detailed instructions for skippers of deep draft vessels will be given at the back of this chapter in the Navigator's Notes.

NOAA Chart No. 11374 covers the island, its surrounding waters, and approaches from the mainland in the Pascagoula area. Boaters coming from Biloxi or Ship Island and other points west will also need NOAA Chart No. 11372.

Leaving Biloxi or Ocean Springs between Deer Island and the mainland, the western tip of Horn Island lies just over 10 nautical miles to the southeast. Kayakers and others wanting to make the shortest possible crossing to Horn Island might want to leave the mainland at Bellefontaine Point, 8 miles east of the bridge at Ocean Springs. From this point, the crossing on a due south heading takes you to the northernmost point of Horn Island, just over 5½ nautical miles away.

Another option to avoid a long, exposed crossing is to leave from the Gautier or Pascagoula area and go to Horn Island by way of Round Island, which makes a good stopover for a rest or a lunch break, or even an overnight camp. Round Island lies just 3½ nautical miles due south of the mouth of the Pascagoula River, and from there it is just a little over 4 nautical miles to the eastern end of Horn Island.

A solo sea kayaker landing on a deserted beach on Horn Island

Horn Island can also be quickly reached from either Petit Bois or East Ship Island, if you are visiting the other islands during your trip. Remember that the crossings between the islands expose you to the open Gulf, and keep an eye on the weather before leaving. There are shoal areas far from land between the islands, so pay attention to where you are on the chart at all times. The distance from Petit Bois to Horn Island is 3 nautical miles; from East Ship it is a bit less than 5 miles.

Because of the island's size, most boaters visiting Horn Island will only explore part of it on a given trip, unless several days are available for hiking and camping. More than once, I have paddled out from the mainland in my sea kayak and circumnavigated the island. This is usually a three- or four-day trip, depending on the amount of stopping and exploring done along the way. Sea kayaks are probably the best boats for exploring the exposed south shore of the island, since a skilled paddler can land on the beach through breaking surf, which occurs much of the time on this shore. By paddling around either the east or west tip and then landing through the surf on parts of the island where there is no path across from the sound, kayakers can almost be assured of finding a deserted, inaccessible campsite on the beach. It pays to keep an eye on the size of the breakers when doing this though, as the surf on this beach can build into powerful dumping breakers more than ten feet high. It is much easier to judge the size of breakers from the beach when facing them than it is from seaward when all you can see is the curling backs of the crests moving away from you. I was quite inexperienced with surf on my first kayak trip to Horn Island.

Overconfident, after a successful solo crossing to the island the afternoon before, I paddled around the eastern end of the island after breaking camp and proceeded to follow the south shore, staying about a mile out, where there were big swells but no breaking waves. When it was time to go ashore for lunch, I pointed my bow toward the beach and, before I realized how big they were, suddenly found myself in 8 to 10-foot rollers. One of these caught the kayak just right and the boat instantly accelerated to three or four times my top paddling speed and plunged down the waveface ahead of the cascade of whitewater curling off the top. I managed to ride it for a few exhilarating seconds before my stern got swept around, causing the boat to go broadside to the wave and roll before its fury like a spinning log. I couldn't stay in the boat, much less do an Eskimo roll, so I came up spitting seawater and gasping for air, separated from my kayak, and still a couple hundred yards from shore. I made it in with no problem, and luckily the waves carried the kayak ashore as well. The boat and I were undamaged. The only thing lost was a 70-dollar diving mask and snorkel that had been stored behind the seat. What I gained was a new respect for the power of breaking waves.

Despite this incident, kayaks are quite able in the surf zone when handled by experienced paddlers. After that dumping, I went on to paddle thousands of coastal miles in all kinds of weather and sea conditions, and so far have only been capsized one other time, off the coast of Puerto Rico, by a rogue wave that had to be more than 15 feet tall.

I have, on occasion, seen breakers of more than 10 feet on the south shores of the barrier islands, and I'm sure, in the right conditions, there could be much higher waves. The size of the waves is not the only factor, though, since much smaller waves can be dangerous if they are closely spaced and dumping rather than spilling in gentle crests as they break. These "dumpers" can break boats in half and smash the occupants into the sand beneath them. Such a surf zone is no place to be in any boat. Only with experience can kayakers learn the limits of what they are able to handle as far as surf is concerned. Anyone venturing around the south shore of Horn Island should be aware that surf is a reality of this exposed shore. Though it may be calm when you arrive there, and the weather may be settled and benign, ocean rollers generated in storms far out in the Gulf can advance upon the islands with little warning. I have been stormbound more than once on the south shores of the islands when I made camp on a calm day and woke up to hear raging surf smashing into the beach in the middle of the night.

Most of the above comments about boating in the surf zone apply only to sea kayaks, as they are about the only watercraft capable of handling large breakers without damage. Some of the smaller, beachable sailboats like Hobie Cat catamarans can negotiate moderate surf, as can a few power-boat designs. The outboard-powered Boston Whalers that the National Seashore rangers use as patrol boats are quite capable in rough water, and I have seen the rangers come in through the surf on occasion.

Skippers of larger craft are advised to stay well off the south coast of the island in all but the most settled conditions. In calm weather, or during periods of north winds, it may be safe to anchor overnight off this south shore, but those doing so should keep a close watch to seaward for a change in conditions and the possibility of building swells from the Gulf.

Vessels that draw more than a couple of feet can only get around to the south side safely by two routes. These are Dog Keys Pass off the western tip, or the Horn Island Pass Channel, which is 2½ miles east of Horn Island and just off the western end of Petit Bois Island. There are extensive shoal areas near the eastern end of Horn Island and these are always subject to change due to the tidal currents and wave action that is constantly moving the sand beneath these waters. Those in seaworthy small boats or kayaks should exercise caution rounding this eastern tip of the island as well. With shallow draft, you may be able to skim over the bottom, but strong tidal currents, Gulf swells, and wind can create steep, unpredictable waves that are extremely difficult to handle. Often you can see these disturbed areas from a distance, or hear the roar of the waves. In these conditions, it is best for even smaller vessels to use the deepwater passes where the seas will generally be smoother.

ASHORE ON HORN ISLAND

The entire south coast of Horn Island consists of wide, white, sandy beaches. In most areas there are large dunes covered with sea oats just inland from the front beaches. The treeline of the forested interior of the island begins well back from the beaches, several hundred yards in some areas. There are no large trees near the water's edge as there are on the north shore of the island, so shade is hard to come by on a sunny day without hiking a bit. What these beaches do offer is seemingly endless hiking and exploring, and mountains of washed-up debris, both natural and man-made, for those inclined to beachcombing and collecting. Inland from the open beaches, there are large areas of pine-forested dunes with equally good hiking and exploring opportunities. There are areas of marsh near the south side of the island that make reaching the interior difficult or impossible without a long detour. Walter Anderson used to spend days neck-deep in these marshes studying the birds and other wildlife. I'm less inclined to do so after seeing the size of some of the alligators that inhabit them, not to mention the cottonmouths.

On one late November morning, as I was kayaking along the south shore of the island about a hundred feet out from the beach, I rounded a sandy point and came upon three full-grown alligators stretched out on the open beach like sunbathing tourists. You can usually find tracks in the sand to verify the fact that alligators like the beach, even if you are not lucky enough to see such an unusual sight.

Other than the tracks of shorebirds, the most abundant animal tracks found on the island are those of raccoons and rabbits. You will see the tracks of these animals practically everywhere on Horn Island, and the animals themselves if you go out for some night hiking, which I highly recommend. There is nothing quite like walking miles of deserted beach at night, far from the city lights of the mainland. On moonlit nights the white sand glows so brightly that hiking even in the forested interior is quite easy. At night one realizes that the Gulf is not quite so empty as it appears in the daylight, as the southern horizon is usually dotted with the lights of commercial fishing vessels working offshore.

Unless there is a strong onshore wind from a southerly direction, those camping on Horn Island in the warmer months might find the insect population unbearable in the middle reaches of the island where the marshes and forests are found. The best strategy for avoiding mosquitoes and no-see-ums is to camp on the long, barren sand spits found at either extreme end of the island. In these areas a light breeze from almost any direction will help keep insects at bay. Strong winds can make camping on these exposed ends difficult though, unless you have a tent designed to withstand the forces and know how to stake it down properly in the deep sand (refer to chapter 4 for more on this). Most everyone camping on the island during warm months can be found on these ends, so on the weekends, you probably won't be alone here. These beaches at each end are over a mile long though, so there is room for quite a few campers to spread out without being crowded.

The wooded sections of the north shore offer the best protection during colder months and high winds, as there are deep, protected pockets to be found between the high dunes where you can camp away from the exposed beach. Along this north shore, many of these dunes are quite close to the water's edge, so these campsites can be reached without having to carry gear too far. Most of these dunes are quite stable, being held together by the pines and other vegetation growing on them. Areas of palmettos and prickly pear cactus among the dunes lend a subtropical or desert island feel to this area. The hiking along the north shore is just as interesting as the south side of the island, though the beaches are much narrower and in some places you might have to scramble over fallen trees or skirt around dunes that reach right to the water.

About three miles from the western end of the island, there are ruins from a World War II era military facility where chemical weapons were supposedly manufactured and stored. These ruins mainly consist of concrete rubble and a prominent brick chimney that can be seen from some distance out in the sound. Other rubble and ruins like this can be found throughout Horn Island, as it was occupied by large military units during the war.

This area near the chimney is not a bad place to camp or at least land for a day trip, as there is a good, easily followed path just west of the ruins that leads over the dunes and through the woods to the Gulf side of the island. This is one of the few places where the island is easily crossed, the others being at the ranger station in the middle of the island and in a couple of places near the eastern end. There is also a good anchorage area in the waters south of these ruins, with depths of fifteen feet fairly close to shore.

Just east of the ruins, hikers walking the north shore will come to an impasse unless they are willing to get their feet wet. Here is found an inlet from the sound into a large interior lagoon. The inlet won't be too hard to wade at low tide though, and parts of the lagoon may be accessible to kayakers at high tide. The area around this and other lagoons on the island is a good place to see the variety of bird life that inhabits these barrier islands. Some of the most impressive birds are the ever-present ospreys that build huge nests in the tops of pine trees and can be seen diving into the sound and flying back to their nests with fish in their talons.

Most boaters visiting Horn Island will want to return after discovering how much there is to see and do there. Since one small portion of the island can easily take a weekend trip to explore, the island easily lends itself to multiple visits, and those returning again and again will undoubtedly find something new each time. Such a beautiful island wilderness so close to home is one of Mississippi's finest treasures and is a rare commodity in today's overdeveloped world. Mississippi residents who have not visited this island should make every effort to do so, whether in their own boats or by charter vessel. Experienced boaters who have been to many other islands and faraway shores will realize that Horn Island is as good as or better than most places they might care to visit.

NAVIGATOR'S NOTES

Approaches to Horn Island
(Use NOAA Charts No. 11374 and No. 11372)

The most direct deepwater route from the mainland to Horn Island is the marked channel from Biloxi Bay between Deer Island and Ocean Springs that leads out to the Gulf at Dog Keys Pass off the western tip of the island.

This channel begins 1 mile southeast of the Highway 90 drawbridge that crosses the mouth of Back Bay between Biloxi and Ocean Springs. From green daybeacon #35 and flashing red beacon #26, at the junction of the channel from Point Cadet and the side channel to Ocean Springs harbor, the Biloxi Bay Channel leads southeast out into the Mississippi Sound on a course of 140 degrees.

After a straight run of 3 nautical miles on this course, at lighted red beacon #14, the channel begins to turn more to the south, and then at lighted red beacon #10, the course turns to due south. The marked channel then continues another 3 nautical miles to green daybeacon #1 and flashing red #2, located at a point about one half mile north of the ICW.

The ICW here lies 2½ nautical miles north of Horn Island's western tip. From this point, continuing south on a heading of 180 degrees will take you to Dog Keys Pass and the open Gulf, or it is safe to set a course to the southeast and head directly for the western half of Horn Island.

Those heading out of Dog Keys Pass must be sure and pass to the east of floating green can buoy #3, which is located about a half mile north of the west tip of Horn Island. West of this floating buoy lies an area of charted shoals where breakers frequently occur. Southwest of #3, flashing red beacon #2 lies off the tip of the island. Pass to the west of this marker, keeping it and the tip of the island off your port beam, and south of this point you will be in the open Gulf.

Horn Island can be approached from the east by way of the ICW for those coming from Pascagoula, Petit Bois Island, or points farther east. The Pascagoula Ship channel intersects the ICW north of Petit Bois's western tip and just over 3 nautical miles east-northeast of Horn Island's eastern tip.

From this intersection of channels, it is possible to lay a course directly for the north side of this eastern tip of Horn Island. This area offers good anchorage behind the long, barren sand spit that is the end of the island, with 13 to 19 feet of water right up close to the beach. Deep water can be found close to shore on much of the north side of Horn Island's eastern half.

Midway along the island's north shore a charted area of shallow water lies in the area between the ICW and the beach. This area can be safely bypassed by staying in the ICW or carefully plotting a course to the south of it in the 10- to 11-foot depths shown on the chart.

Approaching Horn Island from the west requires staying well to the north of the many shoals that lie between Horn Island's western tip and East Ship Island. This area was once the location of the now-submerged Dog Keys, and dangerous shallows and man-made obstructions abound.

Staying in the ICW until north of Horn Island's western tip is a sure way of avoiding these shoals. It is also possible to save some distance when crossing between East Ship Island and Horn Island by running an easterly course along the latitude of 30 degrees, 16 minutes north, which is over a mile south of the ICW.

The south coast of Horn Island can be safely navigated so long as care is taken to stay out of the surf zone. Deep water reaches within a half mile of most parts of this shore, but mariners should be on the lookout for breakers, which indicate isolated shoal areas.

13

EAST SHIP ISLAND AND WEST SHIP ISLAND

East and West Ship Island were simply known as Ship Island prior to August 17, 1969. That is when Hurricane Camille struck the Mississippi coast with a fury sufficient to cut an island in half and forever alter a landscape devastated by her passing. Since the storm made the cut, the two islands have been steadily drifting apart because of the erosion effects of the long-shore currents that sweep from east to west. The cut caused by Camille separated the densely forested eastern portion of the island from the western section on which stands Fort Massachusetts.

This forested eastern part of the original island is now known as East Ship Island, and the historic site of the fort and Ship Island lighthouse is known as West Ship Island.

As already mentioned in chapter 1, the natural harbor on the north side of Ship Island has been of great importance to the exploration and development of the entire region since Sieur d'Iberville first dropped the hook there in 1699. He first named the island *Surgeres*, after the commander of one of his vessels. The name was changed to *Isle aux Vausseaux* or Ship Island, in 1701, when a magazine and barracks were built there and the island was established as a harbor for French ships.

The French retained control of the island until they were defeated by the British in the French and Indian War in 1763. British warships used the

An armada of pleasure craft anchored for the night in the harbor off Fort Massachusetts

anchorage at Ship Island during the American Revolution to protect British interests from Pensacola to Natchez. In 1781, Spain claimed the territory after defeating the British with the help of American merchant Oliver Pollock. The British again took control of Ship Island in 1814 when General Packenham amassed a fleet of 30 British men-of-war, plus many more supply ships and a force of more than 10,000 soldiers in Ship Island harbor. They sailed into Lake Borgne on December 14, 1814, and overwhelmed a U.S. Naval force of 5 ships but were later defeated in the Battle of New Orleans. The British left Ship Island for good the following March.

FORT MASSACHUSETTS

Because of the harbor's strategic importance to the region, American military leaders felt it was of vital importance to fortify the island, especially with the possibility that Spain would try to recapture New Orleans and gain control of the Mississippi Valley. In 1857, President Franklin Pierce signed a bill authorizing the construction of a fort to be built on the island.

Construction began in 1859, and from the beginning the U.S. Army engineers were beset with problems. Living conditions were difficult for the workers. The first superintendent died from yellow fever. Storms destroyed partially completed sections. From the beginning, the lower level of the fort was built too close to sea level, and it has always flooded in the storm surges of hurricanes.

The fort was built of brick, with walls up to 5 feet thick and many beautifully designed archways. There were 21 gun casements at ground level and an additional 14 guns mounted on the top of the walls. Circular granite stairwells provided access between the two levels. Since the fort was not completed when the Civil War broke out, it was of little value. Mississippi militiamen did occupy it for a time and cannons were mounted to use against Union forces but were later removed to be used in the defense of New Orleans. The Union blockade ship USS *Massachusetts* later landed at the abandoned fort and named it after their ship.

This resulted in Ship Island becoming one of the most important posts for the Union. It was used as a headquarters for the blockade fleet and as a hospital and repair facility. Confederate prisoners of war were held there, as well as other southern sympathizers. Thousands of Union soldiers were funneled through this base, and disease accompanied them. During the war, 250 Union soldiers and 153 Confederates, civilians and sailors, were buried on the island.

The fort was used as a federal military prison until 1870. It was further strengthened and completed in 1871 and its cannons were in place by 1872. Today only one cannon remains, a 15-inch Rodman cannon that was the largest gun ever used in the Civil War. This 43,000-pound weapon could fire a 315-pound shell 3 miles, effectively protecting the pass between Ship and Cat Island. But just as the fort was finally completed, it was already obsolete in the new era of ironclad vessels that carried weapons of their own that could penetrate the brick walls of the fort.

Another landmark that stood not far from Fort Massachusetts since 1886 was the Ship Island Lighthouse. The first lighthouse built on the island was a

This replica of the original Ship Island Lighthouse was
built by "Friends of the Gulf." Photo by Michelle Calvert.

45-foot brick tower erected in 1853. In 1886, this structure was condemned
and a square open-framed lighthouse of 12-by-12 timbers was built to
replace it. This wood-framed tower survived four major hurricanes, including
Camille. It was destroyed in a fire set by campers in June of 1972. Recently,
a replica of the original wood tower was built on site by an organization
called "Friends of the Gulf" to honor this historic edifice.

After the Civil War ended, Ship Island was used as a quarantine station
during an outbreak of yellow fever. The National Board of Health set up the
station near the east end of the island, and all incoming vessels were
inspected and fumigated. Citizens on the mainland protested this station and
claimed that winds could carry the disease ashore. It was then moved to

Chandeleur Island, 12 miles farther south, but a hurricane in 1893 wiped that station out and it was reopened on Ship Island, remaining until the 1930s.

In 1933 the federal government granted possession of three portions of the island to the Joe Graham American Legion Post for use as a "National Recreations Park." In 1964 the Mississippi Park Commission bought the former quarantine station. The island was cut in half by Hurricane Camille in 1969, and then in 1971, both parts became part of the newly formed Gulf Islands National Seashore.

Ship Island has been a popular destination for beachgoers since 1926, when excursion boats began taking large numbers of visitors to the island. The tour boats still come, but since the division of the island in 1969, West Ship Island, the site of Fort Massachusetts, gets all the crowds, while East Ship Island sees only those visitors who can get there in private or chartered vessels.

EAST SHIP ISLAND

East Ship Island is now as deserted and natural as Petit Bois Island and Horn Island. The only inhabitants are the many ospreys that nest in the tall pines along the beach and the otters, raccoons, rabbits, and alligators that make their homes in the marshes and thickets.

Since camping is prohibited on West Ship Island, when I began sea kayaking to the islands many years ago, East Ship was always one of my favorites. While Horn Island may be the centerpiece of the Gulf Islands National Seashore, and the main attraction for many, its very size and scale can be overwhelming for a first-time visitor. East Ship Island is much smaller and easier to get to know on an intimate level. East Ship is an island one can walk all the way around in a few hours, whereas a similar hike around the perimeter of Horn Island would take most people two or more days. This island lends itself easily to hiking and exploring, and offers a variety of all the different Gulf coast ecosystems to sample. There are broad beaches of white sand and windswept dunes, as well as stands of mature island pine forests, and a mix of swampy marsh and brackish lagoons. The island is as deserted and desolate as Petit Bois, as there is no ranger station, dock, or any kind of permanent man-made structure to be found.

On the south side of East Ship Island, the Gulf beaches look quite different than those of the other barrier islands. This is because tall pine trees grow right down to the high tide line in places and provide shady spots just out of reach of the surf for resting or camping. Other vegetation in the undergrowth beneath the pines consists of dense bushes and palmetto thickets. This growth makes the beach a haven for wildlife, and just after dark, one can often see large numbers of rabbits and raccoons as they come out for the night. One evening, as I walked along this beach, weaving in and out among the pines, I was startled by a large black animal that raced across the beach and plunged straight into the breaking surf. In the darkness, it was hard to tell what it was. It looked catlike, but I knew a cat wouldn't behave like that. Closer inspection of the animal's tracks in the sand confirmed that it was an otter. Where it went, I did not find out, as I never saw it resurface.

The pines along this beach are also a favorite nesting site for several pairs of ospreys every year. Campers should take care not to set up tents too close to trees with these nests in them. The ospreys get quite excited when someone approaches too near a nest, and they often dive and swoop low overhead while sounding their sharp warning cries to stay away. From a respectful distance, one can watch the ospreys returning to their nests after their fishing trips, often with their squirming prey clutched in their talons.

At times of the year when the ospreys are not nesting, these pines close to the beach make an idyllic setting for a camp on the Gulf side. As on any of the exposed Gulf side beaches on the barrier islands, anyone who camps on this side must be watchful of the weather and surf conditions. Sea kayaks are the boats most suited for landing on these beaches, and for those traveling in kayaks, camping on the south side of the island is the surest way to avoid other boaters and campers. If there is any surf running at all, most boaters in other types of vessels will avoid cruising anywhere near these beaches.

The pines provide secluded, shady campsites, and if you happen to have a hammock in your gear, you can suspend yourself between two pines and enjoy lazy afternoons of sea breeze and rolling surf. I have spent many days like this reading good books and trying to figure out ways to postpone my return to the hectic life I left behind on the mainland.

The downside of all these trees and other vegetation on the beach is that when the winds are calm, or from the wrong direction, biting insects will drive anyone camping there back out to sea. For a detailed description of how bad these pests can be, refer back to the section on camping in chapter 4, in which I relate my experiences from my first night spent on East Ship Island.

Because of its proximity to West Ship Island, campers who get bored with the perfect isolation of East Ship Island can simply paddle, sail, or motor the short distance across the cut to enjoy the diversions found there. I have often kayaked over to West Ship to refill my water jugs or to enjoy a burger and a cold drink or ice cream after days of wilderness camping.

I have also used East Ship Island as a convenient halfway stopover point for a kayak trip from Biloxi to Chandeleur Island. On one such trip, as I was approaching the beaches on the north side of East Ship Island, I noticed something long and dark, undulating as it floated in the clear waters about a half mile from shore. I expected it to be the usual piece of rope hawser from a ship or barge that one often finds littering the beaches. Instead, as I paddled closer, I was astounded to discover that it was an alligator, at least 8 feet long. The seagoing reptile swam swiftly and purposefully, and I wondered how far out it had been as it headed towards the shore. I knew there were alligators on the islands, and they had to get there somehow at some point in time, but I did not expect to see one crossing the sound in the broad daylight.

The waters around East Ship Island are often quite clear compared to other areas of the Mississippi Coast. Sometimes when conditions are right, you can see the bottom in depths of 5 feet or more in the sound off the north beaches of the island. Skimming along in my kayak, I have often seen huge stingrays cruising along over the submerged expanses of white sand here. Once when sailing into the lee of the island on my catamaran, I was surprised to see several sharks of 5 to 6 feet in length traveling together near the shore in about 5 feet of water.

Clear waters and palmettos lend a tropical island feel to
this East Ship Island beach.

EXPLORING EAST SHIP ISLAND

On very clear days, East Ship Island is visible from the mainland beaches
between Biloxi and Gulfport. On many of my kayak trips to the island, I
simply found a place to park along the shore and launched from the beach
to paddle directly to the island. At its closest point to the mainland, in the
vicinity of the Old Biloxi Lighthouse, East Ship Island is 9 nautical miles
to the south. From Gulfport, the island is 12 nautical miles to the south-
southeast. This makes for a 3- to 4-hour paddle in a sea kayak, depending
on where you launch. Some of my kayak passages to and from the island
have taken me up to 6 hours if I was fighting against a strong headwind.

East Ship Island is just over 3 nautical miles long, and its western tip is about three-quarters of a nautical mile from the eastern tip of West Ship Island. Before Ship Island was cut in two, the total length of the island was 7 nautical miles. The distance from East Ship Island's eastern tip to the west end of Horn Island, its nearest neighbor to the east, is just under 5 nautical miles. The distance to Cat Island, the closest neighbor to the west, is also just under 5 nautical miles from the western tip of West Ship Island. The north end of Chandeleur Island, which is part of Louisiana, lies 11 nautical miles to the south-southeast of West Ship Island. This makes East and West Ship Island about as centrally located as they could be in relation to other features on the Mississippi Gulf coast. Both islands and the approaches to them are charted on NOAA chart No. 11372. Instructions for navigation are given in the back of this chapter in the *Navigator's Notes*.

While I have made a direct rhumb-line passage from Horn Island to East Ship Island on more than one occasion in a kayak or my shoal-draft catamaran, this passage is fraught with shoals and not recommended in any but the most settled weather conditions. Chart 11372 shows several submerged poles, pilings, and other obstructions, as well as depths of 2 to 3 feet on this passage. In any sustained wind from a southerly direction, breaking waves of dangerous size are likely to be encountered on the shoals here.

Two navigable passes to the Gulf exist between East Ship and Horn Islands. Dog Keys Pass, described in the previous chapter, is by far the safest. Little Dog Keys Pass is marked with private aids to navigation and is most suitable for those with local knowledge.

The cut made by Camille between East and West Ship Islands is not suitable for navigation except for kayaks and other very small craft. Depths average 2 feet, shoals are constantly shifting, and breakers frequently occur in this pass.

WEST SHIP ISLAND

West Ship Island looks different from the other barrier islands, mainly because there is no forest. Its landscape instead consists of broad expanses of white sand beaches, dunes cloaked in sea oats, and areas of marsh in the interior.

The island offers little in the way of natural protection from the elements. On the undeveloped parts of the island, there is no shade from the scorching sun in the summer or the biting north wind in winter.

But the main thing that makes this island different from the other barrier islands of Mississippi is the presence of man-made structures. Fort Massachusetts, of course, is the oldest and most prominent of these. Then there is the replica of the old Ship Island Lighthouse. Next to this wood-frame tower stands a modern steel tower with a range light 84 feet above sea level. This navigation range lines up with the Gulfport Ship Channel. A long pier also extends into the sound north of the fort and is used as dockage for the large excursion boats that make several trips to the island each day during the season from March to October. This pier also has a docking area for private boats, but depths decrease dramatically inshore of the area designated for the excursion boats. The National Park Service keeps a patrol boat suspended and ready for use on davits on the east side of the pier.

In addition to the fort and pier, there are several other buildings on West Ship Island. The Park Service maintains living quarters and offices on the island, as well as storage buildings for maintenance equipment. A broad boardwalk continues south from the foot of the pier and provides a walkway across the island to the beaches on the Gulf side. This boardwalk crosses an expanse of marsh in the middle of the island, and interpretive signs and rest areas are provided along the way. Public restrooms and a covered picnic area are located just south of the fort along the walkway. On the Gulf beach side, another building houses a concession stand and store, as well as a large covered picnic area and restrooms. Outdoor showers are provided for beachgoers who wish to rinse off the sand and salt water after leaving the beach.

The concession offers such food as hot dogs and hamburgers, as well as cold drinks and a variety of snacks. T-shirts and other souvenirs are sold in the store, along with sunscreen and various beach supplies.

On the beach there is a lifeguard tower with a lifeguard on duty when the excursion boats are running. Beach chairs and umbrellas are also available for rent. For those who would rather not hang out with the crowds on this main beach, deserted beaches are just a short walk away to the east or the west.

It is slightly less than a mile to the west tip of the island, from which you can watch freighters steaming in and out of the Gulfport ship channel and see the beaches of Cat Island clearly on the other side of the pass.

The east end of the island lies almost 2 miles from the main beach and offers similar seclusion. West Ship Island has in recent years become popular with those who prefer to sunbathe in the nude, so be aware of this if you wander off to the more deserted beaches. The Park Service has no regulation against this, so if you prefer to swim and enjoy the beach without the encumbrance of clothing, feel free to do so as long as you are away from the family beach areas near the concession stand and the fort. The other islands are also popular with nudists who have their own boats to reach the secluded beaches.

SHIP ISLAND EXCURSIONS

The vast majority of visitors to West Ship Island get there on one of the tour boats operating out of Gulfport harbor (see chapter 7). Ship Island Excursions has been operated by the Skrmetta family since 1926, when Croatian immigrant Peter M. Skrmetta established a ferry service to the island. The business started with locally built wooden passenger vessels, the *Pan American* and the *Pan American Clipper*. The *Pan American Clipper*, a 65-foot vessel certified to carry 200 passengers is still in service during the peak of the summer season. Two more modern aluminum vessels have been added to the fleet in recent years: the 110-foot *Gulf Islander*, certified to carry 374 passengers, and the 100-foot *Captain Pete*, which is certified to carry 308 passengers. The latter vessel is named after Captain Pete Skrmetta, whose sons, Kenny, Louis, and Steven, pilot these vessels from Gulfport to the pier at West Ship Island. In the peak months of May through August they are often filled to capacity and make several trips per day. The excursion boats offer indoor, air-conditioned spaces for those who want this comfort during the trip, as well as a snack bar. Those who prefer the view and the chance to see dolphins and other marine life can find ample outdoor space on the upper decks and side decks.

With these modern vessels, the trip to the island takes about one hour, dock to dock. Cruising speed is up to 20 knots. Once the boat is docked at West Ship Island, passengers who wish to visit the Gulf side beaches must be prepared to walk across the island on the boardwalk. Since passengers must carry any coolers or other baggage they bring, they are advised to bring only necessities for the visit. Glass bottles, large bulky items, and pets are not permitted on the boats. For more information on Ship Island Excursions, call 228-864-1014 or toll free, 866-GO-MS-FUN. The excursion boats typically operate on a daily basis from March 1 through October, unless bad weather is forecast.

Those who visit West Ship Island in their own boats will find good places to anchor in Ship Island Harbor but should pay careful attention to the charted depths and not try to approach too closely. Despite the availability of charts and the ample deep water in the harbor, boaters run aground on an almost daily basis at West Ship Island. This is partly because of the sheer number of boaters who visit the island, but it is completely unnecessary and could easily be avoided with a little care. Most of the groundings are the result of trying to get too close to the beach. The charted line of 4-foot depths shown on chart No. 11372 is no misprint. The depths outside this line range from 9 to 26 feet, and the transition to shallows is abrupt. Depths of 1 to 2 feet extend quite far from the beach in places within the charted 4-foot line. Most groundings occur when deep draft vessels try to approach the middle section of the pier for docking or anchoring close in. This area is absolutely too shallow for anything drawing more than 2 feet, and the deeper areas near the end of the pier are reserved for the excursion boats and are therefore off-limits. I once stood on the pier and watched the skipper of a 27-foot sailboat drive his keel hard into the sand despite my shouted warnings. When he found himself quite solidly stuck and unable to power off with his engine in either forward or reverse, he gave up hope of getting off without assistance. I suggested that he wing the boom out perpendicular to the boat so that he could get his weight out there to heel the boat over while his female first mate manned the helm and gunned the engine. This method has always worked for me when I have found myself aground on *Intensity*. Demonstrating the

This sailboat is anchored just outside the line of shallow waters
near the beaches of West Ship Island.

common lack of interest in self-sufficiency prevalent among boaters these
days, the skipper ignored my advice and instead asked the park ranger, who
had by now walked down to the end of the pier to see what was going on,
to pull him off with his powerboat. It is not the responsibility of the park
ranger to assist stranded boaters, but since it was 9:30 A.M. and the grounded
sailor was in the way of the excursion boat, which was due in a half hour, the
ranger agreed to help. This involved lowering his patrol boat from its davits
and getting a line on the sailboat. The powerful outboards on the Boston
Whaler were able to pull the boat off, but the whole procedure took a half
hour. The grounding was unnecessary, but even more unnecessary was the

assistance of the ranger. Why the skipper did not want to even try my idea and learn a valuable technique in the process is a mystery to me.

Although West Ship Island gets a lot of visitors who arrive on the excursion boats and sometimes large numbers of private boaters, the anchorage is still a nice spot to spend the night. Since camping is not allowed on West Ship Island, and boaters are required to be off the beach between sunset and sunrise, overnighting here requires a self-contained boat that you can sleep aboard. The anchorage can occasionally get crowded at times such as summer holiday weekends, but at other times of the year tranquility can be found. I have often spent nights anchored there in the fall and winter with only one or two other anchored boats for neighbors.

Once, on the night of the full moon in October, I was sitting alone on deck smoking a cigar after dinner and watching the moonrise. When the moonlight began to illuminate the harbor, suddenly the water around me erupted in loud splashes. I was spellbound as I realized that dozens, perhaps as many as a hundred, bottle-nosed dolphins were cavorting in the moonlight around me, some turning somersaults in midair as they leaped in what appeared to be a celebration of the moonrise. This went on for at least an hour. I have yet to see a phenomenon like this since, but it is one experience at West Ship Island I will never forget.

NAVIGATOR'S NOTES

Approaches to East and West Ship Islands
(Use NOAA Chart No. 11372)

Being centrally located off the coast of mainland Mississippi, East and West Ship Islands can be conveniently approached from several ports or from the ICW.

Those coming from the east on the ICW can stay in this channel until directly north of either East or West Ship Island, and then turn south to the anchorage areas. It is also safe to set a more direct course from Horn Island to East Ship by staying along the latitude of 30 degrees, 16 minutes north until north of the eastern tip of East Ship. This course avoids the shoals that lie more to the south directly between the two islands.

East or West Ship Island can also be approached directly from the harbor of Biloxi by taking the West Biloxi channel out into the Mississippi Sound. This channel is described in detail in chapter 7. Once out into the open waters of the sound past the entrance to this channel at green daybeacon #1 and flashing red beacon #2, continue south on a course of 180 degrees to East Ship Island, about 7 nautical miles south of this entrance. If West Ship Island is your destination, you can angle off of this route and go directly to it once you see the island. On clear days the fort is the most visible landmark on the island and can be seen for many miles.

From Gulfport, West Ship Island is nearer than East Ship, but both can be approached by way of the well-marked Gulfport Ship Channel. Follow this channel to the southeast after leaving the Gulfport Small Craft Harbor. The Ship Channel changes course to the south and heads out to sea about a mile and a half south of where it crosses the ICW. From red beacon #36 on the ship channel, which marks this southerly turn, continue on the same southeasterly course toward the range tower on West Ship Island, which is located just east of the fort.

This course takes you right through the 21- to 24-foot depths of Ship Island Harbor. Anchorage can be found east or west of the pier that extends out north of the fort; just be sure to stay out of the shallows that lie inshore of the end of the pier.

Approaching West Ship Island from points west is best done by staying in the ICW until reaching the intersection with the Gulfport Ship Channel. It is also possible to plot a course from Cat Island to West Ship Island without going north to the ICW, but care must be taken to avoid charted shoal areas that lie outside the ship channel in the spoil areas created by dredging. Ship Island Pass is an easily navigated deepwater route to the open Gulf and is heavily used by commercial freighters entering and leaving the port of Gulfport. The ship channel through the pass lies just off the western tip of West Ship Island.

No navigable pass exists between West and East Ship Islands, as this area is shallow and subject to change. Good depths reach quite close to the beaches on the south side of both islands, but as always on the outside of barrier islands, stay well off the beach and look for shoals that are marked by areas of breaking waves.

The area immediately east of East Ship Island should be avoided, and those unfamiliar with Little Dog Keys Pass should stick to the more clearly marked Dog Keys Pass, near Horn Island.

14

CAT ISLAND

Cat Island is the westernmost of the long chain of barrier islands that begins with Dauphin Island in Alabama. When seen on a nautical chart or map, Cat Island looks quite different than the other barrier islands. All of Mississippi's other barrier islands are long and narrow and are more or less straight, their length running east to west. Cat Island is sort of T-shaped and has multiple coves and points to add interest for boaters. This shape makes for a variety of anchorages for those in shallow-draft vessels that can traverse the thin waters surrounding the island.

The island is heavily wooded throughout its interior but also has beaches that rival those of the other islands for wide expanses of unspoiled white sand. Wildlife is abundant on this island, which gets its name from the large population of raccoons that inhabit its forests. Since the raccoon is a mammal native only to the Americas, the French explorers who first visited the island thought these animals were a type of cat, and so named the island for them.

Although the island is now uninhabited, this has not always been the case. Due to its location and proximity to the mainland, there was an early interest in the acquisition and settlement of Cat Island. The first to petition the French Council for it was Sieur Hubert, who in 1717 described it as a "small island of sand that is subject to overflow in part and on which nothing but rabbits can be put."

During the time that the Spanish possessed the region, Cat Island was granted to Nicholas Christian, who had been raising cattle on it for sometime before moving there in 1745. He lived there for 35 years. Juan Cuevas became the lighthouse keeper on Cat Island and married Nicholas Christian's daughter, thus inheriting the island on which he became prosperous raising cattle. He became a hero when he refused to lead British warships anchored off Ship Island through the tricky passes of the sound in 1814. The British arrested him and insisted that he lead them to New Orleans, but he stubbornly refused, thus buying General Andrew Jackson time to prepare for the ensuing Battle of New Orleans, which proved to be a decisive victory in U.S. history.

Juan Cuevas sold Cat Island to Judah P. Benjamin in 1837, with the stipulation that the Cuevas homestead would be left for the benefit of his descendants. In later years a shipyard was located on Cat Island and the 35-sloop *Creole of Cat Island* was built there. The Boddie family acquired the island in 1911 and retained ownership until recently.

The island became popular with sport fishermen, and two lodges, the three-story Sportsmen's Hotel and the Goose Point Tarpon Club, were built there prior to the 1930s. They were later destroyed by fire.

The U.S. Army set up training camps on both Cat Island and Ship Island during World War II. Cat Island was ideal because it was similar in topography and vegetation to the tropical atolls of the Pacific. The army was experimenting in using dogs to sniff out the Japanese forces that occupied the jungles of those remote islands. Since all Japanese-Americans were interred in camps during the war, there was a ready supply of Japanese volunteers to be used in training the dogs. They were outfitted with heavy protective clothing and then told to run and hide in the interior of the island. The dogs were set loose to sniff them out, but because the diet of the Japanese-Americans was different than that of the enemy soldiers they later encountered in the war, the dogs proved to be of less value than anticipated.

When the Gulf Islands National Seashore was established in 1971, Cat Island was seen as the potential "crown jewel" of the park. The Boddie family was not convinced to sell the island at that time, however. Over the years the owners were approached by many developers who had their eyes on the 2,200-acre island, which was the largest privately owned island remaining in the Gulf. The Park Service approached the owners again in 1998 and again offered to buy the island for inclusion in the park. The Boddie family agreed to sell most of the island this time, for the sum of $25 million, under the condition that they retain 150 acres. The deal was to acquire the island in two phases, and funds to support the first phase were appropriated by Congress with the strong support of the Mississippi congressional delegation, especially Senators Trent Lott and Thad Cochran and Representative Gene Taylor. The Boddie family was pleased with the outcome, having long wished to keep the island in its natural state, despite the numerous enticements from casino developers who wished to get their hands on it.

At the time of this writing, the latest edition of the brochure and map published by the Gulf Islands National Seashore shows the areas of Cat Island shaded in green that are now included in the park. This includes the long point extending to the western tip, as well as the southern shorelines, including Smuggler's Cove. The central portions and the northeast pointing tip are not included as of yet.

EXPLORING CAT ISLAND

In describing the features of Cat Island, it is probably simplest to divide the island into three segments. First is the north coast, which has a shallow bay or cove lying between the western and northeastern tips. Then there is the long southeastern shoreline, which fronts directly on the Gulf. And finally, the southwestern shore, which makes up the rest of the island and includes deep coves and marshes.

In his *Cruising Guide to the Northern Gulf Coast*, Claiborne Young dismisses Cat Island as a destination for visiting boaters because of the extensive shoals found around much of the island. He says that due to the navigational difficulties, the other islands are more appropriate for visitors. It is true that the shoals require special attention to navigation, but in my experience, navigating around Cat Island is no more difficult than in any of the other shoal-water areas described in this book. The waters around the island and its approaches are well charted on NOAA chart No. 11372. The island is certainly popular with local sailors, and on almost any fair-weather weekend the masts of numerous boats will be seen at Cat Island's anchorages. Fishermen also frequent the island, and the proximity to the mainland has made it attractive to sea kayakers in recent years since the sport has begun to catch on in Mississippi.

At its closest point to the mainland, between Long Beach and Pass Christian, the western tip of Cat Island lies just slightly over 6 nautical miles away. The northern point of the island is just under 7 nautical miles from Gulfport and Longbeach. On a clear day the forested island is easily visible from Highway 90 anywhere between Pass Christian and Biloxi. Its western location also makes the island convenient for boaters in the Bay St. Louis area and for visiting boaters from the New Orleans area.

Many boaters arriving at Cat Island from the mainland visit the north side of the island. Depths of 2 to 4 feet extend a half mile from the shore along most of this north coast. Though it makes for a rather long dinghy ride, I have often anchored off this coast in the line of 8-foot soundings beyond these shallows. Any area north of the west point of the island makes for a sheltered anchorage from the prevailing southeast breezes that are usually encountered. The shoreline on this north side is heavily wooded, and much of the forest is overgrown with palmetto thickets and other undergrowth. Near the extreme western tip of the island the trees are mostly pine and the forest is more open. Most overnight boaters anchor off the natural cove formed on the north shore where the island starts to turn off to the northeast. This curved shoreline is shown on the chart as Little Bend. Though it looks like a perfect sheltered cove to anchor in, depths of 1 to 2 feet still prevail out to a half mile from the beaches. Most cruising-size boats will have to anchor out in the more exposed waters beyond this line of shallows. Those in smaller boats and kayaks, however, can approach this shore and enter the bayous that lead into the interior of the island from Little Bend. The largest of these is marked with a line of private aids to navigation that leads into a wide channel opening in the marsh. All others approaching this part of the island must pay close attention to the depth sounder and to their

Scattered pines provide welcome shade on the beaches of Cat Island.

position on the chart. Drop the hook in the 9- to 10-foot depths found outside the shallows and use the dinghy to go ashore.

The entire north point of the island is a beautiful area of white sandy beaches and open, undergrowth-free pinelands. This makes for some inviting hiking and beachcombing, and many who come to the island in smaller boats camp in this area. Since most of this north point is dry rather than marshy and the woods are so open, it is easy to cross the island to the beaches on the Gulf side.

Boaters who want to round the north tip to cruise around to the Gulf side will do well to pay strict attention to the charted shoals that extend north and east of the point. It is a good idea to give this point a wide berth because shoals off of a narrow point of land like this are always subject to change due to wave and current action.

A SHORTCUT TO AVOID

In an accidental grounding off this north tip of Cat Island, I found myself in deep trouble due to a series of events following the first mistake. I had made a late afternoon passage to the island with my longtime friend Dek Terrel of Baton Rouge. We had sailed to the island on *Lightning Struck* from Discovery Bay Marina and arrived to drop the hook off the Little Bend cove area described above just before sunset. The purpose of the trip was not to go to Cat Island but rather to sail offshore into the open Gulf to get some more bluewater experience. Dek was just getting into sailing and wanted to learn all he could.

We decided not to stay anchored at Cat Island that night but rather planned to head on out to sea and navigate all night using a system of 4-hour watches. I hauled in the anchor and raised the mainsail and jib while Dek steered us back to the north so we could round the north point of the island and then make our way to deep water. The wind was steady at 15 knots, so as soon as the sails were sheeted in we were under way and soon at cruising speed. We had studied the chart and plotted a course around the shoals north of the point. Thinking that perhaps we could save a little distance off the backtracking we were having to do to the north, Dek steered us a little closer to the beach than I was comfortable with.

One minute we were sailing at 5 knots and the next the boat shuddered and came to a complete stop. I asked Dek what the depth sounder showed, and he said 2 feet. He had watched the readings go from 8 to 10 feet to 2 feet without warning. Since sounder readings are often inaccurate during groundings, I doubted that the depth was really only 2 feet. I thought that in such a strong wind we could use the full sails to heel the boat over enough to free the keel. This was my first strategy, and it had worked in the past, but this time the boat did not budge. The next step was to start the engine and try to power off, while still leaving the sails set and sheeted in an attempt to get some heeling action. I hung on to the boom and tried to rock the boat while Dek gunned the engine in reverse. Nothing happened. We tried to power forward, hoping that the sandbar was small and that deep water would be found on the other side. Still nothing happened, and I was beginning to realize we were hard aground. This was not good, as the wind was increasing and the tide had just started to ebb. The sun was setting as well, so I was anxious to do something fast.

Meanwhile Dek had already jumped overboard, thinking that perhaps he could shoulder the 6,500-pound vessel off the sand. This could work in some circumstances when lightly grounded in calm conditions, but not in this situation. Dek found deep water just a few feet away from where the boat was stuck, so I went to the bow to free the main anchor, which I passed to him with instructions to set it in deeper water. I had hoped that with the anchor firmly set, we could kedge the boat off using the sheet winches. This might have worked except the winches were worn out and merely slipped when I attempted to crank them under such an extreme load. Dek climbed back aboard, and the two of us pulled and tugged at the anchor rode to no avail. We alternated our efforts with gunning the engine, but we still had not managed to move. I wanted to leave the anchor set since if we did get off this shoal, the increasingly strong wind could blow us right onto another. I decided it was time to make a more serious effort to heel the boat over, this being our only hope of decreasing our draft enough to float free. I lowered and furled the sails and then winged the boom out perpendicular to the hull and lashed it securely in place. Dek once again manned the engine. I had to get my full 190-pound weight as far out on the boom as possible to act as a lever, so I grabbed hold and swung hand over hand out to the end, dragging my feet in the water. Dek kept the engine at full throttle and churned up a cloud of mud and silt beneath us. I could feel the boat beginning to move, but I could tell we were still plowing a furrow through the bottom. Already exhausted from all the struggling with the anchor, I let go of the boom, expecting to find myself in waist-deep water. Instead, I went completely under and my feet did not touch bottom. My sunglasses were swept away as I submerged, and I could feel a strong tidal current rushing past the point of the island. I dove for the glasses several times but failed to find them. By this time I was exhausted from all the effort and when I surfaced the last time, I was a good 30 yards away from the boat. I could see that the boat was floating free, but the anchor was now firmly set and Dek was struggling with all his might to retrieve it. The wind was so strong he could not pull the boat forward to the anchor. I started swimming to get back on board and help him, but in the current I felt as if I were on a treadmill. I redoubled my efforts and swam with all my might. I was not getting any closer, and I was physically exhausted. Dek was fighting the anchor and was unaware of my predicament. I floated for a minute to rest, and within seconds I was even farther away from the boat. Despite the fact that we had run aground, I could not find the bottom anywhere with my feet. I yelled at Dek to get his attention and asked him to throw me a boat cushion. These cushions double as U.S. Coast Guard–required Type IV throwable PFDs. I was steadily losing ground in the current, and wondered if he could throw it close enough for me to reach it, but our boyhood games of backyard football paid off and he put it right on top of me at probably 60 yards. This was right on time, as I was now so tired I could barely stay afloat. I thought that with the cushion under me I could kick my way back to the boat, but this effort proved hopeless and I was still drifting. Dek was back at work on the anchor, but I knew that he couldn't get it up alone. The sun had set and I was on my way out to the open Gulf, riding the tide out to sea on a 2-foot square cushion. This was no longer an inconvenience but a potential disaster. I was now more than a hundred yards from the boat and would soon be out of shouting distance. I yelled at Dek to cut anchor, but then thought he probably didn't have a knife. I saw him disappear down below in the cabin while I drifted in helpless anticipation. He reappeared, and I could see him bending over the anchor line with something. Then he went back to the helm and started the engine. He had cut the anchor loose, and was now underway again heading towards me. I cringed as I thought of all the other shoals that were likely scattered between his position and mine, but miraculously, he did not run aground again, and I was able to climb back on board when he reached me. He had found a butcher knife in the galley. *Lightning Struck's* best anchor along with 25 feet of chain and maybe another 25 feet of half-inch nylon rope were lost, but it was a small price to pay for a valuable lesson learned. This incident taught me how quickly an inconvenience such as running aground can deteriorate into a potential disaster. And, of course, this incident shows the importance of paying strict attention to the charts and to your vessel's position in relation to potential hazards shown on them.

CAT ISLAND'S SOUTH SIDE

Beyond this northernmost point and its treacherous shoals, the southeast side of Cat Island fronts on the Gulf, and here is found the longest and broadest expanse of beach on the island. On the Gulf side of Cat Island, the shoreline is much straighter than any other side of the island and extends a little over three miles to the southwest. Water depths of 7 to 8 feet edge much closer to shore here than on other parts of the island, and I have spent the night anchored off this unprotected coast in times of settled weather.

This side of the island offers good beach hiking, and there are also old sand roads leading into the interior in places. Most likely these will revert back to nature once the remainder of the island is incorporated into the Gulf Islands National Seashore. Large sand dunes can be found near the south end of this beach, so high that they are clearly visible from West Ship Island.

Boaters following this coastline to the southernmost point of Cat Island will have to give this point an even wider berth than the north point if they wish to round it and explore the southwest side of the island. Shoals shown on the chart as South Spit carry only 2 feet of water a mile and a half to the southwest of the land. Flashing red beacon #2 marks the southern limit of these shoals and should be kept to the starboard of any vessel drawing more than 3 feet when rounding the point. Beyond this long area of shallow water, one can stay within the charted area of 7- to 8-foot depths to the west of the shoals and approach Smuggler's Cove on a northeast heading. Smuggler's Cove is a deep indentation in the south coast of the island west of the southern point. According to local history, it was used at various times by smugglers and pirates alike, being a natural hideaway close to, but just far enough away from, the Mississippi mainland. Today the cove is still favored by weekend sailors and powerboaters who are looking for a secluded and protected anchorage. The only drawback to the cove is its shallow depth, with 4 to 5 feet available on the outer reaches and only 2 to 3 feet closer inshore.

West of Smuggler's Cove, much of the south shore of Cat Island is a mix of beaches and marshlands. There are lots of shallow areas that carry only

1 foot of water and some places even less than that. Navigators exploring this side of the island will have to be quite careful and proceed at their own risk. A privately marked channel of white and brown day markers leads into the narrow cove north of Middle Spit. Depths may be unreliable here, and exploration this close to shore is best left to sea kayakers and others in shallow draft boats. Those in larger vessels wishing to sail back into the Mississippi Sound from the south side of Cat Island have the option of taking the charted Cat Island Channel, which leads back to the west-northwest about 2 miles south of the island. This is a much more direct route for those westbound on the ICW for New Orleans and points beyond.

NAVIGATOR'S NOTES

Approaches to Cat Island
(Use NOAA Chart No. 11372)

Navigation to the island from Longbeach is the most straightforward approach. Mariners leaving this harbor can simply set a course toward the island, to the south or south-southeast depending on which part they care to visit. The ICW transits the sound between Cat Island and the mainland just south of latitude 30 degrees, 19 minutes north. Other than the need to watch for passing barges and other commercial vessels on the ICW, there are no special hazards for mariners on this route.

From Gulfport one can follow the Gulfport Ship Channel out of the harbor and then turn off on a course to Cat Island, or wait and make the turn at the junction of the ICW with the ship channel. Those approaching from the east should stay in the ICW channel until west of the island's north tip if the destination is the north side of the island. Extremely shoal waters extend well out from this north tip, and their limits may not be accurately charted.

Mariners bound for Cat Island from Bay St. Louis will have to be careful to avoid the shallows of Square Handkerchief Shoal, which is also mentioned in chapter 6. This shoal, and the smaller Tail of the Square Handkerchief, lies along the rhumbline between Bay St. Louis and Cat Island. A long line of shoal water also extends out south of Pass Christian Harbor. These obstacles make it safest to approach Cat Island from the west via the ICW or by staying close inshore and detouring into the Pass

Christian Harbor channel and exiting its east entrance before laying a course for Cat Island.

There are other routes, such as Pass Marianne, which is charted south of the Tail of the Square Handkerchief, but close attention to your exact location at all times is the key to negotiating these shoal waters.

Cat Island Channel is a well-marked route that passes south of Cat Island and its shoals, providing a more direct route to the open Gulf for mariners coming from Lake Borgne and other points west on the ICW. This route diverges off the ICW at flashing green marker #1, about 8 miles west of Cat Island, and just 1 mile southwest of charted mile marker St M 55. At this point the ICW takes a turn to the northeast and the channel leading south of Cat Island runs in a general easterly direction, gradually curving to the southeast to pass between Cat Island and Isle au Pitre, which lies to the southwest, in Louisiana waters.

APPENDIX A

Boating Safety Equipment

U.S. Coast Guard requirements for vessel safety equipment vary greatly depending on the type and size of the vessel, as well as its use. A comprehensive description of these requirements is available in the publication titled *Federal Requirements for Recreational Boats*. Questions regarding boating safety can be directed to the Coast Guard Boating Safety Hotline: 800-368-5647.

In addition to U.S. Coast Guard requirements, individual states may impose regulations and restrictions. Questions regarding local regulations for Mississippi's coastal waters can be directed to the Marine Patrol at 228-432-7708. The following is a list of equipment required by the Marine Patrol:

VESSEL EQUIPMENT CHECKLIST
(Marine Patrol will inspect for these items)

- Registration number (canoes and sea kayaks exempted)
- Wearable life jackets for each person on board (children 12 and younger are required to wear a lifejacket at all times while aboard a vessel under 26 feet in length)
- Ventilation (on vessels with enclosed compartments)
- Backfire flame arrestors (on vessels with inboard engines)
- Throwable life preserver (on vessels over 16 feet in length)
- Sound producing device
- Closed trash container
- Navigation lights (all vessels after sunset)
- Fire extinguisher (on vessels with enclosed fuel compartments)
- Visual distress signals (on vessels under 16 feet in length at night; on larger vessels at all times)

APPENDIX B

Marinas of the Mississippi Gulf Coast

LaFrance Marina
3200 LaFrance Drive
Bay St. Louis
228-467-9180

Bayou Caddy Marina
Hancock County
Bay St. Louis
228-463-0368

Bay Marina and RV Park
100 Bay Marina Drive
Bay St. Louis
228-463-0368

Bayou La Croix Marina
11060 Hwy. 603
Bay St. Louis
228-466-4300

Bordages Brothers Marina and Shipyard
6149 Central Avenue
Bay St. Louis
228-467-0650

Diamondhead Ship Store and Marina
Harrison County
Pass Christian
228-255-7055

Pass Christian Harbor
Harrison County
Pass Christian
228-452-3315

Pelican Cove Marina
103 W. Bayview Street
Pass Christian
228-452-7390

Pepper's Discovery Bay Marina and Resort
24616 Yacht Club Drive
Pass Christian
228-452-9441

Long Beach Harbor
Harrison County
Long Beach
228-863-4795

Gulfport Small Craft Harbor
Harrison County
Gulfport
228-868-5713

Rivers Bend Marina
1400 Mill Road
Gulfport
228-896-8300

Broadwater Resort Marina
President Casino
Biloxi
228-385-4097

Keesler AFB Marina
Harrison County
Biloxi
228-374-0002

D'Iberville Marina
D'Iberville Port Commission
Biloxi
228-392-7966

Beau Rivage Marina
875 Beach Boulevard
Biloxi
228-386-7580

Biloxi Small Craft Harbor
Harrison County
Biloxi
228-436-4062

Point Cadet Marina
119 Beach Boulevard
Biloxi
228-436-9312

Bay Point High and Dry
169 5th Street
Biloxi
228-374-7766

Ocean Springs Harbor
1320 Harbor Drive
Ocean Springs
228-875-4696

Harbor Pointe Apartments and Marina
2421 Beachview Drive
Ocean Springs
228-875-8801

Paige Bayou Marina
3400 Rouses Marina Road
Ocean Springs
228-826-4444

Mary Walker Marina
3328 Mary Walker Drive
Gautier
228-497-3141

Inner Harbor Marina
Jackson County
Pascagoula
228-938-6627

Choctaw Marina
3301 Hemlock Avenue
Moss Point
228-475-6100

Little River Marina
3200 Dumas Road
Moss Point
228-475-5244

APPENDIX C

Marine Services of the Mississippi Gulf Coast

BOATYARDS

Jourdan River Marina and Boat Repair
1739 Blue Mead
Bay St. Louis
228-467-4771

Kremer Marine Inc.
1408 Cowan Lorraine Rd.
Gulfport
228-896-1629

Bay Marine Boat Works
151 5th Street
Biloxi
228-432-2992

Rebel Boatworks Shipyard
161 5th Street
Biloxi
228-435-2762

Covacevich Yacht and Sail
336 Bayview Avenue
Biloxi
228-436-6401

Pitalo's Marine
704 Sandstone Street
Gautier
228-497-9900

BOAT TOWING/ ON-THE-WATER SERVICES

Sea Tow Services of South Mississippi
228-374-1092
(or VHF channel 16)

APPENDIX D

Island Camping Checklist

Tent with "no-see-um" netting

Tarp or rainfly

Extra line or cordage for securing tarp

Tent stakes and mallet

Machete or hatchet

Knife

Sleeping bag

Self-inflating sleeping pad

Inflatable pillow

Crazy Creek or similar folding seat

Hammock

Campstove

Stove lighters or matches

Stove fuel

Stainless steel cookware (skillet, coffee pot, cook pot, spatula, etc.)

Stainless or plastic dishes (bowls, plates, cups) and utensils

Compact can opener

Trash bags

Biodegradable liquid soap, scrub pad

Cooking and drinking water in leakproof containers

Waterproof flashlight

Spare bulbs and batteries for light

Insect repellant

Duct tape (for misc. repairs to tent, etc.)

Rain jacket and pants, or poncho

Hiking boots or shoes

Layered clothing for cold weather

Long-sleeve cotton shirt and trousers for hot weather
Shorts, T-shirts, beach sandals
Hat for sun protection
Swimsuit
Basic first-aid supplies
Snakebite kit
Benadryl (for stings)
Prescription medication if needed
Sunscreen (SPF 30 or higher)
Towel
Toothbrush, toilet paper, etc.
Camera
Binoculars
Sunglasses with retainer cord or strap
Notebook and pencils or pens
Walkman CD or cassette player (optional)
Reading material for long days in the hammock (optional)

APPENDIX E

Sea Kayak Touring Checklist

Appropriately designed kayak for intended trip
Strong, lightweight touring paddle
Two-piece spare paddle
Sprayskirt
Coast Guard-approved personal floatation device
Paddle float (for reentry after a capsize)
Bilge pump
Bailing sponge
Duct tape (for emergency repairs)
RTV silicon sealant (for emergency repairs)
Pocket-sized multitool (for repairing rudders, etc.)
Sharp rescue knife
Deck-mounted navigation compass
Backup hand-bearing compass
Handheld GPS receiver
Handheld VHF radio
Compact waterproof binoculars
Waterproof chart pouch
Appropriate charts
Dividers (for chartwork)
Watch (for navigation)
Handheld aerial flares or 12-gauge flare gun
Red marker dye
Sunglasses with retainer cord or strap
Collapsible wide-brimmed hat
SPF 30 or higher sunscreen
Waterproof dry-storage bags

Benadryl (for jellyfish stings)
Readily accessible high-energy snacks for long crossings
Readily accessible water supply sufficient for duration of crossing

- *For overnight trips to the barrier islands, the items on the Island Camping Checklist should also be added to this list.*

APPENDIX F

Resources

LIST OF NATIONAL OCEANIC AND ATMOSPHERIC ADMINISTRATION NAUTICAL CHARTS FOR MISSISSIPPI WATERS

Chart No. 11367 Intracoastal Waterway-Waveland to Catahoula Bay (covers the extreme western end of the Mississippi mainland, the waters of Lake Borgne, and the lower Pearl River)

Chart No. 11372 Intracoastal Waterway-Dog Keys Pass to Waveland (covers the mainland coast from Bay St. Louis east to Ocean Springs, including St. Louis Bay and Back Bay of Biloxi, as well as Cat Island and West and East Ship Islands)

Chart No. 11374 Intracoastal Waterway-Dauphine Island to Dog Keys Pass (covers the mainland coast from Davis Bayou east to include the Pascagoula River and Grand Bay, as well as Horn Island and Petit Bois Island)

Chart No. 11373 Mississippi Sound and Approaches, Dauphin Island to Cat Island (smaller scale chart showing offshore waters, passes between the islands, and approaches to the mainland)

Chart No. 11371 Lake Borgne and Approaches, Cat Island to Point Aux Herbes (small-scale chart like No. 11373, showing western approaches to the Mississippi Sound and Lake Borgne)

These charts can be purchased at most Gulf coast marine supply dealers, fishing tackle dealers, and some sporting goods stores. Charts may be ordered directly from the National Oceanic and Atmospheric Administration. Call 1-800-638-8972.

SAILING INSTRUCTION AND CLASSES

Mid-South Sailing Center Inc.
Gulfport
228-863-6969

North Star Sailing Charters
Biloxi
228-594-6834

Note: Most local yacht clubs also provide sailing instruction for members, and other licensed captains operating out of various marinas in the area can provide differing levels of instruction.

KAYAK RENTAL, SALES, AND INSTRUCTION

Da Beach House
604 S. Beach Blvd.
Bay St. Louis
228-467-1108

Wolf River Canoe and Kayak
21640 Tucker Rd.
Long Beach
228-452-7666

H 2O Sports MS LLC
10470 D'Iberville Blvd.
D'Iberville
800-292-6864

INFORMATION ON FISHING RULES AND REGULATIONS

Mississippi Department of Marine Resources
1141 Bayview Avenue
Biloxi, Mississippi 39530
800-374-3449 or 228-374-5000
www.dmr.state.ms.us

APPENDIX G

Bibliography/Recommended Reading

Akin, William N. *Mississippi: An Illustrated History*. Windsor Publications Inc., 1987.

Alvord, Douglas. *Beachcruising*. International Marine Publishing, 1992.

Anderson, Agnes Grinstead. *Approaching the Magic Hour: Memories of Walter Anderson*. University Press of Mississippi, 1989.

Burch, David. *Fundamentals of Kayak Navigation*. Pacific Search Press, 1987.

Cardwell, J. D. *Sailing Big on a Small Sailboat*. Sheridan House, 1997.

Casey, Don. *Sensible Cruising: The Thoreau Approach*. International Marine/Ragged Mountain Press, 1990.

Craighead, Frank C. *How to Survive on Land and Sea*. United States Naval Institute, 1984.

Daubert, Ken. *Kayakfishing: The Revolution*. Coelacanth Publishing, 2001.

Dowd, John. *Sea Kayaking: A Manual for Long-Distance Touring*. Douglas and McIntyre LTD., 1986.

Dunaway, Vic. *Sport Fish of the Gulf of Mexico*. Wickstrom Publishing, 2000.

Gibbons, Euell. *Euell Gibbons' Beachcomber's Handbook*. David McKay Co., 1973.

Hansen, Gunnar. *Islands at the Edge of Time: A Journey to America's Barrier Islands*. Island Press, 1993.

Harvey, Derek. *Multihulls for Cruising and Racing*. International Marine/Ragged Mountain Press, 1991.

Herndon, Ernest. *Canoeing Mississippi*. University Press of Mississippi, 2001.

Herring, Mack R. *Way Station to Space: A History of the John C. Stennis Space Center*. National Aeronautics and Space Administration, 1997.

Higginbotham, Jay. *The Pascagoula Indians*. Colonial Books, 1967.

Hutchinson, Derek C. *Derek C. Hutchinson's Expedition Kayaking*. Globe Pequot Press, 1999.

Iberville's Gulf Journal. University of Alabama Press, 1981.

Jenkins, Peter. *Along the Edge of America*. Mariner Books, 1997.

Jones, Thomas Firth. *Multihull Voyaging*. Sheridan House Inc., 1994.

Kinton, Tony, and Bill Dance. *Fishing Mississippi*. University Press of Mississippi, 2002.

Kirkpatrick, Marlo Carter. *Mississippi: Off the Beaten Path*. Globe Pequot Press, 1999.

Little, Ida. and Michael Walsh. *Beachcruising and Coastal Camping*. Wescott Cove Publishing Company, 1992.

Maloney, Edward S., and Charles Frederic Chapman. *Chapman Piloting: Seamanship and Boat Handling*. Sterling Publications, 1999.

Marine Resources and History of the Mississippi Gulf Coast, vols. 1-4. Mississippi Department of Marine Resources, 1998.

McGinnis, Helen. *Hiking Mississippi: A Guide to Trails and Natural Areas*. University Press of Mississippi, 1995.

Mississippi Atlas and Gazetteer. Delorme, 1998.

Mississippi Road Atlas. University Press of Mississippi, 1997.

Moitessier, Bernard. *A Sea Vagabond's World*. Sheridan House, 1998.

Rousmaniere, John. *The Annapolis Book of Seamanship*. Simon and Schuster, 1999.

Saltwater Fishing Tactics: Learn from the Experts at Saltwater Sportsman Magazine. Creative Publishing International, 1999.

Schueler, Donald G. *Adventuring Along the Gulf of Mexico: The Sierra Club Travel Guide to the Gulf Coast of the United States and Mexico from the Florida Keys to the Yucatan*. Sierra Club Books, 1986.

Sugg, Redding S., ed. *The Horn Island Logs of Walter Inglis Anderson*. University Press of Mississippi, 1991.

Tighe, James. *Following the Water, Working the Land*. Quail Ridge Press, 1999.

Wells, Mary Ann. *Native Land: Mississippi, 1540-1798*. University Press of Mississippi, 1994.

Young, Claiborne S. *Cruising Guide to the Northern Gulf Coast: Florida, Alabama, Mississippi, Louisiana*. Pelican Publishing Company, 1998.

INDEX